MW00489452

Introduction to Afro-American Studies
Post-Reconstruction to the 21st Century
Volume 2

LaVonne Jackson Leslie
Howard University

KENDALL/HUNT PUBLISHING COMPANY
4050 Westmark Drive   Dubuque, Iowa 52002

Cover photo courtesy of Library of Congress.

Copyright © 2005 by LaVonne Jackson Leslie

ISBN 0-7575-2473-7

Kendall/Hunt Publishing Company has the exclusive rights to reproduce this work,
to prepare derivative works from this work, to publicly distribute this work,
to publicly perform this work and to publicly display this work.

All rights reserved. No part of this publication may be reproduced,
stored in a retrieval system, or transmitted, in any form or by any
means, electronic, mechanical, photocopying, recording, or otherwise,
without the prior written permission of Kendall/Hunt Publishing Company.

Printed in the United States of America
10 9 8 7 6 5 4 3 2 1

Dedication

Dedicated to the loving memory of my mother, Christine Shelton Chriesman, and my dearly departed grandmother, Jennie V. Shelton Parker, who inspired me to strive for the very best in life in spite of obstacles.

Contents

Foreword

Abdul Karim Bangura
Howard University and
American University

Invest in a human soul. Who knows? It might be a diamond in the rough.
  —Mary McLeod Bethune

Readers are leaders, Thinkers succeed.
  —Marva Collins

Education is the key to unlock the golden door of freedom.
  —George Washington Carver

As the preceding quotes from three great African American teachers--Mary McLeod Bethune, Marva Collins and George Washington Carver--suggest, it is only through education and selflessness that the next generation of leaders can be prepared. Consequently, a thorough education calls for an equally thorough understanding of our past and present. Professor LaVonne Jackson has presented us in her two volumes of Introduction to Afro-American Studies the tools to help us begin this challenging and exciting journey.

Indeed, what Professor Jackson has done in this work is to help render obsolete the pervasive and pernicious myth of African Americans as inactive agents in history. Although the role of African Americans in contemporary society is evident to anyone who reads today's newspapers, listens to the radio, or watches television, many people still believe that African Americans are a people devoid of a sophisticated philosophy. In recent years, however, there has been a resurgence of interest in the philosophical thought of African Americans among scholars. Today's movement of African Americans has turned to history for a "usable past"— a definition of the African American. After almost five decades during which schools and colleges across the United States have rushed to institute courses and programs dealing with the history of African Americans, newspapers, magazines and television stations have produced expensive series on the history of African Americans, and publishers have reproduced long out-of-print monographs, too many White Americans still know far too little about the sophisticated contributions of their fellow citizens—i.e. African Americans. The contemporary crisis in race relations, moreover, has made Americans more aware than ever of the ethnic dimension of their history, and interest in the past of African Americans has gone hand-in-hand with a desire to study the history of immigrants, Native Americans, and other ethnic groups.

Despite the fact that African American and White scholars have been writing about the educational thought of African Americans for many years, the Afro-American Studies field is in many ways still in its infancy. This is partially because almost every phase of the past of African Americans has been shrouded in myths and misconceptions, one of the most pervasive and pernicious of which, as I alluded to earlier, is the notion of African Americans as inactive agents in history. Moreover, there has not been a corresponding increase in the number of texts and anthologies suitable for an introductory course on Afro-American Studies, and teachers have been forced to require their students to purchase numerous books and to spend a good deal of time in their library reserve rooms reading additional material. Professor Jackson's work will go a long way to remedy this problem.

Even more disappointing is the fact that available works on the subject often lack a proper appraisal of the real nature of the thoughts of African Americans, and they are based on a concept that fragments African American life derived from a Eurocentric division of labor theory which separates education from politics, religion, economics, and the social institutions of family, or group, or people. This fragmentation theory emanates from Eurocentric epistemology and a fundamental approach to existence which has its genesis in Greco-Roman and subsequently Judeo-Christian thought.

Thus, one of the major tenets that guide Professor Jackson's work is that before we attempt any description of the sophisticated thoughts of African Americans, it will be necessary to locate its total personality within the boundaries of its own self-perception; this means delineating African American philosophy and its view of the world, both visible and invisible, its fundamental habits of thought, and its attitude towards its physical and spiritual existence.

The African American life concept is holistic—i.e. it is based on an integrative world view. All life to the

African American is total; all human activities are closely interrelated. This has as its underlying principle the sanctity of the person, her/his spirituality and essentiality. This essentialist view of the person confers value to her/his personhood. All else—her/his labor and achievements—flow from this value system. Even personal failure cannot invalidate it.

As can be gleaned from Professor Jackson's work, for African Americans, politics defines duties and responsibilities alongside obligations and rights. All these relate to the various activities that have to do with survival. The survival concept is continuing, dynamic and dialectical. The fundamental principle that is at the basis of this conception is a moral one.

The African American moral order never defined rigid frontiers of good and evil. Good and evil exist in the same continuum. Whatever is good, by the very nature of its goodness, harbors a grain of evil. This is a guarantee against any exaggerated sense of moral superiority which goodness by itself may entail. The notion of perfection, therefore, is alien to African American thought. Perfection in itself constitutes a temptation to danger, an invitation to arrogance and self-glorification. The principle of balance defines the relationship between good and evil. As life operates in a dialectics of struggle, so also does good balance evil and *vice-versa*.

Thus, the essence of Professor Jackson's work is that it is imperative and urgent for African American educators to be concerned about broader education as well as training and to be concerned about approaches to learning and teaching which are conducive to the kind of educated African American needed today and in the future. Educated African Americans are needed who

(a) can deal with cultural and technological changes, uncertainties, and ambiguities;

(b) are sensitive to and capable of working with diverse values;

(c) will continue to learn and develop their professional and intellectual skills;

(d) can work with colleagues and facilitators in constructive and open ways while sustaining a strong sense of character, ethics, and professional commitment;

(e) are flexible, open minded, and capable of finding new information on their own, absorbing new information and insights, and correcting their paths when what they learn calls for that; and

(f) are largely self-directed, creative, and have a proper sense of autonomy as well as responsibility.

If the primary purpose of African American educational processes is to help learners become such citizens, it is obvious that *andragogic* (student-directed) approaches must be built into the procedures for fulfilling our educational responsibilities. Teachers must be sensitive to the socialization effects and self-fulfilling nature of different educational assumptions, philosophies, principles, and practices. African American educational programs do not want to teach learners to act as mindless cogs in academic machinery of common characterization.

African American learners cannot afford to function solely according to the behavioral and intellectual patterns of dependence and passivity that are encouraged and inculcated by pedagogic (institution or teacher-directed) assumptions, principles and practices.

To the contrary, the autonomy, self-directedness and creativity encouraged by the principles and practices of *andragogy* are the characteristics most needed in the next generation of educated African American. When *andragogy* is considered along with the idea of the socialization effects of educational environments and the possibilities of a reinforcement of these notions and contexts, the implications for an African educational process appear vital.

Indeed, no book can be all things to all readers. My guess is that what follows will strike a responsive chord in some and leave others untouched; this is preferable to a wide, but tepid, acceptance.

Acknowledgments

"Those who have no record of what their forebears have accomplished lose the inspiration which comes from the teaching of biography and history."

These are the words of Dr. Carter Godwin Woodson, distinguished Black author, editor, publisher, and historian (December 1875 - April 1950). Carter G. Woodson believed that Blacks should know their past in order to participate intelligently in the affairs in our country. He strongly believed that Black history—which others have tried so diligently to erase—is a firm foundation for young Black Americans to build on in order to become productive citizens of our society. Known as the "Father of Black History," Carter G. Woodson holds an outstanding position in early 20th century American history. Woodson authored numerous scholarly books on the positive contributions of Blacks to the development of America. He also published many magazine articles analyzing the contributions and role of Black Americans. He reached out to schools and the general public through the establishment of several key organizations and founded Negro History Week (precursor to Black History Month). His message was that Blacks should be proud of their heritage and that other Americans should also understand it. In order to accomplish this mission, it is necessary to provide a body of scholarship on the history of African Americans. In meeting these criteria, *Introduction to Afro-American Studies I: Post-Reconstruction to Twenty-First Century* will focus on the significant contributions of African Americans from the past to the present with emphasis on accomplishments and challenges within the context of U.S. and global affairs in the 21st century.

Introduction to Afro-American Studies, Volume I: Post-Reconstruction to Twenty-First Century depicts African Americans at the center of their own history, highlights African Americans actively constructing their own destinies through difficult times and hostile environments, and combines chronological structure with thematic perspectives. It begins with the participation of African Americans in events in the post-reconstruction era beginning with the Spanish-American War and concludes with their cultural, economic, political, and sociological experiences in contemporary times. By providing an analysis of African American life over time and by relaying the history within the context of American society, it will encourage students to examine major controversies and facts on the contributions and experiences of Africans in America.

In preparing *Introduction to Afro-American Studies, Volume 2,* I am thankful for assistance and support from colleagues, librarians, friends, and family. I wish to thank Abdul Karim Bangura at both Howard University and American University for his invaluable contribution in critiquing, editing, and typesetting the manuscript. My students, Dwight Saunders, Victoria Ricci, and Adebayo Idamakin, provided assistance in collecting necessary articles and books. My son, Sharrod Perry provided valuable administrative assistance. The librarians at Howard University aided in locating important documents and research material. Special thanks to my family and friends for moral support and understanding, particularly my husband, Randolph William Leslie; daughter, Christina Roberts; and friends Nannie Barnes, Meshelle Days-Lewis, and Celia Daniel. I thank my brothers and sisters; Lorenzo Chriesman, Robert Chriesman, Loretta Chappelle, Glenda Turner, Jennie Chriesman, and Susie Lloyd, for providing inspiration and expressing pride in my accomplishments. I gratefully acknowledge essential support from Heather Austin and the editorial team at Kendall-Hunt. Indeed, it has been a challenge and pleasure working with and learning from the staff. Finally, I am grateful to my students at Howard University for expressing interest in my lectures and providing insights into subject matters relevant to the African American experience.

Chapter 13

African Americans in Spanish-American War and Segregation Era

This chapter focuses on African Americans during and after the Spanish American War, with emphasis on their military experiences and race relations on the home front. America began to focus on expanding its presence in other parts of the world. It was influenced by the imperialist actions of Europeans in Africa in their pursuit to dominate the region in the name of colonization.

During the late 1800s, with the closing of the frontier, many Americans thought that expansion elsewhere would be an efficient way to meet the continuing demand of the country's industries. It was believed that new lands and colonies would help to strengthen America's military power. Industrialists were interested in building industries and expanding businesses in new countries with people of color. The Hawaiian Islands were among the territories that interested America. America saw the value of this territory as a site for a naval base, coaling station, and for cable landing. In 1884, America leased Pearl Harbor as a naval station to provide protection for American-owned industries. As a result,

American investors put more capital into the islands. In 1875, sugar and other Hawaiian products gained free entry into America. The Wake, Midway, Palmyra and Howland islands in the Pacific held special interest for American investors. America also showed interest in Islands controlled by Spain while the country declined as a major imperial power. America enforced its policy most vigorously in South America and the Caribbean.

By 1900, the U.S. had acquired Hawaii, Guam, the Philippines, and Puerto Rico in the name of imperialism. Prior to this period, American businesses had extended their activities to islands in the Caribbean, Latin America, and the Pacific, partly due to the activities in Africa of France, England, Belgium, Italy, and Germany. David Livingstone, Cecil Rhodes, and Henry M. Stanley were Europeans who had emphasized the importance of Africa to an industrialized world. Leopold of Belgium, Wilhelm of Germany, and Queen Victoria of England were prominent Europeans responsible for the partition of Africa. George Washington Williams, an African

1

Jornee' de l'armee d'Afrique et des troupes colonials. French soldiers with Black soldiers from Africa during colonization. Library of Congress.

American historian, vehemently criticized the invasion of Africa.

At the Paris Peace Conference in Berlin between 1884 and 1885, European nations partitioned Africa and this became labeled the "Scramble for Africa." The Paris Peace Conference helped pave the way for the European colonization of East Africa, Southwest Africa, and West Africa.

As a result of European colonization in Africa, America decided to acquire its own dark empire outside of Africa, specifically in areas in Spanish America under Spain's control. America exploited conditions in Cuba, through its use of yellow journalism, emphasizing the inhumane treatment the Cubans received from the Spaniards, which helped encourage them to demand independence from Spain. With support from the American government, the Cubans, led by Antonio Maceo, a mulatto general, and Quentin Bandera, known as "The Black Thunderbolt," carried out a revolt against Spain, marking the advent of the Cuban Revolution.

The Cuban War for Independence that broke out in 1895 was a continuation of an earlier revolt (1868-78) against Spanish rule. Spain brutally halted the revolt. To maintain order in Cuba, Spain sent General Valeriano Weyler to suppress the insurrection. Weyler confined many Cubans to concentration camps behind barbed wire fences. Starvation and diseases took such a toll on Cuban lives that Americans dubbed the Spanish leader "Butcher" Weyler. Americans protested the war and encouraged involvement in liberating the Cubans from Spain's dominance. The *New York Journal* of William Randolph Hearst and Joseph Pulitzer's *New York World* newspaper instigated war fever by publishing sensational accounts of events in Cuba. Many Americans believed that it was the destiny of the United States to expand beyond its continental boundaries. They favored war with Spain. But President William McKinley and his Cabinet remained calm. Spain began to take steps to grant Cuba limited independence when sympathizers in Havana, Cuba, rioted.

On January 25, 1898, the U.S.S. Maine arrived to protect American lives. About the same time, Spain's ambassador to Washington, Enrique Dupuy de Lome, had expressed concern in a letter to a friend about McKinley's intentions. The letter fell into American hands and on February 9, and it was printed in the *New York Journal.* Six days later came the fateful explosion in Havana Harbor.

Spanish American War and African Americans

America's opportunity to engage in the conflict occurred on February 15, 1898 when the battleship "Maine" was blown up with a loss of 260 officers and crew. This incident led to war between the United States and Spain known as the "Spanish-American War," or the "Splendid Little War." The cause of the blast was never definitely known. The Spaniards claimed that it had occurred in one of the ship's boilers. A United States Navy board of inquiry ruled that the blast had come from an underwater mine fastened to the ship's hull. Whatever the cause, the explosion caused what John M. Hay, United States ambassador to Britain, called "a splendid little war."

From the beginning, African Americans were involved in the war against Spain. At least 30 of them lost their lives on the ship when it exploded. A majority of African Americans were anxious to help America acquire independence and freedom for the Cubans, whom they regarded as Blacks and mulattoes. Many were enthusiastic about enlisting in the military. African American leaders were divided over their support of the war. Some African Americans were anti-imperialist and, thus, they identified with the Cuban rebels who believed that Spain had imposed a racial caste system on them. Therefore, they supported the war. African Americans who refused to support the war did so because they believed that they were being used to help promote America's imperialistic agenda. African American Reverend George W. Prioleau, chaplain of the Ninth Cavalry, criticized the war as being hypocritical. He stated:

> Talk about fighting and freeing poor Cuba and of Spain's brutality...Is America any better than Spain? Has she not subjects in her very midst who are murdered daily without a trial of judge or jury? Has she not subjects in her own borders whose children are half-fed and half-clothed, because their father's skin is Black....Yet the Negro is loyal to his country's flag.

In 1898, four African American outfits, all of which had participated in wars against Native Americans in the West, fought in the Spanish-American War. The Ninth Cavalry regiment, known as the "Buffalo Soldiers," had scouted 34,420 miles of western desert, laid hundreds of miles of new roads and telegraph lines, protected the mail coaches, and carried out military actions against the great Apache chiefs, Victoria and Geronimo, prior to the war. Buffalo Soldiers won 19 medals of honor and had a remarkably low desertion rate, as compared to one-third of their White counterparts. They may have received their nickname from the Kiawa, Cheyenne, and Apache forces they encountered on the western Plains. There is the possibility that the name might have been derived from the thick overcoats African American soldiers wore on the cold Plains, or the soldier's hair that reminded the Native Americans of a buffalo's hide. A third and the most accepted theory is that it was a moniker of respect based on Native Americans' appreciation for the buffalo that served as a source of clothing, food, fuel, and shelter, as well as many other uses. African American soldiers, including Henry Flipper, the first Black graduate from West Point in 1877, might have regarded it as a compliment.

During the War, the first African American commander of Black troops, Charles Young, the second Black West Point graduate and Buffalo soldier, rose from 2nd Lieutenant of the 10th Cavalry to Major of the 9th Ohio Regiment. The Ohio battalion led by Major Young was comprised of an all-Black unit. In all, 16 Black regiments fought in the Spanish-American War. They fought in all of the major battles and made significant contributions. African American infantrymen fought with valor in the battles of El Caney, Las Guasimas, and San Juan in Puerto Rico. They were nicknamed "Smoked Yankees" by the Cubans, in contrast to White soldiers led by Theodore Roosevelt, known as "Rough Riders." Black soldiers mounted magnificent assaults against the Spaniards. They marched with White regiments against the

Spaniards in the city of Santiago de Cuba during the war, thereby winning a major victory. The Rough Riders battled with them, causing Commander Roosevelt to praise their performance. A few African American soldiers were recognized for their bravery. Elijah Tunnell, a cook on the U.S.S. Winslow, became the first African American to die for the United States during the War. Due to his actions, he earned the highest medal of honor awarded to any African American soldiers during the war.

The 3rd North Carolina, an African American cavalry stationed in the Pacific, was a Black volunteer regiment commanded by all Black officers. In spite of their bravery in the war, Black soldiers still suffered from discrimination, segregation, and racial insults. Some Black soldiers protested unfair treatment received from fellow White soldiers. They attempted to challenge the abuses heaped upon them. Most African Americans exercised restraint. They hoped to strengthen race relations by participating in the war. Despite constant problems from fellow White soldiers, Black soldiers remained determined to be central in the war efforts. By the time the war ended, seven Black soldiers had received the Congressional Medal of Honor and 100 had received commissions as officers. In spite of contributions made by Black soldiers in the war, some Whites, especially those in the South, neither wanted Blacks to fight in the war, nor did they want them to receive recognition for their achievements in enabling America to defeat the Spaniards.

In the Philippines, the leader, Emilio Aguinaldo, led a revolt against the Spaniards and agreed to cooperate in the Spanish-American War with assistance from the United States. The joint effort ended Spanish rule in most of the Philippine Islands. The Philippines gave to the United States the foothold it needed in Asia to compete against Britain, France, and Russia. It was very important for the United States to control the areas, which were populated by darker people, as mandated by manifest destiny. This empire includes Black, White, and yellow, or mixed people, to represent the United States. In Cuba, more than 600,000 Blacks and persons of African descent lived there; and in Puerto Rico, more than 300,000 Blacks lived there. The Americans soon invaded Puerto Rico and controlled the island. Blacks lived even in Hawaii and the Philippines. When the United States acquired the Canal Zone in 1903, many Blacks lived in Panama and many more came from the Caribbean islands to work on the Panama Canal. Spain's military setbacks in the Caribbean left other islands in American hands.

At the end of the war, the United States was regarded as one of the great powers of the world. Almost overnight it acquired a colonial empire of 120,000 square miles and 8,000,000 people. The Treaty of Paris, on February 6, 1899, ended the war and required (1) Spain to relinquish all claim to sovereignty over Cuba; (2) Spain to surrender to America, the Island of Puerto Rico, and other Spanish insular possessions in the West Indies, including Guam; and (3) upon payment of $20 million from America, Spain was to relinquish the Philippines. Thus, it appears that for the first time in American history, a treaty acquiring new territory did not confer U.S. citizenship on the residents, nor did the treaty mention future statehood. America's now owned territories with no prospect for statehood and whose residents lacked the rights of American citizenship. America had become a colonial power.

Many Americans, including African Americans, opposed the treaty because of its colonial implications. Lewis H. Douglass (son of Frederick Douglass) stated: "That whatever this government controls, injustice to dark races prevails....It is hypocrisy of the most sickening kind to make us believe that the killing of Filipinos is for the purpose of good government and to give protection to life, liberty, and pursuit of happiness." African Americans repeatedly debated this issue. They could not believe America's noble plans for Filipinos while they themselves were denied equal citizenship in the United States.

Post-War and Race Relations

After the war, Filipinos, like the Cubans, had expected to gain their independence. However, the treaty that had ended the war simply took their country out of Spanish hands and placed it under American control. Throughout the country, small bands of Filipinos began to rebel. Incidents between American and Filipino soldiers grew into island-wide armed conflict. On February 4, 1899, the Philippine-incurred war began against the Americans and lasted until 1902. American soldiers fought the rebels for two years. Their leader, Aguinaldo, was forced into hiding in the mountains. Order was finally restored in 1902. It cost $400 million, and 4,200 Americans and 220,000 Filipinos lost their lives during this conflict that resulted in the Philippines coming under America's control.

America considered the color problem it had at home when it passed its policy toward the new possessions. The United States did not want to upset the race equilibrium within its boundaries. In Puerto Rico, one-third of the population had African ancestry, and many White Puerto Ricans had Black blood. So, the United States passed the Organization Act to restrict their political rights and to prevent them from influencing African Americans to fight for greater political opportunities. Therefore, in order to maintain economic and political control over the people, the United States acquired the right to appoint all major officials on the islands.

An expansion of America's Black empire also came with the purchase of the Danish West Indian Islands in 1917. The Treaty acquired, for the United States, the Virgin Islands from the Danish in August of 1916 for $25 million, and established a military government that lasted until 1931 when President Hoover created a civil government for the islands that became the Virgin Islands. In 1937, President Roosevelt appointed William Hastie to be the Federal Judge of the islands. In 1946, President Truman designated Hastie as governor of the islands.

America also acquired control over Santo Domingo, which changed its name to the Dominican Republic. After its separation from Haiti in 1844, this country, made up mainly of Blacks and mulattoes, failed to establish stable political and economic conditions. It, therefore, succumbed to American "dollars diplomacy" established during Taft's presidency. Such a policy supported U.S. commercial interests abroad for strategic purposes, especially in Latin America. The Roosevelt Administration took control of the

Dominican Republic's customs service and used the proceeds to repay its European creditors. In March of 1917, the United States stationed Marines on the islands. They remained there until 1924. In the long run, it provoked resentment in Latin America.

Haiti's experience with the United States resembled that of the Dominican Republic. During World War I, in 1915, the United States negotiated a treaty with Haiti that allowed it to have control over the country's finances and politics for 10 years. In 1917, the county was placed under complete military rule, and the treaty of 1915 was extended for another 10 years. Many Haitians resented American occupation. A revolt soon broke out. The American Marines killed more than 2,000 Haitians in order to restore order. The opposition continued until 1934. After 19 years of occupation, American troops finally left Haiti.

Another country, Liberia, was regarded as a protectorate of America. In 1909, at the request of Liberia, the United States sent three commissioners to settle boundary disputes between that country and Great Britain and France. During World War I, America's interest in Liberia increased. The Firestone Rubber Company of Akron, Ohio leased 2,000 acres of land for $5 million and had been given the opportunity to lease up to one million acres of rubber land.

Since post-reconstruction, Blacks had assumed an important part in extending the empire of the U.S. American ministers to Haiti were Black. In 1877, John M. Langston went to Haiti and officially served as the American representative. Frederick Douglass became the American minister to Haiti in 1890. From 1871 until the present, most of America's ministers to Liberia have been Black.

Blacks had hoped that a new era would bring prosperity. Instead, they experienced an increase in social and political problems in urban areas. Hopes had increased with Black soldiers in the Spanish-American War, but they soon faded. President Theodore Roosevelt had led Blacks to believe that he favored equality. He invited Booker T. Washington to the White House. He was criticized by Southerners for this action. He also appointed William Crum, an African American, to the collectorship of the Port of Charleston, South Carolina. Once more, Southerners attacked the president.

Between 1897 and 1911, President William McKinley had appointed twice as many African Americans to federal positions as any previous president. In Theodore Roosevelt's second term (1901-1909), African Americans realized that conditions had not improved; instead they encountered new problems with the rise of cities. In 1900, approximately 72 cities had more than 5,000 Blacks.

Upon their arrival to urban centers, Blacks faced segregation and violence.

Race Riots in America

Race riots swept the country early in the century. In August of 1904, in Statesboro, Georgia, two African Americans were accused of murdering a White farmer, his wife, and three children. They were convicted and sentenced to be hanged. A mob came in and dragged them out and burned them alive. This signaled terrorism against African Americans. Many had their homes destroyed during the riots. Events in Statesboro indicated that all African Americans were susceptible to racial violence.

The South's most sensational riot occurred in Atlanta in September of 1906. Whites attacked African Americans at random, killing four, injuring many more, and destroying many homes. In the same year, another riot occurred in Brownsville, Texas, involving three companies of the 25th Regiment comprised of African American soldiers. They were discharged from the military for their actions without the benefit of hearings, by order of President Roosevelt. His actions convinced African Americans that he had no interest in their welfare.

The South did not represent the only area in America hostile to African Americans. Whites frequently attacked African Americans in large northern cities. Rioting in the North was as vicious as in the South. The most sensational riot in the North occurred in 1908, in Springfield, Illinois. A mob of whites lynched two African American men, injured others, destroyed Black-owned businesses, and dispersed only when five thousand troops from the state militia appeared. In the North and South alike, little effort occurred to prosecute the leaders of such attacks. Throughout the nation, riots occurred on a regular basis. Black leaders expressed concern and discussed methods to protect the rights of Blacks.

Race Relations and Lynching

In the midst of lynching and violence against African Americans, Jim Crow laws emerged to segregate and to strip African Americans of their civil rights. The emergence of Black communities in urban areas and a significant African American labor force in major industries presented a new challenge to White Southerners. They could not control African Americans in urban communities in the same informal ways they had been able to use to control rural African Americans, who were more dependent on White landowners and merchants than their urban counterparts.

Jim Crow statues passed by the legislatures of the Southern states created a racial caste system in the American South. They were named after an ante-bellum minstrel show character. The minstrel show became one of the first indigenous forms of American entertainment. The tradition began in February of 1843 when a group of four White men from Virginia, billed as the "Virginia Minstrels," applied Black cork to their faces and performed a song-and-dance act in a small hall in New York City. The performance was such a success that the group was invited to tour other cities and imitators sprang up immediately. These troupes were successors to individual performers who imitated African American singing and dancing. One of the earliest and most successful individual performers was Thomas Dartmouth "Daddy" Rice.

Rice, a White actor, was inspired by an elderly slave in Louisville, Kentucky. He saw crooning and dancing to a song that ended with the same chorus:

Weel about and turn about and do jis so,
Eb'ry time I weel about I jump Jim Crow.

Rice's imitation of the slave's song and dance routine took him from Louisville to Cincinnati to Pittsburgh to Philadelphia and finally to New York City in 1832.

Jim Crow laws started in 1880s and imposed legal punishments for consorting with members of another race. In 1883, The U.S. Supreme Court declared unconstitutional the Civil Rights Act of 1875. This act prohibited racial discrimination in the selection of juries and in public transportation and public accommodations. The Court also ruled that the Fourteenth Amendment prohibited state governments from discriminating against people due to race but did not restrict private organizations or individuals from doing so. Thus, railroads, hotels, theaters, and other public facilities could legally practice segregation. Eventually, the Court also validated state legislation that discriminated against African Americans. In 1896 it legitimized the principle of "separate but equal" in its ruling on *Plessy v. Ferguson*. The Court ruled that separate accommodations did not deprive African Americans of equal rights if the accommodations were equal. In other words, according to the Court, "separate but equal" facilities did not violate the equal protection clause of the 14th Amendment. In 1899, the Court went even further by declaring in *Cumming v. County Board of Education* that laws establishing separate schools for Whites were valid even if they provided no comparable schools for African Americans.

Along with discrimination and segregation, the lynching of African Americans occurred nationwide. Between 1882 (when reliable statistics were first collected) and 1968 (when the classic forms of lynching had disappeared), 4,743 persons died of lynching, 3,446 of them Black men and women. Mississippi (539 Black victims, 42 White) led this grim parade of death, followed by Georgia (492, 39), Texas (352, 141), Louisiana (335, 56), and Alabama (299, 48). From 1882 to 1901, the annual number nationally usually exceeded 100; 1892 had a record 230 deaths (161 Black, 69 White). Although lynchings declined somewhat in the 20th Century, there were still 97 in 1908 (89 Black, 8 White), 83 in the racially troubled postwar year of 1919 (76, 7, plus some 25 race riots), 30 in 1926 (23, 7), and 28 in 1933 (24, 4).

George Henry White, the last former slave to serve in Congress and the only African American in the House of Representatives, proposed a bill in January of 1901 that would have made lynching of American citizens a federal crime. He argued that any person participating actively in or acting as an accessory in a lynching should be convicted of treason. White pointed out that lynching was being used by White mobs in the Deep South to terrorize African Americans. He illustrated this by showing that of the 109 people lynched in 1899, 87 were African Americans. Despite White's passionate plea, the bill was easily defeated.

African Americans fought against lynching in various ways, but especially by publicizing the record of brutality. One of the most prominent opponents of lynching was Ida B. Wells. Born in Mississippi in 1862, she attended a school set up by the Freedmen's Bureau and worked as a rural teacher from 1884 to 1891. In 1891, in Memphis, Tennessee, she helped to found, and began to write for, the black newspaper, *Free Speech*. She attacked lynching, arguing that several local victims had been targeted as a means of eliminating successful Black businessmen. In response, a mob destroyed her newspaper office. She moved north and, throughout the 1890s, spent most of her time crusading against lynching, speaking in the North and in England, and writing a pamphlet, *A Red Record* (1895).

The NAACP also fought a long campaign against lynching. In 1919, it published *Thirty Years of Lynching in the United States: 1889-1918*. The NAACP also paid for large advertisements in major newspapers to present the facts about lynching. To show that the members of the organization would not be intimidated, it held its 1920 annual conference in Atlanta, considered at the time to be one of the most active Ku Klux Klan areas in America.

Lynchings increased, with Mississippi, Alabama, Georgia, and

Louisiana leading the nation. In 1900, more than 100 African Americans were lynched; and by World War I, it had increased to more than 1,100. African Americans, regardless of gender, faced constant assaults and violence. Marie Thompson, an African American woman in Lebanon, Kentucky, killed a White man in self-defense, and while jailed was captured by a White lynch mob. According to the *Louisville Courier-Journal*, Thompson fought the mob to the end:

> The woman was struggling and fighting like a tiger all the time, but the mob was too much for her, and a minute later she was swinging in the air, with her feet several inches from the ground. All of a sudden she twisted around and grabbed a man by the collar, jerked a knife from his hands and cut the rope that was choking the life out of her.

Despite her gallant efforts, Thompson while escaping was "shot down in a hail of gunfire."

The high court rulings led to a profusion of Jim Crow laws. By 1914, every Southern state had passed laws that created two separate societies: one African American, the other White. Blacks and Whites could not ride together in the same railroad cars, sit in the same waiting rooms, use the same washrooms, eat in the same restaurants, or sit in the same theaters. African Americans were denied access to parks, beaches, and picnic areas; they were barred from many hospitals. What had been maintained by custom in the rural South was to be maintained by law in the urban South.

Beginning in 1915, victories in the Supreme Court began to chip away at the Jim Crow Laws. In *Guinn v. United States* (1915), the Supreme Court supported the position that a statute in Oklahoma law denying the right to vote to any citizen whose ancestors had not been enfranchised in 1860 (grandfather clause) was unconstitutional. In *Buchanan v. Worley* (1917), the Court struck down a Louisville, Kentucky law requiring residential segregation. African American leaders discussed outrage against increased violence toward African Americans and discussed ways to devise solutions to address race problems. In 1905, W. E. B. DuBois and other Black leaders met secretly in Canada, near Niagara Falls, and drafted demands for racial equality, including civil rights and equality in job opportunities and education and an end to segregation. The Niagara Movement grew steadily, despite opposition from Booker T. Washington, T. Thomas Fortune, and their allies.

Members of the Niagara Movement met again in Boston in 1907, and later they convened in Odenton, Ohio. The Springfield riot compelled White progressives in 1909 to sponsor a biracial conference with members of the Niagara Movement to seek ways to improve race relations. The conference led to the founding in 1910 of a new organization, the National Association for the Advancement of Colored People (NAACP), destined to provide important leadership in the fight for black equality.

The NAACP established a biracial board of directors and pledged to work for the abolition of forced segregation, equal education for all, the complete enfranchisement of African Americans, and for the enforcement of the 14th and the 15th Amendments. Among those who participated in its founding were Jane Addams, Mary White Ovington, William Dean Howells, Oswald Garrison Villard, William English Walling, Henry Moskowitz, Ida B. Wells, John Dewey, and W.E.B. DuBois, who became Director of Publicity, responsible for editing the organization's magazine, *The Crisis*. African American radical and editor of the *Guardian* newspaper, William Monroe Trotter, refused to support the NAACP because he distrusted the motives of the White founders.

In its first year, the NAACP launched programs to increase industrial and economic opportunities for African Americans, to oppose lynching, and to provide greater police protection in the Black community. It also fought for the rights of African Americans in the judicial system. It won two important court cases beneficial to African Americans: *Guinn v. U.S.* (1915) and *Buchanan v. Warily*, (1917). In *Guinn v. U.S.*, the Supreme Court ruled that states could only establish literacy standards that would not violate the 15th Amendment. The *Buchanan v. Warily* case dealt with city ordinances seeking to segregate African Americans in residential districts. The court held that a law to prevent the sale of property to a person because of his race would overstep the states' police power, since it would directly violate a clause in the 14th Amendment, prohibiting state interference with property rights except by due process of law.

Racist Propaganda and Race Relations

Anti-Black newspapers increased to promote White supremacy. The writings often portrayed African Americans as inferior and submissive; thus, they were destined to be controlled by Whites. The writers used their works to justify discrimination and segregation against African Americans. The writings of Thomas Dixon, a White supremacist, resulted in the most notable racist motion picture produced, *The Birth of a Nation*. Scholarly and popular literature, newspapers, and journals reinforced social injustice.

White writers produced a variety of racist works to degrade African Americans. Frederick L. Hoffman's *Race Traits and Tendencies of the American Negro* (1896), Philip Alexander Bruce's *The Plantation Negro as Freeman* (1889), Charles Carroll's *The Negro, A Beast* (1900), Robert A. Shield's *The Negro, A Menace to American Civilization* (1907), and Thomas Dixon's *The Leopard's Spots* (1902) and *The Clansman: An Historical Romance of the Ku Klux Klan* (1905) negatively affected race relations. These writers expressed the opinion that different races had certain "fixed traits" that nature had ordained through "years of evolution." According to Dixon, African Americans represented an "inferior species to Whites, and nothing could be done to change that reality."

Many of these writers believed that freedom had produced a new generation of young African Americans who had not known the discipline of slavery and were now retrogressing into a state of "heathenism and brutishness" that threatened not only the South but also White society. The African American man as a rapist and murderer emerged at the core of racist propaganda. Consequently, these writers justified and promoted White violence as a means to discipline "unruly" African Americans.

Political and Economic Strategies to Obtain Equality

African Americans undertook efforts to make political and economic gains to improve their status in society, in the midst of violence, White supremacy, and increased segregation. With increased racial violence, restrictions multiplied to ostracize African Americans from the political process. The Ku Klux Klan used violence to keep Southern African Americans from voting. In efforts to strengthen their party's power, Republicans continued to solicit votes from Southern African American voters. However, in most cases, African Americans failed to gain substantial political rights, but they managed to succeed in establishing their own businesses in the Black community.

Black businesses patronized African American clients because many White establishments would refuse services to them. Therefore, African Americans managed to establish prosperous businesses. Alexander Hamilton established a successful construction enterprise in Atlanta. Alonzo Herndon had an upscale barbershop in Atlanta that patronized well-to-do White men. He also founded the Atlanta Life Insurance Company, the largest African American owned stock company in the world. H. A. Loveless in Montgomery, Alabama, owned a funeral home, a hack and dray company, a coal and wood yard, and a real estate agency.

African American women also succeeded in business ventures. Maggie Lena Walker and Madame C. J. Walker were among the most successful women business owners. Maggie Lena Walker, secretary-treasurer of the Independent Order of St. Luke, a mutual benefit society, organized and founded St. Luke Bank and Trust Company of Richmond, Virginia. She made significant accomplishments in the society and the banking industry. The purpose of the Order of St. Luke was to provide assistance to its members in sickness, in old age, and in meeting funeral expenses. Mrs. Walker collected the dues and maintained the books. She encouraged members to save and invest their money. When she became secretary-treasurer, the order had only 3,408 members, no reserve funds and no property. By 1924, she had increased the organization's membership to 100,000, acquired a home-office building valued at $100,000, organized an emergency fund of $70,000, and had established a newspaper, *The St. Luke Herald.* In 1902, she founded and became president of the St. Luke Penny Savings Bank, later renamed The St. Luke Bank and Trust Company, a depository for gas and water accounts and for city taxes. Ms. Walker not only excelled in business, but also in the community for helping those who helped themselves.

Madame C. J. Walker may have been the most successful African American business owner. Sarah Breedlove Walker, born in 1869, on a Louisiana cotton plantation, became a millionaire cosmetic manufacturer. She married C.J. Walker at age 14 and became widowed at 20. She took in laundry to make a living and experimented in her spare time with a concoction of oils to condition her hair so that she could remove the kinky curls. In 1905, she developed a hot iron, or straightening comb, which would remove the tight curls. Her comb appealed to millions of African American women. She opened a cosmetology school to train her operators, employed agents to sell her products, and built a factory to make her products. She employed more than 2,000 agents, maintained a payroll of more than $200,000, and acquired a substantial fortune from her factory and school in Indianapolis. At a cost of about $250,000, she built a mansion at Irvington-on-the-Hudson, New York. She was deeply concerned with the poverty of others and became a philanthropist. She bequeathed $100,000 toward an academy for girls in West Africa and granted donations to African American institutions and charities.

African American family around the turn of the century. Library of Congress.

Social Clubs and Organizations in the Black Community

The Black community benefited from organizations founded to improve social and economic conditions for African Americans in urban centers. The Committee for Improving Industrial Conditions of Negroes in New York and the National League for the Protection of Colored Women merged to form the National League on Urban Conditions among Negroes. It was later named the National Urban League, with George Edmund Haynes and Eugene Kinckle Jones as executive officers. It received support from Julius Rosenwald, Booker T. Washington, and Kelly Miller, a professor at Howard University. The

League undertook efforts to assist newly arrived African Americans in their adjustment to urban centers. It developed a program for the training of young men and women for social work, established scholarships, and offered training programs.

The YMCA and YWCA also assisted urban African Americans. By 1906, branches were established for African Americans in Washington, D.C., Philadelphia, New York, and Baltimore. They provided education and social improvement programs. Efforts also occurred to improve housing, as exemplified by the Octavia Hill Association in Philadelphia. In urban centers where African Americans migrated, they benefited from cultural and social organizations that helped them to sustain a quality of life while coping with economic, political, and social problems.

Conclusion

The late 19th Century presented new complex challenges for African Americans. They were compelled to participate in America's quest to dominate new territories populated with people of color controlled by the Spaniards. The Spanish-American War involved African Americans who desired to help liberate the Cubans, Filipinos, and Puerto Ricans under Spain. Their participation helped America defeat Spain and become a world power. African Americans hoped that their status would improve in America due to their contributions toward the war efforts. However, they were disappointed because race relations had worsened. Lynchings and violence against African Americans, including Black soldiers, spread nationwide. Obstacles to economic and social equality persisted; however, African Americans managed to progress.

Black businesses were founded in the Black community, as well as cultural and social organizations evolved to help African Americans cope with injustices. The National Association for the Advancement for Colored People (NAAC) addressed discrimination and segregation. The Urban League assisted African Americans in urban centers with economic and social needs. African Americans were able to deal with nes challenges in a racist society due to their efforts to uplift themselves.

Review Questions

1. Why did African Americans support the Spanish-American War?

2. How did the Spanish-American War affect the status of Blacks in America and race relations?

3. How and why did Jim Crow laws emerge in the South as the Black population in urban centers increased?

4. What actions did the NAACP take to improve conditions for African Americans?

5. Why did lynching seem to increase during and after the war?

6. What Black businesses emerged in the Black community?

Chapter 14

African American Pursuit for Education and Social Uplift

This chapter is about Black education, economics, and social activities that affected African Americans while struggling to deal with discrimination and segregation. African Americans stood at the forefront in guiding and supporting education for the advancement of the race. Progress in education served as their strongest weapon in the struggle for equality.

The Black church assumed a primary role in providing education in the Black community. Church affiliated denominational boards existed to promote education for African Americans. In many instances, primary assistance for Black schools came from organizations associated with denominational boards, such as the American Missionary Association that provided co-education at Berea College in Kentucky and the Freedmen's Aid Society of the Methodist Episcopal Church which, by 1878, included secondary schools, a college, two medical schools, and three theological schools that accepted

Blacks. The Home Mission Society aided Black Baptists, Presbyterians, Episcopalians and Catholics, and supported activities to aid Black education. They often provided schools, supplies and teachers, as well as school buildings. Black denominations also helped to establish secondary schools and colleges.

Not only did African Americans benefit from the Black church in terms of education, they also gained from financial support granted by wealthy White philanthropists. Many White donors had ties with African American leaders acceptable to White society, such as Booker T. Washington, an eminent African American spokesman.

Education and Black Leadership of Washington and DuBois

Booker Taliaferro Washington was one of the foremost Black educators of the late 19th and early 20th

Tuskegee Institute offered classes in domestic training and the industrial trades.

Centuries. He had a major influence on Southern race relations and was a dominant figure in Black public affairs from 1895 until his death in 1915. He was born a slave on a small farm in the Virginia backcountry in 1858 or 1859; he wasn't sure which. "I know nothing of my ancestry beyond my mother," he later wrote. Washington moved with his family after emancipation to work in the salt furnaces and coal mines of West Virginia.

With 50 cents in his pocket, he went to Hampton Institute in 1872, in search of an education. After acquiring a secondary education at Hampton Institute, he taught at a common school and experimented briefly with the study of law and the ministry, but settled for a teaching position at Hampton. In 1881, Washington founded Tuskegee Normal and Industrial Institute patterned after the Hampton model in the Black Belt of Alabama. He fused practical and academic training in his new educational methods with emphasis on agricultural and vocational training. He excelled in establishing Tuskegee as a major learning institution for African Americans.

White society embraced Washington because he encouraged African Americans to work hard to earn acceptance from the White majority and to stay in their place without conflict. Washington fully expressed his sentiments regarding the role of African Americans in a famous speech delivered at the Cotton States Exposition Fair in Atlanta in 1895. The statements he made persuaded White society and African Americans to acknowledge him as the leader for African Americans.

Washington advised African Americans to acquiesce in disfranchisement and social segregation to insure that Whites would encourage Black progress in economic and educational opportunities. He eloquently outlined his philosophy in the speech. Black people, he told his segregated audience, would find genuine opportunities in the South: "When it comes to business, pure and simple, it is the South that the Negro is given a man's chance in the commercial world." Washington added that African Americans should not expect too much but should welcome menial labor as a first step in the struggle for progress: "Nor should we permit our grievances to overshadow our opportunities."

Washington reassured White society that cooperation between the races should exist in the interest of prosperity, and that it would not endanger segregation. He stated: "In all things that are purely social, we can be as separate as the fingers, yet one as the hand in all things essential to mutual progress." Finally, he implied that African Americans should not protest denied rights that White men possessed. Instead, he urged them to struggle steadily rather than make defiant demands. His speech was praised by both White and Black listeners and by those who read it when it was widely reprinted. He received extensive and mostly positive coverage in Black newspapers. Some of that popularity stemmed from admiration for his leadership and agreement with his ideas. T. Thomas Fortune, African American editor of the *New York Age*, stated that Washington had replaced Frederick Douglass (who died in 1895) as a leader. Washington further increased his popularity with the founding of the National Negro Business League in 1900, his widely read autobiography, *Up from Slavery* (1901), his celebrated dinner at the White House in 1901 with President Theodore Roosevelt, and control of patronage politics as the chief African American advisor to Presidents Theodore Roosevelt and William Howard Taft.

Washington elaborated on his Atlanta speech in 1896 when he accepted an honorary degree from Harvard University, thereby becoming the first African American to receive that honor. "During the next half century and more," Washington told his Harvard audience, "my race must continue passing through the severe American crucible. We are to be tested in our patience, our forbearance, our perseverance, our power to endure wrong, to withstand temptations, to economize, to acquire and use skill and our ability to compete, to succeed in commerce . . . . This is the passport to all that is best in the life of the Republic, and the Negro must possess it, or be debarred."

Activist African American leaders, among them William Edward Burghardt DuBois, believed that Washington had surrendered the principles for which they had struggled to acquire. Five months after Washington's Harvard speech, John Hope, the president of Morehouse College, responded: "If we are not striving for equality, in heaven's name, for what are we living? I regard it as cowardly and dishonest for any of our colored men to tell White people or colored people that we are not struggling for equality. If money, education and honesty will not bring to me as much privilege, as much equality as they bring to any American citizen, then they are to me a curse and not a blessing. . . ." Despite such criticism of Washington, he continued to establish his reputation as a leader for the Black community and, in doing so, he not only promoted education, but also farming and business programs for African Americans.

Washington's commitment to agricultural and industrial education served as the basis for his approach to "the problem of the color line." By the beginning of the 20th Century, he was convinced that African American men and women who had mastered technical and vocational skills at institutions like Tuskegee and Hampton would be recognized, if not welcomed, as productive contributors to the Southern economy. He believed that economic acceptance would lead, in due course, to political and social acceptance.

Washington became extraordinarily powerful. In the words of his assistant, Emmett J. Scott, Washington was "the Wizard of Tuskegee." He was especially effective in dealing with prominent White businessmen and philanthropists. William H. Baldwin, vice president of the Southern Railroad, was so impressed with Washington's management of Tuskegee that Baldwin agreed to serve as the chairman of Tuskegee's board. He also acquired support from the major industrialists, including steel magnate Andrew Carnegie and Julius Rosenwald, the head of Sears, Roebuck and Company. They had faith in his decisions and regularly consulted him before contributing to Black colleges and universities.

Washington advised African Americans to avoid politics, but oftentimes he ignored his own advice. Although he never ran for office, nor was he appointed to a political position, Washington influenced politics for African Americans.

In 1901, President Roosevelt invited Washington to dinner at the White House, where the president's family and a Colorado businessman joined them. African Americans highly praised Washington, but the White South, alarmed by such a flagrant breach of racial etiquette (African Americans did not dine with White people), resented such action.

Washington and Roosevelt regularly consulted each other on political appointments. In the most distinguished case, Washington convinced Roosevelt to appoint William D. Crum, a Black medical doctor, as the collector of customs for the port of Charleston, South Carolina. With Washington's persuasion, Roosevelt appointed African American attorney and former all-American football player William Lewis as U.S. District Attorney in Boston.

Most of Washington's political activities were not revealed. He secretly helped finance an unsuccessful court case against the Louisiana grandfather clause, which disfranchised African American male voters whose grandfathers had not acquired the right to vote. Washington provided funds for two cases that challenged Alabama's grandfather clause to the U.S. Supreme Court, which ultimately rejected both on a technicality. He attempted to persuade railroad executives to improve conditions on segregated coaches and in-station waiting rooms. He worked covertly with White attorneys to free an African American farm laborer imprisoned under Alabama's peonage law. In many of these secret activities, Washington used code names in his correspondence to hide his involvement. In the Louisiana case, he was identified only as X, Y, Z.

Washington was a complex man. Many people found him unassertive, dignified, and patient. Yet he was ambitious, aggressive, and opportunistic, as well as shrewd. As a conservative leader, he did not directly or publicly challenge White supremacy. He was willing to accept literacy and property qualifications for voting if they were equitably enforced regardless of race. He also opposed women's suffrage. He attacked lynching only occasionally with trepidation. African American leaders continued to express disappointment with Washington and disputed his leadership. William Monroe Trotter, Harvard educated publisher of the Boston *Guardian*, became an outspoken opponent of Washington. The main purpose of the *Guardian* was "propaganda against discrimination based on color and denial of citizenship rights because of color." Trotter opposed all compromises on civil rights, whether they were proposed by Washington or the president. He described Washington as "the Great Traitor," "the Benedict Arnold of the Negro Race," and "Pope Washington." Trotter hated Washington's leadership and compromising position, and joined forces instead with William Edward Burghardt (W.E.B) DuBois, Washington's most critical adversary. Prior to joining forces with DuBois, Trotter was arrested at a 1903 National Negro Business League in Boston when he attempted to enter the stage to confront Washington. He

remained in jail for this incident referred to as "the Boston Riot."

Another critic of Washington, Du Bois graduated from Fisk University in 1888, a historically Black institution at Nashville, Tennessee. He became the first African American to earn a Ph.D. (in history) from Harvard University in 1895. His doctoral dissertation, *The Suppression of the African Slave-Trade to the United States of America, 1638-1870*, was published in 1896. Although DuBois had earned an advanced degree in history, he was well trained in the social sciences; and at a time when sociologists were theorizing about race relations, he was conducting empirical inquiries into the condition of African Americans. He expressed little tolerance for African Americans unwilling to demand their civil and political rights.

Du Bois often clashed with Washington, who preached a philosophy of accommodation and urged African Americans to accept discrimination for the time being and elevate themselves through hard work and economic gain to win the respect of the Whites. In 1903, in his famous book, *The Souls of Black Folk*, DuBois argued that Washington's strategy, rather than freeing the Black man from oppression, served only to perpetuate it. This attack revealed opposition to Booker T. Washington among many African American intellectuals. It divided the leaders of the African American community into two wings—the "conservative" supporters of Washington and DuBois' "radical" companions.

DuBois attacked Washington for failing to stand up for political and civil rights and higher education for African Americans. He found even more infuriating Washington's willingness to compromise with the White South and Washington's apparent agreement with White Southerners that African Americans were not their equals. DuBois stressed that he agreed with Washington on some issues, but disagreed even more about significant ones and that on these issues it was necessary to oppose Washington, especially when it came to education and suffrage for African Americans.

Both leaders, Washington and DuBois, stressed the importance of education for African Americans, albeit their views differed in terms of the best type of education for African Americans. DuBois supported higher education in the liberal arts with an educated "talented tenth" responsible for leading the race, whereas Washington promoted vocational training and the skilled trades. They may have differed in their promotion of education for African Americans; however, they understood the importance of education in order to make gains. Thus, education became a major concern in the African American community.

Philanthropy and Black Education

In 1928, America had 560 African American teachers; from 1900 to 1928, more than 1.5 million African American children attended school. Thirty-four institutions for African Americans offered collegiate training. A large number of African Americans attended universities and colleges in the North. Virginia, Arkansas, Georgia, and Delaware provided state colleges for African Americans. By 1900, more than 2,000 African Americans had graduated from institutions of higher education.

Many Southern Whites wanted to limit education for African Americans to elementary schooling. Others felt that African Americans should not have special consideration as a group for which a designated amount or kind of education should be provided. Despite such concerns, large educational foundations supported by philanthropists funded education for African Americans in the South. Grants in aids for Black education stimulated self-help, helped improve public education and, as a result, supplemented teachers' salaries, brought equipment and school supplies, and provided school buildings. Grants were also used for common school education.

The General Education Board was incorporated to support education programs for African Americans. Its major objective was to improve education in the South by providing assistance to private and public institutions to educate African Americans.

Large foundations affiliated with wealthy White industrialists gave major contributions to assist Black education. Robert C. Ogden, H. H. Rogers, Collis P. Huntington and William Baldwin, railroad businessmen, and Andrew Carnegie, steel industry founder, were among the primary donors. John Rockefeller donated $1 million to promote education, regardless of race, sex, or creed.

The Peabody Education Fund, John F. Slater Fund, Anna T. Jeanes Fund, Julius Rosenwald Fund, and the Phelps-Stokes Fund served as the leading foundations. George Peabody founded the Peabody Institute of Baltimore. He established museums at Harvard and Yale; in 1861, he established an education fund for destitute areas in the Southern and Southwestern states. Most importantly, Peabody assisted in the establishment of a permanent system of public education in the South.

John Slater donated $1 million to improve education for African Americans in the South. Between 1882 and 1911, he assisted both private and church schools in teacher training programs and made donations to public schools. In 1911, he funded country training schools.

Anna T. Jeanes donated $200,000 to the General Education Board. This fund was known for supporting Black rural schools in the South. Julius Rosenwald in 1910 donated money to improve education among African Americans. He displayed a special interest in rural Black schools. Caroline Phelps-Stokes also showed a special interest in African American education. She donated funds to improve existing schools.

Philanthropists did little to encourage equitable distribution of public funds for the education of all Southern children. White Southerners felt that if philanthropists supported Black education, then public taxes ought to be used for White education.

Church philanthropy addressed the social needs of African Americans and supported agencies to promote its own interests. On the other hand, educational foundations were primarily interested in gaining recognition in mainstream society.

Labor and Migration of African Americans from the South

African Americans migrated from Mississippi, Louisiana, Alabama, and Georgia, and moved to the North and West to seek better opportunities. Nearly 50,000 African Americans went to Kansas and other Northern areas, but tens of thousands were forced back to the South by armed White men who patrolled the riverfronts and roads. Many Southern Whites did not want African Americans to leave because they needed to keep them as laborers.

By the mid-19th Century, nearly 1,000 African Americans worked in the California mines; by 1860, there were more than 4,000. African Americans lived in the mining sections of Nevada and Colorado in the 1850s. Some African Americans became important and influential members in their communities. Mifflin W. Gibbs was a successful businessman who started California's first Black newspaper; Biddy Mason was an ex-slave who became a nurse and famous for her charity work in Los Angeles.

Black farmers played an important role in the West. George Washington Bush, a freeborn mulatto, joined an overland emigrant party in 1844 and moved to the Pacific Northwest where he helped to build the region's first American-owned gristmill and sawmill, and he introduced the first mower and reaper. His son, William Owens Bush, also a master farmer, served two terms in the Washington state legislature. George Washington, another successful African American farmer, founded the town of Centralia, Washington, in 1872.

The development of the Western cattle industry in the 1860s offered another opportunity for Blacks. African Americans comprised nearly one-fourth of the cowboys on the cattle drives. When the long drives ended, many worked as ranch hands or became rodeo performers. Some were outstanding. Nat Love performed in Wild West shows and wrote the only autobiography of a Black cowboy. Bill Pickett invented the rodeo event of "bulldogging." John Wallace acquired his own land and became a member of the Texas and Southwest Cattle Raisers Association.

By the last half of the 19th Century, an African American group known as "Exodusters" moved to the west to build homes and communities. They came out of the Egypt of the South to what they hoped was the promised land of Kansas. Benjamin "Pap" Singleton of Louisiana, Henry Adams of Louisiana, and Edward P. McCabe of Tennessee were leaders in the "Exodus" to the Midwest. Pap Singleton headed the Tennessee Real Estate and Homestead Association. He was a former slave and U.S. Army veteran. According to Singleton, "The reasons for the Exodus were White violence, peonage, abuse of Black women, inadequate education facilities, and political intimidation." Adams claimed to have persuaded 98,000 African Americans to migrate westward. Edward P. McCabe established economically viable and politically independent all-Black towns in Kansas and Oklahoma. Nicodemus in Northwest Kansas became the most successful and permanent of the Exoduster settlements, and it still exists today.

Urban Migration and Labor Challenge

Urban African American workers, both in the North and the South, made attempts to join labor unions and were prevented from joining. They often faced prejudice against them and denied adequate job training necessary for craft union membership. White workers claimed that African Americans were unfit for skilled mechanical work.

The Knights of Labor became the first White labor union to accept African American workers. The American Federation of Labor adopted a resolution to accept membership regardless of color or race. African Americans organized independent unions such as the National Association of African American Steam and Gas Engineers.

African Americans exhibited the belief that conditions for them would improve as a result of Theodore Roosevelt's Presidency in 1901, as well as Washington's influence as a leader as exemplified by his importance in the appointment of William Crum to collectorship of Port of Charleston, South Carolina. They changed their positions during Roosevelt's second term when they realized that he did not intend to resolve issues concerning the civil rights of African Americans.

African Americans in urban centers had to deal with serious conditions. Upon their migration, slums increased and juvenile delinquency grew rampant in areas populated by African Americans. As their presence increased, restrictions were placed in many facets of life. They faced discrimination and segregation throughout the nation.

African American leaders took action to address problems in the Black community that resembled those in other urban areas due to migrations from Southern and rural areas. News reporters, identified as "Muckrakers" by Theodore Roosevelt, supported legislation to correct urban social ills (slum conditions, unemployment, crime, drugs, corruption, etc.). Violence in the cities disproportionately affected African Americans. In the latter part of the 19th and early 20th Centuries, lynching and race riots increased. More than 100 African Americans were lynched in the first year of the new century. Racial conflicts escalated into race riots, with the most famous ones occurring in August of 1904 in Statesboro, Georgia; September 1906 in Atlanta, Georgia; and August 1906 in Brownville, Texas, that involved African American soldiers. Race riots also erupted in Northern cities. The worst Northern riot occurred in Springfield, Illinois in 1908. White mobs roamed the Springfield streets for two days in August, killing and wounding African Americans, wrecking homes, and causing many to leave the city. White homes marked by white handkerchiefs were not attacked.

Black leaders held a meeting to discuss methods to address problems facing African Americans. In 1905, the Niagara Movement headed by W.E.B. DuBois evolved from this meeting. Later, it led to the founding of the National Association for the Advancement of Colored People (NAACP) in 1909 that included among its board of directors W.E. B. Du Bois, Ida B. Wells, Jane Addams, William Dean Howells, John Dewey, Mary White Ovington, Oswald Garrison Villard, and William English Walling. DuBois served as Director of Publicity and Research and became responsible for editing the organization's publication, *The Crisis*. Jesse Fauset served as the managing editor. The first edition of *The Crisis* appeared in November of 1910. The magazine's name came from James Russell Lowell's poem, "The Present Crisis." The magazine aimed to "set forth those facts and arguments which show the danger of race prejudice...."

The Committee for Improving Industrial Conditions of Negroes in New York and the National League for the Protection of Colored Women were formed to protect the rights of African Americans. In 1911, the National League on Urban Conditions, renamed the National Urban League, was founded, with Eugene Kinckle Jones as Executive Secretary. It offered assistance and provided programs to help African Americans adjust to urban life, developed programs for young men and women, and offered social work training. The Young Mens' Christian Association (YMCA) and the Young Women's Christian Association (YWCA) established local branches for African Americans. Some organizations established settlement houses to aid destitute people; two of these are the Octavia Hall Association of Philadelphia and the Model Homes Company of Cincinnati.

Although many cultural and social programs existed to uplift African Americans, economic challenges continued to persist. It was difficult for African Americans to make a living. In 1880, more than 75% of African Americans in the U.S. still resided in the South, and they had to accept agricultural work. They were forced to engage in sharecropping and tenancy farming, which did not allow them to prosper, since they were not paid with money and remained indebted to the White landowner. Those who received compensation were paid low wages.

It was also difficult for African Americans to acquire farmland, even if they had the funds, because many Whites were reluctant to sell land to them since they did not want to share power associated with land ownership in the South. Thus, Black farm owners were few in number. In the South, they owned 158,479 farms, while Whites in South owned 1,078,635 farms.

Booker T. Washington addressed this problem at a conference at Tuskegee for African American farmers. They received literature on farm improvement. After 1907, with contributions from philanthropists, the Southern Board of Education hired demonstration agents to provide training in farming. Regardless of Southern reliance on farming, it failed to appeal to many African Americans; and since farming did not provide a decent living, many opted to move to the Midwest and urban areas for better opportunities, as well as to escape unfair and cruel treatment from White landlords and merchants. They looked forward to a better quality of life.

Some African Americans considered going to Africa and solicited support from the American Colonization Society. African American leaders debated among themselves over leaving the South. Frederick Douglass opposed the exodus because, as he said, "The government would protect Blacks wherever they lived and that emigration offered no permanent remedy." He also feared that "Blacks would become nomads and lose possible strength in the South where they were concentrated." Despite such concerns, African Americans elected to leave the South to secure jobs in factories created due to industrialization. For the most part, African Americans in Southern towns were prevented from securing jobs in industries and factories. However,

they would acquire them in Midwestern and Northern cities.

By 1910, the African American labor force had increased to more then 350,000. Most African Americans generally had to accept lower paying jobs.

Black Entrepreneurs and Black Inventors

African Americans entered the fields of business and industry. They embarked upon a program of Black business enterprise. African Americans established many types and sizes of businesses. They operated grocery stores, drug stores, restaurants, shirt factories, lumber mills, co-operatives, and real estate agencies. They also founded banks and insurance companies. In 1888, Rev. W. W. Browne organized in Richmond the first bank solely administered by African Americans, the Savings Bank of the Grand Fountain United Order of True Reformers. African Americans established other banks, such as the Capital Savings Bank of Washington and the Alabama Penny Savings Bank. A majority of the banks did not survive because African Americans could not sustain them with adequate capital.

African Americans contributed to industrialization as scientists and inventors. Scientific contributions were made by George Washington

Carver, a chemurgist (a scientist using chemical and industrial skills to make organic raw materials), made over 300 synthetic products from peanuts including women's cosmetics, 100 products from sweet potatoes, and 75 products from pecans. He also created dehydrated foods. Carver never patented any of his discoveries, refused to accept any profits, and donated his discoveries to humanity. Inventions made by African Americans during the time included the following:

Toggle harpoon created by Lewis Temple (1848)—that revolutionized the Whaling Industry, Sailing Apparatus by James Forten (1850), Automatic Lubrication System for Railroads and Heavy Machinery by Elijah McCoy (1892), Gas Mask by Garrett A. Morgan (1914)—saved many lives during WWI, Automatic Traffic Signal by Garrett A. Morgan (1923), Automatic Shoe Making Machine by Jan Matzeliger (1883)—revolutionized the making of shoes, First Open Heart Surgery by Dr. Daniel Hale Williams (1893), Automatic Car Coupling Device by Andrew Beard (1897), Mechanical Seed Planter by Henry Blair (1834), Mechanical Corn Harvester by Henry Blair (1836), Sugar Refining System by Norbett Rillieux (Dec. 6, 1846)—revolutionized the Making of Sugar; Multiplex Telegraph system by Granville Woods (Oct. 11, 1887)—allowed messages to be sent and received from moving trains, Railway Air Brakes by Granville Woods (Apr. 10, 1903)—provided the first safe method of stopping trains, Elevator by Alexander Miles (Oct. 11, 1888), Steam-boiler/radiator by Granville Woods (June 3, 1884), Folding Bed by L. C. Bailey (July 18, 1899), Curtain Rod Support by W.S. Grant (Aug. 4, 1896), Overshoes or galoshes by A. L. Rickman (Feb. 8, 1898), Lantern or lamp by M.C. Harney (Aug. 19, 1884), Telephone by Granville Woods (Jan. 7, 1885)—which was far superior to Alexander Bell's invention, and the Trolley Car by Granville Woods (May 29, 1888).

Social and Cultural Life in the Black Community

In the new century, African Americans continued to relocate for better economic opportunities. As a result of their migration, Black communities evolved in the cities. In 1900, 72 cities reported a population of more than 5,000 African Americans. In Charleston, Savannah, Montgomery, Jacksonville, Shreveport, Vicksburg, Baton Rouge, and other Southern cities, African Americans outnumbered Whites.

African Americans faced difficulty in securing employment in cities. This difficulty existed because employment opportunities were inadequate to satisfy the number of people coming into the urban areas. Therefore, African Americans were excluded from jobs reserved for White workers. Furthermore, most of the jobs in the factories and industries required labor union membership, and many organized labor unions restricted African Americans. White industrialists would exclude African American workers and imply that they were inefficient. However, in most cases, African American laborers were not hired due to discrimination from White employers.

Housing problems also arose for Blacks. Segregation ordinances established White blocks and Black blocks. Extreme congestion created small unsanitary homes with large families that led to poor health and high mortality rates.

African Americans believed it was more important for them to remain separate from Whites socially and culturally more so than economically. To reflect their independence, they founded fraternal orders of truth, with secret rituals and benefit associations, such as the Masons, Odd Fellows, Black women's Order of the Eastern Star and Sisters of Calanthe. These secret orders and others offered sickness and death insurance and provided aid to members' widows and orphans.

Beneficial and insurance societies grew during this period. The Young Mutual Society of Augusta, Georgia and the Beneficial Society of Virginia represented benefit societies in the Black community. Mutual benefit societies led to the establishment of Black insurance companies. The National Benefit Life Insurance Company became the largest African American insurance company. In 1898, North Carolina Mutual Life Insurance Company was founded, and next was Atlanta Life Insurance Company. African Americans undertook efforts to help the underprivileged by establishing orphan homes, hospitals, and sanitaria. The Carrie Steel Orphanage, organized by a Black woman, was supported exclusively by Blacks.

Literary and Social Activism

The result of social and cultural strivings led to the emergence of African American intellectuals and writers. In 1881, Frederick Douglass wrote *The Life and Times of Frederick Douglass* and, in 1900, Booker T. Washington wrote *Up From Slavery*. African American historian George Washington Williams wrote *History of the Negro Race From 1619 to 1880* published in 1882.

In 1896, the first scientific historical monograph, *The Suppression of the African Slave Trade*, was written by renowned African American leader W.E.B. DuBois. In 1892, African American women wrote significant works. Ida B. Wells published *Southern Horrors: Lynch Law in all Its Phases* in support of anti-lynching legislation, Anna Julia Cooper wrote *A Voice from the South: By A Black Woman of the*

South, and Frances Ellen Watkins Harper wrote *Lola Leroy, or Shadows Uplifted,* the first novel published by an African American in the post-bellum years of the Reconstruction period. It included poetry and short stories.

African Americans also wrote fiction with emphasis on race. In 1880, William Wells Brown published *My Southern Home.* Paul Laurence Dunbar was the best known African American author of the period. He wrote many novels, including *Sport of the Gods* (1902); two books of short stories, *Folks From Dixie* (1898) and *The Strength of Gideon* (1900); and several volumes of poems, including *Majors and Minors* (1895) and *Oak and Ivy, Lyrics of the Lowly Life* (1896). Charles Waddell Chestnut's novel and short stories were also popular; they included *The Conjured Woman* (1899), *The Wife of His Youth and Other Stories of the Color Line* (1899), *The House Behind the Cedars* (1900), and *The Marrow of Tradition* (1901). More so than Dunbar, Chestnut focused on life behind the color line as well as interactions across the color line

Black magazines also became prevalent. *The Southern Workman* and *the AME Review* addressed education, literary and religious matters. Black newspapers also became prevalent. In 1901, George Forbes and William Monroe Trotter published *The Guardian.* Another popular newspaper, *The Baltimore Crusade,* denounced Washington's programs and demanded equality for African Americans. At the turn of the century, African Americans were in a stronger position due to educational, business, social and cultural activities.

Community Service and Activism

The emergence of the club movement among Black women and other self-help organizations enabled more prosperous African Americans to aid those suffering from poverty and prejudice. African American women decided that they needed an organization within the church that would provide them with a similar degree of independence.

By the 1890s, a significant number of women's clubs evolved across the country, including a parallel movement among upper-middle class African American women. The Colored Women's League of Washington, organized in 1892, established a kindergarten for African American children. African American women discovered that they were neither allowed to become members of the General Federation of Women's clubs, nor could they be represented at the 1893 World's Fair. Inspired by the ability of national clubs to tackle national issues, in 1896, they decided to create the National Association of Colored women (NACW). It established girls' homes, hospitals, and other social agencies.

Membership in the NACW came mainly from the urban elite, teachers, wives of professionals, ministers, and businessmen. Mary Church Terrell became a leading figure in the NACW. As a graduate of Oberlin College in 1884, she was among the first African American women to complete a college education. After graduation, she taught at Wilberforce, Ohio, and then at the Preparatory School for Colored Youth in Washington, D.C. Mary became one of the first women Presidents of the Bethel Literary and Historical Association. The association discussed major issues and questions of the day. There was negative reaction to her leadership, but it was concluded that "she could preside with ease and grace, plan with foresight and execute with vigor." After marrying Robert Terrell, Mary resigned her teaching post to spend the rest of her life as a lecturer, women's rights activist, and leader of the Black women's club movement.

The NACW adopted the motto "Lifting as We Climb" with the intention of demonstrating to "an ignorant and suspicious world that our aims and interests are identical with those of all good aspiring women." Terrell established an ambitious and forward-thinking agenda for the organization that focused on job training, wage equity, and childcare. The organization raised funds for kindergartens, vocational schools, summer camps, and retirement homes. In addition, the NACW opposed segregated transportation systems and was a strong and visible supporter of the anti-lynching movement.

Ida B. Wells-Barnett became the most outspoken member against lynching. As editor and co-owner of the newspaper, *Memphis Free Speech*, she critiqued Southern injustice and lynching. In 1892, she was forced to flee to Chicago, when her newspaper office was destroyed, where she continued to carry out a militant campaign against violence toward African Americans.

Founded in 1900, the Women's Convention brought many African American women into the emerging Women's Club Movement. The National Association of Colored Women grew from 5,000 members in the late 1890s to 50,000 in the 1910s and 100,000 a decade later. The members stood at the forefront in confronting issues affecting the Black community.

Toward the end of the century, African American leaders held conferences that included women to address African American issues. At Lake Mohonk, they held a conference to discuss education, religion, and economic problems affecting African Americans. In 1890, the African American League of the United States was founded to promote Black self-help and to fight segregation and discrimination. It also sponsored conferences on race matters. Between 1896 and 1914, W.E.B. DuBois sponsored the Annual Conference on Negro Problems. To address concerns in the Black community, African American intellectuals produced scholarly studies on African American life. DuBois wrote the *Encyclopedia on the American Negro Problems*.

Growth of the Black Church

The Black church served as an important agent to maintain group unity and self-help. African American conservative members who controlled the churches clashed with progressive, especially among the Baptists. The progressive members withdrew from the Baptist and Methodist denominations and joined Congregational, Presbyterian, Episcopalian and Catholic churches.

African American Baptists congregations also clashed with Whites over control of the Black Baptist Association and Conventions. In 1886, African Americans organized the National Baptist Convention to reduce the influence of the White national associations. They founded their own publishing house, the National Baptist Publishing House. It distributed its own Sunday school literature.

The Black church also promoted education, encouraged Bible reading, functioned as a welfare agency, offered community service projects, established or supported homes for the aged and orphans, organized day care centers, served as an employment

agency, and provided domestic training. African Americans undertook additional efforts to become socially self-sufficient. They focused on cultural, musical, and social activities to reflect their talents.

Music and Dance (Cakewalk, Minstrel Shows)

African American entertainers publicized their many talents during the period. They depicted exceptional musical skills. Madame Marie Selika (real life name Mrs. Sampson Williams), whose stage name was chosen to honor the heroine of Meyerbeer's *L'Africaine*, became recognized as an outstanding soprano singer. Henry F. Williams, a renowned cornetist and violin player, as well as a composer, played in the famous Jubilee Orchestra of Boston as well as the Gilmore Band. Boston musician, Frederick Elliott Lewis was a pianist, organist and violinist. Justin Holland played the guitar and flute. He published more than 300 pieces of music. His arrangements of popular songs at that time, such as "Home Sweet Home," were widely distributed. Thomas Green Bethune, known as "Blind Tom," was the most famous African American pianist of the period. He played music from memory on the piano. A contemporary of his remarked: "He is a sort of doorkeeper besides: and when he opens the portals, music

Minstrel show characters in black face comedy provided popular
entertainment with negative stereotypes of African Americans.

seems to issue forth to waken the soul to ecstasy."

African American musical companies prospered during this period—among them the Progressive Musical Union of Boston and the Philharmonic Society of New Orleans. African Americans excelled as dance performers in cities such as Boston, Philadelphia, Detroit, and New York. James Bland, a former Howard University student, wrote popular minstrels and songs.

The Minstrel shows portrayed African Americans as irresponsible, happy-go-lucky, wide-grinning creatures who laughed loudly, rolled their eyes, danced, played the banjo, ate watermelon, sang songs, and kept their audience in hysterical laughter through the use of slapstick comedy. The princes of comedy, Bert Williams and George Walker, made the cakewalk famous. Both men starred in the famous Williams and Walker shows. They set the tone for comedy portraying African Americans. In addition to entertainment, African Americans identified with their own in sports.

Sports (Jack Johnson)

At the turn of the century, boxing became the athletic arena in which highly guarded claims existed to substantiate the superiority of White manhood. Since 1882, White boxers had refused to fight African American boxers for fear that their notions of superiority would be undermined if they were defeated. In 1903, the reigning White champion, Jim Jeffries, refused to fight African American challenger Jack (John) Johnson, stating that "When there are no White men left to fight, I will quit the business....I am determined not to take a chance of losing the championship to a Negro." In 1908, Jim Jeffries defeated Tommy Burns in Australia to become the world's heavyweight boxing champion. Upon Jeffries' retirement, Tommy Burns, the new champion, was defeated by Johnson who threatened the image of White males with his outstanding boxing talents. In 1908, Jeffries came out of retirement to regain the title, but he faced defeat from Johnson. Angry and disappointed, Whites attacked African Americans throughout the nation partly in response to this episode.

Johnson, born in Galveston, Texas, in 1878, exhibited an attitude unacceptable to White society in the midst of discrimination and segregation. He was portrayed as the rebel who challenged White authority with flair even in potentially dangerous situations. He consorted openly with White women, eventually marrying two of them while champion. As the world heavyweight boxing champion, Johnson dominated the boxing field to the extent that a long search was conducted for a "great White hope" to defeat him. To many African Americans, Johnson was an icon in

Black society. He won 57 bouts against his White opponents. In 1912, he was arrested for violating the Mann Act, known as the White Slave Law, which made it illegal to transport women across state lines for immoral purposes. He had been traveling with his White fiancée. Although found guilty through the courts, Johnson refused to go to jail and, instead, fled to Canada and later to France with his new wife. In 1915, he lost his title to Jess Willard in Cuba, in a controversial bout. Many believed that Johnson "threw" the fight to avoid jail time in America. He eventually served 10 months in jail in 1920 for his conviction under the Mann Act.

Conclusion

African Americans faced insurmountable challenges in the late 19th and early 20th Centuries, as they attempted to take their rightful places in American society. Discrimination and segregation continued throughout the nation. Jim Crow laws set the tone for Southern society that relegated African Americans to second-class citizenship. African Americans faced lynching, race riots, segregation, as well as unemployment. To cope with these obstacles, they refashioned their lives in many ways. African Americans placed great emphasis on education and religion. They made significant gains in both fields due to their own efforts and support from White philanthropists. The Black church had an important role in supporting Black education. African Americans also improved their status by leaving Southern rural areas for better opportunities. Migration to urban centers helped African Americans improve their quality of life by securing jobs in the industries, establishing businesses, and creating viable cultural and social agencies in the Black community. They also achieved recognition in sports, with boxing at the forefront. Upon these achievements, African Americans should have been prepared to face challenges forthcoming in the new century. The advent of events leading to World War I provided them with a new perception of American society.

Review Questions

1. What efforts did African Americans make to promote Black education?

2. How did Black education benefit from philanthropy and denominati onal efforts in the early years of the century?

3. Compare and contrast the philosophies of Black leaders Booker T. Washington and W.E.B. DuBois. Explain what factors determined their stances on Black education.

4. What circumstances caused African Americans in the South to migrate to Western and Northern states?

5. African American women undertook major tasks to uplift the Black community. What methods did they use to improve conditions for African Americans?

6. How significant was Jack Johnson's athletic career for African Americans, and how did it affect race relations?

Chapter 15

African Americans in World War I and the Aftermath

This chapter focuses on the lives of African Americans in the military and on the home front during and after World War I. The world plunged rather unexpectedly into a universal struggle in 1941. Archduke Francis Ferdinand, heir to the Austro-Hungarian throne, was assassinated on June 28 in Sarajevo, then the capital of Bosnia. Blaming the Serbs for the crime, the Austrian government sent Serbia an ultimatum demanding that the offenders be brought to trial by a tribunal in which Austria should be represented. Serbia refused to yield to this and other Austrian demands and won Russian support. Germany upheld Austria, fearing that if such an act passed unpunished it would threaten the crowned heads of all Europe. Germany argued that the Russian army's mobilization was really a declaration of war against her. She declared war on Russian on August 1 and on France two days later; in return, France declared war on Germany. England resented Germany's violation of Belgian neutrality.

Accordingly, the British Empire entered the war against Germany and Austria, the Central Powers. When Germany disregarded her treaty obligations by invading neutral Belgium, Kaiser Wilhelm lost support from other European and American nations, most of whom eventually joined the Allies in the fight to curb the power of Germany.

While in sympathy with the struggle against tyranny, the United States did not regard the sinking of its neutral ships and interference with its commerce sufficient cause for entering the war. America had begun an unprecedented period of business prosperity as a result of supplying wartime goods for the belligerent countries. Many struggling industries suddenly received an unusual impetus. New enterprises sprang up rapidly. Americans used to a paltry living multiplied their wealth almost overnight through timely investment. The nation's prosperity brought on a new day for the laboring man, and these good times also aided African

Americans. The large influx of immigrant labor which reached American shores each year was promptly blocked by the war. As a result, the domestic supply of workers soon proved too scarce to meet demand. The northern and western industrial centers raised wages to attract more laborers. The man-power needs of the munitions makers and other war production industries were so great that the white labor market could not meet the labor demand. Departing from time-honored custom in the North, the needy employers began to bid for African American workers in the South. Thus, skilled African American laborers gained employment in the wartime industries. Eventually, however, the pressure of the war began to be felt more so than the prosperity, as the United States prepared for its own entry into the conflict. President Woodrow Wilson declared that America was going to war to make the world "safe for democracy." African Americans felt that they would be fighting for greater democracy for people in other parts of the world as well as for themselves in their own segregated nation.

African Americans in the Military in World War I

When Congress declared that a state of war existed with Germany on April 6, 1917. African Americans experienced a new era. Although most American citizens thought that Germany should be destroyed, few were anxious to fight in the war in Europe. They had to be persuaded to support the war effort. Some German sympathizers approached African Americans in the hopes of convincing them to oppose the war. Therefore, a few African Americans expressed support for Germany. Many more insisted that before African Americans should join the fight to support Europe against German imperialism, they should experience the privileges of democracy at home. Some African American leaders, such as Asa Philip Randolph, the young socialist and union organizer, opposed the war. W. E. B. DuBois, an intellectual historian and educator, urged African Americans to support their nation.

Anti-war advocates who expected African Americans to be disloyal to the United States, however, had misjudged them. Many African Americans loved America and would have died readily in its defense. They had clung to the hope that white citizens would one day embrace the ideas of democracy for all men. The war was a "God-sent blessing," one black newspaper insisted, because the conflict would give African Americans the opportunity to earn white regard and advance the standing of their race by valiant wartime service.

Some whites urged the government not to recruit African Americans. These same critics spoke against African Americans with skepticism and questioned their loyalty to America. "I know that a [black] knows nothing about patriotism, love of country or morality," said Robert Y. Thomas, a member of Congress from Kentucky. He further stated: "And if [they are in] the Army at all, they should be commanded by white officers. If they are not, they're going to make trouble wherever they go."

Many white Americans continued to pressure the government to exclude African Americans from military service. Some argued that African Americans would be easily intimidated from fighting. These arguments failed to prevent the War Department from accepting African Americans into the military. African Americans enlisted in high numbers, indeed, and wore their soldier "doughboy" uniforms in slightly higher ratios than did their white countrymen. They comprised approximately 9.4% of the population during the war and approximately 9.6% of the total number of the registrants under the Selective Service Act throughout the duration of the war. A higher percentage of African American-to-white registrants was actually accepted for service: about 36 per cent of the African Americans and 25% of the white registrants were accepted. About two million African Americans registered for the draft, and over 400,000 were accepted into the armed services. Among them were 1,300 commissioned officers, 9 field clerks, and 15 army nurses.

Neither France nor Great Britain hesitated to use Black troops in Europe. A force of 208,000 Senegalese helped to defeat the Germans on the Ourcq and Marne. Another 30,000 Congolese and about 20,000 Blacks from the British West Indies also fought at the Allied front. When the United States finally decided to accept African Americans for the American Expeditionary Forces (AEF), some federal officials tried to prevent their acceptance. Many African Americans had to register at separate induction centers to avoid conflict with white troops. At first, the War Department failed to provide for the training of African American officers. All Black troops served under white officers due to the Army's lack of interest in training or commissioning black officers. Some southern congressmen requested to have African Americans confined to stevedore regiments, where they would be assigned as laborers under white officers.

African American leaders vehemently protested against any such arrangement. They accused the War Department of attempting to restrict African Americans to labor units. Although the Secretary of War assured them that African American soldiers would have similar duties as white soldiers, a majority of African American soldiers in the Army served in service units such as the quartermasters, the stevedores, and the pioneer infantrymen, who were responsible for cooking, loading and unloading supplies, digging latrines, and burying the dead killed in battle. Most were part of the Twenty-Third Division while in training in the United States before being reassigned to the French or the Ninety-Second and Ninety-Third Divisions of the U.S. Expeditionary Forces in France, under General John J. Pershing. There were several all-black units, including the Twentieth Engineer Regiment, Tenth Cavalry, 805th Pioneer Infantry, 315th Pioneer Regiment, Fifteenth Infantry Regiment, and four combat regiments: the 369th, 370th, 371st, and 372nd. Most of these troops were trained at Camp Wadsworth, in Spartanburg, South Carolina, before being sent to France. Nearly three-fourths of the 200,000 African Americans soldiers sent to France served as army laborers. Most African Americans joined the army, despite restrictions, because the Navy, Coast Guard, and Marines refused to accept them. About 10,000 African Americans enlisted in the navy, and most of them served as messmen. Only 24 African American women served in the nurses corps, compared with 21,000 white nurses. Furthermore, African American women had entered the corps just one month before the war ended.

While there were several excellent and ultimately well-honored black combat units in the military engaged in the service supply divisions abroad, most of the Black units were assigned at the English and French ports and at depots like Givres. Millions of dollars worth of American goods were handled by 25,000 passing through vast warehouse corridors to begin a 140-mile trip over interior, railroad lines to the front. African American troops unloaded the transports, prepared the trains to carry supplies to the interior, and built depots for storing them. When American forces found hills and forests in their path, the labor battalions built roads from the port of entry to the front. They also buried the dead, salvaged war materiel, and detonated explosives scattered over France by the enemy.

African American Officers in the War

African Americans were told diplomatically that they would be drafted to fight in the same ranks as other soldiers. But at first, the War Department was not sure that the army could use African Americans as officers. The students and faculty of Howard University launched a nationwide campaign to force it to change its policy. The Central Committee of Negro College men demanded a training camp in which well-educated Negroes could be trained as officers. Many African Americans supported this plan. The War Department finally addressed this issue. After some vacillation, in June of 1917, the Wilson administration established a segregated camp to train African American officers. The training site was Fort Des Moines, Iowa.

Many questioned how the Fort Des Moines experiment would workout. They also wondered whether the army would actually commission a large number of African American officers. Both questions were answered by October 15, 1917. On that date, 639 of 1,200 officer candidates received commissions. It was the largest single group of African Americans ever to reach the rank of second lieutenant. It was believed that the Wilson administration granted African Americans' demands for officers in order to gain support for the war. But the army hardly supported the move. Its handling of the case of one high-ranking African American officer revealed its stance.

Colonel Charles Young, a graduate of West Point, became the highest ranking African American officer during the war. He was confident and persistent in his efforts toward excellence and toward commanding the respect of his men. When white troops once refused to salute him as an army officer, Young stripped off his coat and made them salute the buttons. He later served as a professor of military science and tactics at Wilberforce University. At the outbreak of the Spanish-American War, Young had been assigned to the 19th Ohio Regiment and had participated in the Cuban action. After the war he had served overseas as a military attaché. He was later assigned to the 10th Calvary, commanding a squadron in Mexico in 1915. Early in World War I, Colonel Young was retired with a physical disability, but he vigorously protested his retirement. To prove his stamina, he made a dramatic ride by horseback from his Ohio home to Washington, D.C., but to no avail. The army would not assign him to active duty. Later, however, and before the war ended, he was recalled into the army to train African American recruits in Illinois. After the war, he was transferred to Liberia to help organize that country's army. On vacation in Lagos, Nigeria, he contracted a severe fever from which he never recovered. He died there in 1922 and was buried with full honors in Arlington National Cemetery.

African American officers often suffered discrimination, especially those men in the 92nd Division, the unit in which most of the soldiers trained at Fort Des Moines served. Many regarded the division's commanding general, Charles C. Ballou, as unfit. Surrounded by biased white officers, Ballou shaped his policy accordingly. In a famous incident at Camp Funston, Kansas, General Ballou issued an order insisting that the men of his division not raise the "colored question" and stir up racial antagonism when a black sergeant was not to go where they were not welcome. What caused real bitterness among the troops, however, was the General's feeling that the success of the division depended on the good will of the white public.

Wherever African American officers were stationed, a systematic effort was made to get rid of them. Their superiors brought them before efficiency boards as soon as possible in the hope of speeding their retirement or having them assigned to labor battalions. The same thing happened in all-Black regiments. Such was the case in the New York 15th Infantry where the white commander caused the African American officers to be transferred or released from military service for inefficiency. Many senior officers openly stated that they preferred white officers to be assigned to their regiments.

To rid staffs of black officers, many white commanders filed critical complaints against them. They often charged the officers with cowardice under fire. This was the accusation against four officers in the 368th Regiment who were later praised for their bravery. They received orders at the French front to advance and then to withdraw. They obeyed the orders. Their troops were actually unprepared to attack, lacking maps, hand grenades, adequate ammunition and artillery support. The army's high command had no intention of sending these troops "over the top," orders from headquarters later revealed. In the first phase of this offensive, the troops were reserved as combat liaison units between the United States 77th Division and the French *Chasseurs a*

Pieds. These ill-equipped troops were sent into battle, against orders, as part of the zero-hour assault. The white officer in charge of leading the attack was nowhere to be found during the engagement. Even the battalion commander, Major Max A. Elser, was not near enough to the front to be reached. As a result, two companies of the 2nd Battalion became badly disorganized. After he charged the unit's four African American officers with inefficiency, Major Elser was promoted to Lieutenant Colonel. A later probe ordered by Secretary of War Newton D. Baker, however, showed that Elser had gone to the rear as soon as the fire had become intense. This inquiry also cleared the African American officers of all blame. Secretary Baker took the occasion to praise these and other African American soldiers for their valor at the front. Another white officer, Colonel Allan J. Greer, risked a court-martial in hopes of ridding the army of African American officers. He wrote a letter to Senator Kenneth D. McKellar of Tennessee pointing out weakness he had observed in African American officers. "Now that a reorganization of the army is in prospect," he told Senator McKellar, "I think I ought to bring the matter to your attention that is of vital importance, not only from a military point of view, but from that which all southerners have. I refer to the question of Negro officers and Negro troops." Thus, he implied that

African American officers and troops were questionable in the military.

While some high-ranking white officers like Colonel Greer tried to have African American officers dismissed on charges of inefficiency, the French had nothing but praise for the Black soldiers assigned with them. French officers often intervened to prevent an African American officer from encountering humiliation and or a dishonorable discharge from the military. It was obvious to men like the French General Goybet that the African American soldier's only shortcoming as a soldier was his low morale—a condition caused by white racial bias. The charges of general incompetence among African American troops proved baseless. The 370th Regiment of the 8th Illinois Division, a unit led by Blacks, helped to shatter this myth entirely. Its heroes won 21 American Distinguished Service Crosses, 68 French *Croix de Guerre* and 1 Distinguished Service Medal. Another African American regiment, the 369th was under fire longer than any other United States unit. The entire regiment was honored with the *Croix de Guerre,* and 171 officers and enlisted men were also awarded the Legion of Honor Medal.

African American Soldiers in France

African American soldiers while fighting in France to "make the world safe for democracy" were subjected to the social code of discrimination from their white fellow soldiers. Emmett J. Scott, former Secretary to Booker T. Washington, served as a Special Assistant to the Secretary of War. He documented many examples of discrimination and prejudice toward African American soldiers serving overseas. African American troops were ordered to sail on the battle ship to Virginia. After they had gone aboard, however, the officer in charge removed them on grounds that no "colored troops had ever traveled on board a United States battleship." Where it might have been necessary for officers of both races to eat and sleep in the same barracks, special assignments were made to segregate them. White officers were assigned to their own quarters, and African American officers had assignments to theirs. In preparing for a reception for General Pershing at one of the front-line camps, General Logan ordered all troops except African Americans to be ready for an arms inspection. African American troops not at work were to remain in their quarters or tents.

The white commanders made every effort to keep African American soldiers away from the French people. General James B. Erwin issued an order that the African Americans troops should not associate with French women. The African American soldiers disobeyed the order, although the General tried to enforce it. African American officers in school at Vannes accepted invitations to attend French-American charity dances. These dances charged an admission fee. Upon hearing of the dances, one of the commanders prohibited the African American troops from attending. He declared that no officer of the 167th Brigade should be permitted to attend a dance when a fee was charged. White officers at the same school, however, were allowed to attend.

In a document issued on August 7, 1918, according to Emmett Scott, "American army headquarters sought to extend a racial barrier throughout France." General Pershing's headquarters passed a memorandum entitled "Secret Information concerning Black Troops" to a French mission. It proclaimed that French officers in command of African Americans troops should have an understanding of the racial status assigned to African Americans in the United States. The document described African Americans as "a degenerate menace, tolerable only through the maintenance of an impassable gulf between the two races." The French were cautioned not to treat African Americans with familiarity or indulgence, as this would give affront to white Americans." The United States, the memo went on, "feared that comradeship with French soldiers might stir the Negroes with undesirable aspirations on their return to the States." Only business and service associations between the races

were possible, it said. The Black, the directive added, was noted for his want of intelligence, lack of discretion, and lack of civic and professional conscience."

The French army was then advised to prevent intimacy between French officers and African American officers: to discourage its officers from eating with African Americans, shaking their hands or seeking to talk or meet with them outside of the requirements of military service. The memo also asked the French not to commend African American troops too highly in the presence of white Americans. Although it was all right to single out the good qualities and service of African Americans, it suggested, this should be done in moderate terms strictly in keeping with the "truth." The French did not accept the American view, but insisted on "*liberte, egalite, fraternite.*" Whether in Champagne, the Argonne Forest, or at Metz, the African American soldier distinguished himself. A score of African Americans, like Needham Roberts and Henry Johnson of the New York 15th Division, repelled a German raid in May of 1918, against almost overwhelming odds. These soldiers returned to their homes as heroes, decorated by France with the *Croix de Guerre* for their bravery in action.

The strain on race relations, however, continued. Finally, Secretary of War Newton D. Baker, in conjunction with President Wilson, asked President Robert R. Moton of Tuskegee to go abroad and make an investigation into the problems reported there. One commanding officer had complained of the high incidence of crime among his Black troops. Upon checking the facts, however, Moton learned that out of a total force of over 12,000 men, only six had committed serious offenses. While in France, the Tuskegee president also spoke to the men, counseling them, and reassuring them of the victory that would be theirs when they were fighting to create and to maintain.

African Americans on the Homefront

The African American community supported the war effort in many ways. They purchased more than $250 million worth of bonds and stamps to help finance the war debt. Mary B. Talbert, President of the National Association of Colored Women, reported that African American women alone had purchased more than $5 million worth of liberty bonds. African Americans also helped to conserve food for the war effort. The United States became dependent on African Americans to produce and conserve food, since a significant number of African Americans labored as cooks and farmers. Not only did African Americans labor in these capacities, but they also worked in the

defense industries. The war had created employment opportunities in northern industries and stimulated the Great Migration. During the war, an estimated 700,000 to one million African Americans left the South for northern and western cities. They were determined to benefit from the war by working in the defense industries.

The migration of African Americans to the North increased throughout the period of the war. The North was regarded as the land of promise. Married men often moved ahead of their families. They obtained

Southeast Missouri African American Farm Family

work and housing before sending back or returning for kin and friends. A Burton, South Carolina, migrant stated: "I do not care to move my family before I can locate myself, by coming and spending at least six months." Some African Americans pooled their resources and moved in groups to industrial centers, since ten or more people could obtain reduced railroad rates. African Americans formed numerous migration clubs. African American women also left the

South for their own specific reasons. Upon their arrival to the cities, they sometimes had to accept work as domestics, with long hours and low pay. Whereas African American men often moved through a series of jobs in a variety of southern and northern cities before reaching their final destination, African American women usually made one non-stop trip.

The National Urban League, founded in 1910, offered assistance to newly arrived African Americans in the cities. It offered employment, housing, and training assistance. A major goal of the organization was "to secure and train Negro social workers." On the eve of World War I, the organization sponsored its first social work fellows; and by 1919, it had maintained constant contact with black college women and men, encouraging them to pursue a career in social work. It's magazine, *The Opportunity*, kept the Black community informed on current economic and social issues as the Black industrial class dramatically grew.

African American men acquired jobs in meatpacking, auto, steel, and other mass production industries. In Cleveland, Pittsburgh, Detroit, and Milwaukee, for example, the percentage of African American men employed in industrial jobs increased from an estimated 10 to 20 percent of the Black labor force in 1910 to about 60 to 70 percent in 1920 and 1930, respectively. African American women also gained industrial jobs during the labor shortages of World War I. They acquired employment not only in jobs traditionally held by white women in textiles, clothing, and food production, but also in glass, leather, paper, iron, and steel manufacturing as well. Industrial jobs represented nearly 15 percent of the African American female labor force. Despite gains in employment, African Americans encountered increased discrimination and segregation during and after the war.

Race Relations and African American Reaction

"The problem of the twentieth century," W. E. B. DuBois had prophetically written as early as 1903, "is the problem of the color-line, the relation of the darker to the lighter races of men in Asian and Africa, in America and islands of the sea." This prediction in *The Souls of Black Folk* has particular application to the mood and temperament of the period following World War I.

The war in Europe had been a broadening, if brutal, experience for African American and white soldiers alike. African Americans, however, returned from France and England with a new attitude. They had risked their lives in "the war to end all wars;" yet, the old order of prejudice and exclusion remained at home. Despite the loyalty shown by African American soldiers, they were treated with contempt upon returning to the South. The army uniform on an African American created in "the racist the same reaction as a red cape waved in the face of a bull." African American soldiers shouting for equality and justice were beaten, shot down, lynched—in general, terrorized. They had violated no law; yet, the mobs reasoned that lynching a few African Americans would serve as an example to the rest. The violence would remind them of "their place."

The postwar hysteria finally reached the nation's capital itself. A number of white enlisted men had been antagonized by reports of Negro assaults on white women. Upon hearing a rumor that a marine's wife had been molested, they proceeded, on July 19, 1919, to the southwest section of Washington, DC where they assaulted several African Americans. The next day, white soldiers and sailors joined with white civilians to spread the terror. African Americans were pulled from autos and streetcars and assaulted into unconsciousness. One was seized by a mob and beaten unmercifully, right in front of the White House. Other African Americans were shot and left to die in the streets.

The mob had misjudged the Negroes of Washington, D.C. After the whites tried to invade Negro areas the following day, the Blacks took the offensive. The white mob wounded about 300 Negroes one night; the next night, four whites and two Negroes

died in the fray. A similar riot occurred in Chicago a few weeks later. The white population was incensed to the point of touching off a race war. This was the direct result of Negro migration to Chicago's industrial plants and their invasion of desirable residential districts. The clash took place at a bathing beach, following upon bombing of homes bought during this period by Negroes. The Black population fought back in Chicago, too. A number of whites died in the violence.

A serious riot had erupted two years earlier in Houston after the American Expeditionary Forces entered the war. Negro soldiers based in Texas had been insulted repeatedly by whites. The issue exploded on August 23, 1917, when over a hundred Negro soldiers marched into Houston armed with rifles. This demonstration followed a number of disputes with local patrolmen and military police. The morning after the riot, it was announced that 13 had died (including one Negro) and that 19 were wounded (among them five Negro soldiers). These troops had been sent to guard government property at Camp Logan. The arrival of so many Negro troops alarmed some white citizens in Houston. Six hundred soldiers were expected. Some of the troops resented the segregation rules they had to observe. Prior to the riot, white officers had been regarded as sympathetic to the Negro soldiers. Prohibitionists, however, concerned about soldiers drinking in the local saloons, fomented discord by encouraging a local newspaper to publish an editorial entitled "Remember Brownsville an editorial," which further inflamed tempers.

The mayor of Houston ordered an investigation of the riot and the incidents which led to it. The testimony and other data showed that the outbreak was due to several factors: problems of segregated transportation, mistreatment of Negro women by white police, poor ties between Negro military police and white civilian police, and retaliatory action of a small band of Negro soldiers.

Twenty-five such conflicts broke out in 1919. In a disorder occurring in Elaine, Arkansas, white men fired on a Black church meeting. One white man was killed in the aftermath. Mobs of whites roamed the streets, killing and beating any African American they found. Several African Americans were arrested and another white killed. Finally, federal troops were called in to quell the outbreak. The accused African Americans were tried without the assistance of legal counsel and were found guilty after 45 minutes. The NAACP took the case and entered an appeal to the Supreme Court, which reversed the decision and ordered a new trial.

The riots and other incidents caused by severe prejudice publicized the plight of the Black person in America. Many whites became aware of its severity for the first time. Because of this, the NAACP grew in militancy and in membership. Between 1917 and 1920, dues-paying members rose from 10,000 to nearly 90,000. NAACP branches formed everywhere. They multiplied from 80 in 1917 to 356 in 1920. African American men and women had gone from frustration to hope and back to despair in their struggle for equality. The long period of rioting was a reaction to a seemingly hopeless situation. When it ended, the African Americans began to try once again to find realistic means of obtaining justice for themselves and for their children.

End of World War I

Upon the war ending in 1918, African American soldiers expected better treatment, but they were soon disappointed. Their return from military duty was greeted with joy in the Black community. New York's African American regiment was greeted with a parade in Harlem of approximately one million supporters. Other cities such as Buffalo, New York, St. Louis, Missouri, and Chicago, Illinois welcomed African American troops. African Americans were determined to secure a larger share of democracy. Many Whites felt threatened by this new attitude and feared that African Americans would make demands for first-class citizenship. To prevent, this White supremacist groups became more widespread. Ku Klux Klan membership increased in southern and northern areas. Klan chapters increased to a militant union of more than 100,000. They opposed African Americans, Orientals, Roman Catholics, Jews, and all foreign-born individuals. The Klan made more than 200 public appearances in 27 cities shortly after World War I ended. Membership within the Klan grew nationwide to include the New England states, as well as New York, Indiana, Illinois, Michigan, and other northern and midwestern cities. Klan members held public office. In addition to Klan activities, lynching increased during the post-war period.

More than 70 African Americans were lynched during the first post-war period. Ten Black soldiers, several still in their uniforms, were lynched, mostly in the South. Fourteen African Americans were burned publicly and 11 were burned alive. African Americans reflected a new attitude with determination to defend themselves if necessary. They refused to accept violence and terror against them without fighting back.

The summer of 1919, known as the "Red Summer," was the greatest period of interracial strife the nation had ever witnessed. From June to the end of the year, 25 race riots erupted throughout the nation. Serious problems in race relations intensified due to competition between Whites and African Americans for jobs in urban centers, segregation in housing, and discrimination in accommodations. The most serious racial outbreak occurred in Chicago in July. The African American population in the city had more than doubled. Attempts made to keep African Americans out of White neighborhoods led to a riot in Chicago that started at Lake Michigan Beach—then spread to the South Side—and lasted for 13 days, with 38 people killed, 15 Whites and 342 African Americans. More than 1,000 families, mostly African Americans, became homeless.

Riots occurred in Knoxville, Tennessee; Omaha, Nebraska; and Elaine, Arkansas; and other cities. In 1921, a riot occurred in Tulsa, Oklahoma, with nine Whites and 21 Blacks killed. A riot occurred in Detroit in 1925, when Whites attempted to keep an African American physician from residing in a White neighborhood. The NAACP came to his defense. Many Whites stated that it was foreign influence, especially association on the basis of equality, of the French during the war that caused African Americans to fight back.

Black organizations protested the denial of first-class citizenship to African Americans. The NAACP later passed a resolution addressing the status of African Americans. The National Race Congress passed resolutions of protest. In 1919, the NAACP held a conference on lynching. Later in the year, it took steps toward securing the passage of a federal law against lynching. The bill failed to pass in Congress because southern Senators had organized a filibuster to prevent a vote on the measure.

The NAACP also investigated crimes committed against African Americans and published documents on them. In 1919, it published *Thirty Years of Lynching in the United States 1889-1918*. Walter White, a light-skinned African American, served as an investigator. In 1929, he wrote *Rope and Faggot: A Biography of Judge Lynch* based on his findings over a 10-year period. In 1921, more than 200 meetings were held to address problems encountered by African Americans. The same year, the NAACP brought cases to courts to halt oppression and discrimination. The case of *Nixon v. Henderson* succeeded in having the U.S. declare null and void a Texas statute that excluded African Americans from Democratic primaries in the states.

The Commission on Interracial Cooperation, another interracial organization interested in race problems, organized in 1919, set out to attack racial prejudice. It worked primarily in the South due to the efforts of Will Alexander and other prominent White Southerners who established an educational program on race relations. Through its monthly publication, *The Southern Frontier*, it advocated for equality, the abolition of lynching, and voting rights.

Despite the efforts of the NAACP and the Commission, many African Americans felt excluded, especially those in the lower socio-economic ranks. They appealed to a new leader named Marcus Garvey who created the largest mass movement among Blacks before the 1963 March on Washington. He arrived from Jamaica in the Caribbean in 1916. He preached the doctrine of Black unity and a return to Africa for the Black race. He aimed to establish a Pan-African government. He gave Blacks a new sense of pride in their ancestry by stressing the military, political and artistic triumphs of their African heritage. He emphasized the beauty of Blackness, telling of a Black God, Black Christ, a Black Virgin Mary, and Black disciples. Many African American intellectuals did not support Garvey who used race pride to attract followers. W. E. B. DuBois became Garvey's most powerful opponent.

Garvey headed the Universal Negro Improvement Association (UNIA), which was very popular. He instituted a program to send Blacks to Africa. He applied to the League of Nations for permission to settle Blacks in colonies in Liberia. He sent a delegation to the Versailles Peace Conference and requested the German colonies in Africa to be granted to his African government. When this failed, Garvey warned the European governments that their colonization in

Africa would be brief. He advised Africans to overthrow their colonial rulers.

Garvey's newspaper, the *Negro World*, discussed racial prejudice. He established auxiliary organizations, such as the *Universal Black Cross Nurses*, the *Universal African Motor Corps*, the *Black Eagle Flying Corp*, and the *Black Star Steamship Lines*. Garvey used his steamship enterprise that consisted of three ships to establish commercial relations with Africa, as well as to enable African Americans to migrate to Africa. When it failed, his backers lost large sums of money. Garvey's conduct of his steamship ended his success. He was found guilty of using the mail to defraud and was sentenced to prison for five years. In 1927, President Coolidge pardoned him and ordered his deportation. He was sent back to Jamaica where he died in 1940. His movement had made history as the first mass movement among African Americans.

Another leader, Father Divine, also known as George Baker, led a social and religious movement that began in 1919, with a small group in Sayville, New York. His mission started with charitable work, but this was a temporary solution since he considered welfare degrading to those who received it and a burden on society. Divine's long range goal was to bring prosperity through cooperation and economic opportunity. He established peace missions in many eastern cities and midwestern communities. Peace Mission members in Harlem operated 25 restaurants, six grocery stores, ten barber shops, ten dry cleaning stores and 24 wagons which sold clams and oysters or fresh vegetables. Later, they opened up businesses in upstate New York. The Mission also ran a coal business with three trucks that picked up the coal at the mines in western Pennsylvania and delivered it to Harlem. The foods sold at the grocery stores and on the carts were also bought in bulk for a discount, so that customers ultimately saved money. His sermons promoted business as a calling from God to serve people. "Do not go in business for the purpose of seeing how much you will gain," he said, "but go in it to see how much you can give." He eventually built his peace missions up to 22,000 members across North America and into Europe.

Conclusion

In 1917, America entered into World War I. At the beginning, opposition occurred against allowing African Americans to participate in the military. Many African Americans supported the war with the belief that it would result in democracy and equality in America. African American leaders debated whether they should support the war. Eventually, African Americans became primary participants in the war as soldiers. As civilians they also contributed to the war efforts. They continued to encounter discrimination and segregation, in spite of their contributions. They became determined to gain equality in the military and on the homefront.

The war had created industrial jobs. As a result, African Americans left rural areas to secure employment in the industries, despite opposition from whites. The Great Migration of African Americans to urban centers occurred during the war that enabled many to improve their living standards. The Urban League aided African Americans in urban centers.

They benefited from social programs offered by the organization. Although efforts existed to aid African Americans in their transition, obstacles materialized in the form of violence. The KKK increased attacks against African Americans. Lynching increased during the war. African Americans fought back with a new determination as a result of their war experiences. Black leaders addressed discrimination and segregation toward African Americans. New Black leaders emerged. Marcus Garvey and Father Divine were two such leaders. They made significant contributions toward uplifting African Americans.

Review Questions

1. Compare and contrast the leadership of Marcus Garvey and Father Divine.

2. Why did most African Americans support the War? How did they justify their support or opposition?

3. Did opposition exist against allowing African Americans in the armed forces during World War I? Explain.

4. Why did African Americans leave the rural South during the War? What circumstances caused the migration during this period?

5. What factors contributed to violence against African Americans during and after World War I?

6. What were the homefront experiences of African American women during the war?

Chapter 16

The Black Renaissance

The Black Renaissance, also known as the Harlem Renaissance, represented an astonishing period for African Americans. It was a time when African Americans expressed pride in their heritage and race. They reflected a new awareness in many artistic, cultural, and social arenas. This chapter examines the activities of African Americans to reflect how they exposed their talents to the world and, in doing so, helped to alter negative impressions of African Americans. World War I and events on the home front caused African Americans to leave the rural South for better socioeconomic opportunities.

The Great Migration and African Americans

The "Great Migration" began with World War I, when African Americans began leaving the South in large numbers. They left for many reasons. From 1916 to 1919, nearly 70,000 African Americans migrated from the rural South to northern cities to seek better lifestyles and working conditions. Influenced by accounts of city life, thousands of African Americans left the South without knowing what trials and tribulations awaited them. The combination of word-of-mouth advice, active recruiting by northern labor agents, and promises of free transportation often supplied the reason and mode for migrating North. The Chicago *Defender*, an African American newspaper, published articles exposing the blatant racism of White southerners, political oppression, and the perpetual threat of lynching. Every migrant lost something as soon as he or she left the rural South. Some left behind families and congregations. Others lost the respect of their southern relatives and ministers. In search of social justice and equality, African-Americans sought opportunity in the urban, industrial regions of the North and West and, as a result, gave birth to a mass migratory movement.

Since most southern African Americans engaged in farming, they suffered due to increased mechanization in farming that left them as sharecroppers with little to do. But with its booming cotton economy, the Mississippi Delta still attracted a steady influx of migrants from the rest of the South. At its inception, sharecropping in the Delta held the promise of a decent standard of living and independence. In theory, with a good harvest, everyone stood to make money. In reality, planters exploited the system to their advantage, and sharecroppers often ended up in debt at the end of each year. With no income during the off season, sharecroppers were forced to buy food, clothing and other necessary supplies on credit from the plantation commissaries. Prices were exorbitant, goods were shoddy, and debt piled up. When harvest time came around, tenants were often forced to sell their share of the crop directly to the plantation at below market prices. After the harvest, the tenants often failed to earn enough to cover their debts. While Delta planters enjoyed great prosperity, their tenants were stuck in an endless cycle of debt. As plantations consolidated and centralized, what little opportunities for advancement the croppers once had slipped away. Entrenched in poverty, sharecroppers began heading North for industrial jobs.

Extreme poverty was not the only reason African Americans left the Delta. In the 1920s, the threat of racial violence loomed over the South. The law in the Delta had never offered much protection for African Americans. With the rise of the Ku Klux Klan in the 1920s, the violence

and intimidation only intensified. In fact, there were far fewer lynchings in the Delta than in the rest of Mississippi, but this provided little solace for the Delta African American community, which still lived in fear of mob violence and lynching.

The migration was also spurred by the lack of educational opportunities in the Delta. While the Percy family had ensured that African Americans in Washington County had access to decent education, this wasn't the case in the rest of the Delta. White school boards seldom hired enough teachers for African American students, and the teachers they did bother to hire were almost never college graduates. In one county, there were only three teachers for a population of 350 students. During the harvest season, matters only got worse. Across the Delta, officials refused to open schools until every last bit of the harvest had been brought in. At times, schools didn't open for the year until mid-November.

After the Great Flood of 1927, there was less reason than ever to stay in the Delta. Homes were destroyed, possessions were lost and crops were ruined. One Greenville sharecropper put it succinctly when he explained that he had to "get my family out of this cursed South land—down here a Negro man is not good as a White man's dog." Leaving, however, was easier said than done. Delta planters' fortunes depended on African American labor, and they were determined to keep tenants on their plantations. While some offered better conditions to induce sharecroppers to stay, others resorted to intimidation and brute force to keep tenants from leaving. Tenants wishing to leave generally slipped away under the cover of darkness, not telling anyone of their plans, lest word spread to the plantation house. Train stations were guarded, and African Americans found on trains were pulled off and sent back to their plantations. To escape, croppers fleeing the Delta often walked 10 or more miles to board a train in another town.

For African Americans, the favored destination was Chicago. From 1920 to 1930, the African American population exploded in Chicago, increasing from 109,458 to 233,903 residents in just a decade. The Great Migration of people was accompanied by a musical migration; Delta Blues music traveled to Chicago and put down new roots in the city. Although the North was no promised land, conditions were better for African Americans, and migrants who left seldom returned. With its sizzling Jazz and Blues, substantial middle class, and political clout, Chicago's Black community rivaled Harlem's in the 1920s and 30s. Drawn by the city's meatpacking houses, railway companies and steel mills, the Black population in Chicago skyrocketed from 44,000 in 1910 to 235,000 in 1930. In 1928, the first Black congressman since Reconstruction

Republican, Oscar De Priest, was elected.

The Great Migration increased Detroit's Black population from under 6,000 in 1910 to 120,000 in 1930. Working in the auto and other industries, a Black middle class soon developed, creating an important cultural community. Harlem was the Mecca of urban Black life. If you wanted to write, you went to Harlem. If you wanted to dance, you went to Harlem. If you wanted to create social change, you went to Harlem. If you wanted to compose music, you went to Harlem. If you wanted the best chance at changing your circumstances and you were Black, you went to Harlem. It was considered the heart of the Renaissance in African American letters; hence, the name The Harlem Renaissance. It was also considered the heart of African American life; hence, the designation of Harlem as Home in most Black literature of the time. Harlem stands, then, not only as a designation of a geographical area, but also as a symbol for the best and worst qualities of African American life during the early 20th Century.

The Impact of Migration to Urban Centers

Black Southerners found a second emancipation in the ability to leave when they wanted, to wherever they wanted to go. James R. Grossman contends that "Most ex-slaves traveled only short distances...to prove to themselves and their former masters that they now controlled their own labor and their own family life; the act of moving constituted a test of the meaning of emancipation." These were the baby steps that a toddler took. The adolescent leaps lay in the actual relocation to a new land—a land of opportunity in the North. The push of migration, clearly, was the history of Black oppression in the South coupled with the lack of acceptance of Black emancipation by the racist White infrastructure. Instead of abandoning all forms of slavery and brutality, the South merely sneaked around the laws and continued to maintain a relationship of fear with its former slaves. Grossman argues that "Living in a society that sought to render them as dependent and powerless as possible, they acquired a new source of power over their lives information that a better alternative not only existed but beckoned. They used the information and the network to plan and execute the process of their migration North, as well as to determine their destination."

The pull of migration was opportunity itself. Grossman states that "Analysts who examined the appeal of the North the pull forces also compiled innumerable lists, citing high wages, equality, bright lights, privileges, good schools, and other attractions describing the obverse of what the migrants were fleeing in the South." These pull and push forces

were the culminating influences that set the foundation for a mass movement. Similar to the northern migration to large cities such as Chicago, a westward migration was also taking place. Shirley Ann Wilson Moore states that "The push of racial violence and poverty and the pull of California's reputation for freedom and economic opportunity were important factors in Black migration to Richmond." Hence, migration was a viable factor for the advancement of African-Americans in their nascent freedom. Whether North or West, a Black consciousness was assembling itself en masse.

Harlem, a section of upper Manhattan in New York City, increased in reputation and population during these years. It attracted Blacks with massive talents from all over the United States, the West Indies, and other parts of the world like a magnet. Historian Darlene Clark Hine states, "The decade of the 'roaring twenties,' a pivotal and turbulent one in American history, was also a period of unprecedented flowering of Black culture, encompassing literature, the visual and plastic arts, as well as the performing arts." This Black Renaissance, or the New Negro Renaissance as it was sometimes referred to, was ubiquitous at the time, but it was Harlem that served as a sort of showplace for the cream of the crop of poets, artists, and writers. According to Hine, the basis and quintessence of what Alain Locke baptized in 1925 as the "New Negro Renaissance" was the extraordinary wealth of talent compressed into a small section of the big city.

The Harlem or Negro Renaissance was a time when African Americans and White Americans alike "discovered" the vibrancy and uniqueness of Black art, music and, especially, literature. The decade was marked by exciting nightlife in Harlem's cabarets, particularly the Cotton Club; by the publishing of a great number of novels, short stories, plays, poems, and articles about and by Blacks; by great musicals written by and starring Blacks, most importantly the legendary *Shuffle Along*; and by the production of artwork by talented young artists like Aaron Douglas and Richmond Barthe. What made this period significant was the fact that the "Negro was in vogue," as Langston Hughes writes in his autobiography, *The Big Sea*. For the first time in American history, a large number of Black artists could earn livings and be critically acknowledged in various fields

In all forms of art, African Americans developed a need to identify and utilize both African American folk forms (tales, spirituals, and customs) and African forms. What made this Renaissance pivotal for African Americans, most particularly artists and intellectuals, was the affirmation of a distinct cultural heritage and the *visibility* of that culture's manifestation. The fact

that this phenomenon occurred in the 1920s is easily understood in light of American history of the era. The Black Renaissance was significant in the overall mosaic of the post-war period, often referred to as the "Jazz Age." This label itself reflects the influence of African American culture on the period. Black artists, like noted White artists of the "lost generation" that included Hemingway and Fitzgerald, were influenced by the rejection of traditional moral values which produced a mania for exotic lifestyles. In fact, this post-war generation often "found itself" in a trek to Harlem's entertainment spots!

Although the patronage of Whites was a factor in the Harlem Renaissance (not only did they "patronize" cabarets, but their patronage often extended to supporting young Black artists), the period is notable above all for its Black artistic and philosophical awakening. Why was Harlem the focal point of this movement? Scholars have provided numerous explanations, the most obvious being that New York, the cultural center of America, was the logical center for the genesis of formal African American culture. Harlem's Black population in 1920 was extremely large and continued to increase throughout the decade, reaching 200,000 by 1930, according to James Weldon Johnson's *Black Manhattan*. The Harlem Black community contained not only American Blacks, but also many West

Indians. It was the national headquarters for protest groups such as the National Association for the Advancement of Colored People and the Urban League.

Black pride in Harlem had been exemplified on July 28, 1917 by a parade of 10,000 African Americans silently protesting anti-Black violence. In 1919, Blacks marched again to celebrate the return of the all-Black 369th Infantry from service in World War I. Furthermore, by 1920, Harlem had gained a symbolic significance for Blacks which caused it to be referred to as a "Mecca" by scholars of the period. Harlem was not a ghetto; it was a Black city! The books, *Black Manhattan* (1930) by Johnson and *Negro Metropolis* (1940) by Claude McKay, as well as the essay, "Harlem: The Cultural Capital" by Alain Locke in *The New Negro* offer further evidence that Black intellectuals considered Harlem a Black capital.

Between 1900 and 1920, the number of Blacks in Harlem doubled, as did the Black populations in many other northern cities. This movement, including the further growth between 1920 and 1930, is referred to as the "Great Migration." Blacks left the South in astonishing numbers for many reasons: depression in the agricultural southern economy, the World War I industrial boom in the North, growing oppression in the South, and a thoroughly American phenomenon of striving for a better quality of life. Charles S. Johnson, a

Black sociologist and an important figure in the Renaissance, concluded in his essay, "The New Frontage on American Life": "In ten years, Negroes have been actually transplanted from one culture to another."

Black Leadership in the Movement

The Black Renaissance or "New Negro Movement" was a time of excitement for the younger generation of the Negro intelligentsia, dubbed the "New Negroes" in Alain Locke's collection of the same name published in 1925. As Locke, often termed the "father" of the Negro Renaissance, says in his introductory essay, "The New Negro," "The younger generation is vibrant with a new psychology." This "new psychology" was a freedom of expression hitherto unknown in such a large number of Black artists as well as receptiveness to anything "Black" on the part of many Whites.

Black intellectuals and their White allies and patrons promoted Black culture in the arts and writing by mentoring and supporting the young participants. The "Talented Tenth," a term coined by W. E. B. DuBois to represent educated African Americans responsible for leading the race, stood at the forefront of the movement. Alain Locke, a Howard University professor; W. E. B. DuBois, Director of Publicity for the NAACP and scholar; Walter White, NAACP official; Charles S. Johnson, Urban League official; James Weldon Johnson, author of the national Black anthem; Jesse Fauset, co-editor of the *Crisis,* and Reverend Adam Clayton Powell, Sr., pastor of Abyssinian Baptist Church in Harlem with the largest African American congregation in the U.S. were among the most prominent in the group.

Many Harlem Renaissance leaders and participants wrote for radical magazines like *The Crisis, Opportunity,* and *The Messenger.* W. E. B. DuBois, already a noted scholar, author, and spokesman by 1920, was editor of the NAACP's *Crisis* magazine, founded in 1910 in New York. His editorials were widely read. The Urban League's magazine, *Opportunity,* edited by Charles S. Johnson, also initiated one of the most important series of events in the Renaissance by promoting contests for promising young Black writers. In 1924, *Opportunity* sponsored the first of several dinners honoring young Black writers. C. H. Johnson termed it their "debut" and, as Arna Bontemps recalls in his essay, "The Awakening: A Memoir," "Johnson was pleased to call the dinner a 'coming-out party' for an informal group designated as the 'Writer's Guild.' "

The socialist magazine, *The Messenger,* begun by activists A. Phillip Randolph and Chandler Owen in 1917, also employed some of the Renaissance writers, notably Wallace Thurman. The majority of Renaissance writing was not polemical, but the subtle ties that many writers had with established protest organizations were important in understanding the pervasive feeling of Black intellectuals that all accomplishments were in a sense political. Harlem's Black movement also served as a center for protest organizations. Although the Black Renaissance was fundamentally a cultural movement, it was connected to Black protests of the period that formed an important psychological backdrop. More than anything else, the Harlem Renaissance was a marker of the shift of the Black intellectuals from the South to the North.

It seemed to embody "the best of times," when Blues was hot and Jazz was a growing stay in America's culture; when speakeasies were filled with both Blacks and Whites dancing to the 'rhythms of life' set out by the saxophone, trumpet, and drums; when the "New Negro" was setting his mark in politics, art, literature, music, science, the social sciences and every aspect of American life into which he could win his way; when the industrial North seemed to call forth African Americans out of the agrarian South and when the African Americans responded to the call in droves, fleeing the violence and racism of the KKK and lynch laws and the abject poverty of share-cropping; when it seemed as if the urban North, in cities like New York, Chicago, and Detroit, was a place where the American Negro could finally find respite from racial prejudice, could finally hold a decent job with decent pay, could finally become an unharassed property owner, and could finally go out dancing Saturday night without fear of having men in White sheets shatter his fun.

If it was "the best of times," it was also "the worst of times" though Blacks and Whites joined on the dance floors at night and shared tables at the newest Blues and Jazz clubs, racist policies and sentiments still separated Americans in all aspects of life; and, although Whites went to the hot spots of Negro life, it was often out of curiosity—they wanted to watch Blacks in order to see their "primitive" character and inferior mode of thinking, living, being. Although the African American was making headway in areas formerly denied him such as the arts, literature, sciences, etc., he often did so by repudiating the mores, manners, and lifestyles of the poorer classes of Blacks. As a result, tensions arose between the middle class and poorer Blacks—the former group thought the latter was holding back the race by remaining "common" or "niggerish," while the latter group thought the former was just trying to erase its Blackness by "acting White." And, although African Americans could often find good jobs and good pay, most were forced to become domestics or factory workers with little chance for advancement. The city

life that had promised so much did not deliver.

If one examines the academic and social backgrounds of many of the participants of the Renaissance, one might reasonably conclude that the movement was primarily an elitist or middle-class phenomenon. In some senses, this is true; yet, this is an oversimplification. The men and women prominent in the awakening felt in many cases that they spoke for the "common" Black person. Also, many writers, particularly Langston Hughes, Rudolph Fisher, Claude McKay, and Zora Neale Hurston, glorified the "average" African American in their poetry and fiction.

The fact is that during this period, Black pride for many Blacks (not only those involved directly in the Renaissance) was more evident than in any previous period. Marcus Garvey's separatist "Back to Africa" movement centered in New York was important in the movement.. Although many of the Harlem intellectuals severely criticized Garvey, he was vastly popular with working-class Blacks. Garvey in turn criticized the "New Negroes" as being elitist "talented-tenth" traitors. However, Garvey's racial pride theories, emphasis on African American history, advocacy of a return to Africa, and stress on economic independence for Negroes attracted attention from the masses. In 1921, a massive convention of Garvey's U.N.I.A. occurred in New York. The international extravaganza was held in August and, according to Bontemps, "Nothing quite comparable had ever occurred in the New World experience of Black people." His parades and conventions reflected an increased sense of Black pride and interest in an African heritage on the part of Negroes of all classes. Garvey's movement flourished until his imprisonment for fraud in 1925.

Harlem Renaissance Activities

The Black Renaissance movement depicted an artistic, cultural, and social burgeoning of writing about race and the African American's place in American life during the early 1920s and 1930s. It's hard to put an exact date on this period because what happened during this time—in terms of social criticism, protest, and political advancements, as well as in terms of the growing literati—was a long time in developing. It was an extremely exciting and fruitful period in African American history. Why did such a rebirth or influx of creativity occur, and why did it occur in Harlem? One factor that has been cited was that a large number of southern, rural, Black Americans arrived in Harlem at this time "in search of economic opportunity and a safe haven from racial oppression." And they found a community like this in Harlem. These migrants brought with them their "oral tradition,

regional speech patterns, and rhythms, including the Blues and Jazz." Another reason was that Black magazines such as *Opportunity* and *Crises* held literary contests with prizes, supported by White philanthropists such as Amy Spingarn and the Rosenwald Fund, drew writers from all over the country. Also, there was a White audience for these artists and performers which meant funding. Before this time, there had not been interest backed with monetary means from the White community. There is also the factor of promoters of Black pride to be considered. "Marcus Garvey's charismatic Pan-African movement instilled race pride and a sense of community in Black Americans of diverse social classes and ethnic origins."

Three major events between 1924 and 1926 placed African American literature writers in the mainstream of the Black Renaissance. The first event was the publication of *The Survey Graphic*, a Harlem community magazine, which produced its first issue in 1925. This particular issue focused on the writings of Blacks and was edited by Alan Locke, a literary scholar. The second event was the publication of *Nigger Heaven* (1926), written by Carl Van Vechten, a novelist writing about the Black culture during the Harlem Renaissance. Many African Americans were offended by the contents of the book, but it also created a Negro Vogue that drew thousands to the excitement of Harlem. Finally, in 1926, a group of young writers, including Langston Hughes, Zora Neale Hurston, and Wallace Thurman, eventually took control of the literary Renaissance in Harlem. The men and women prominent in the awakening felt in many ways that they spoke for the "common" Black person. Also, many writers, particularly Langston Hughes, Rudolph Fisher, Claude McKay, and Zora Neale Hurston, glorified the "average" Negro in their poetry and fiction.

African American Women Writers in the Black Renaissance

Black Renaissance women included Jessie Fauset, Nella Larsen, Regina Andrews, May Miller, Georgia Douglas Johnson, and Zora Neale Hurston. These women "were eclipsed by these high-powered talents [their male counterparts] who by virtue of their gender had more social mobility and networks than women did." Thus, we see that within this community that nurtured young artists, women faced adversity. Few women were published. Of course, there were some exceptions like Nella Larsen, Jessie Fauset, and Mercedes Gilbert, but the overwhelming majority found themselves either published privately or solely in Black magazines. As seen throughout history, Black women faced adversity two-fold for their race

and gender. Hine explains the odyssey of a Black woman during this time:

"When Black women, like the men, flocked to New York from the rural South and other parts of the country, they were often perceived by the White community solely as farm laborers, potential cooks, cleaning women, nannies who would work for $2 a week (at one point Zora Neale Hurston accepted work as a domestic). Within the Black community they were contained in other ways, expected to lend moral support to the endeavors of Black men, to dedicate themselves to family and/or church activities, and to uphold an antiquated image of virtuous womanhood. White women were beginning to bob their hair, raise their hemlines, and dance the Charleston while Black sisters were held to nineteenth century codes of conduct."

Black women faced double standards both within and outside of their community. They were excluded most of the time from many social gatherings. Men such as Wallace Thurman would have parties at which only Black and White men would be present. So, in response, Black women began to host their own "literary salons" like the ones Regina Anderson of *Opportunity* would hold at her apartment with prominent women writers of the time. Another example would be A'Lelia Walker (the daughter of Madame C. J. Walker) who held crazy parties at her townhouse called "The Dark Tower."

Zora Neale Hurston's was "a colorful and flamboyant figure in the 1920s and 1930s who created controversy whenever she appeared…she also created a remarkable body of writings—folklore, anthropological studies, plays, short stories, essays, novels, and an autobiography." Hurston began her illustrious career by publishing short stories in *Opportunity*. Then with other writers including Langston Hughes and Wallace Thurman, she edited the "short-lived" magazine *Fire!* She went on to collaborate with Hughes on a play entitled *Mule Bone*, which was a comedy about African American life. *Mules and Men* is Hurston's famous volume of folklore that was followed by a volume of Caribbean folklore entitled, *Tell My Horse*. She also wrote a handful of novels within and after the time constraints of the Harlem Renaissance, which includes *Jonah's Gourd Vine* in 1934, her masterpiece, *Their Eyes Were Watching God* in 1937, *Moses, Man of the Mountain* in 1939, and *Seraph on the Suwanee* in 1948. Her autobiography, *Dust Tracks on the Road* was published in 1942.

Hurston always set her novels within the context of an all-Black or mostly Black background. Within these settings, "Hurston rejects color and race identify as important to her situation, although the implications of these factors were woven skillfully into her work." She often examined the African American rural middle-class world. Although her characters were indeed poor, she did not allow their economic situation to hinder their principles. As noted by one critic, "poverty is not at the core of their problem, as it is for the majority of African Americans. Rather the struggle of African Americans for both spiritual and physical freedom is carried out behind the walls of segregation."

Hurston aimed to speak directly to the African American women of her time. She knew how extremely difficult it was to live under the double oppression that they felt. She wished to teach these women "how to be Black without being limited by that reality; how to be women without the constraints of womanhood; and how to remain true to both of these and still be an educated artist." But this challenge plagued Hurston herself all her life. Another trait that distinguished Hurston from other Black writers of the time is how she treated race relations: "Hurston challenged and contested the notion that the integrity of the African American race needed defending and that the responsibility for this defense must be borne by each individual Black person." She believed that such a burden originated from essentially the same racist ideology: that is, that "Black people were deficient and had to be uplifted for approval by the dominant society and that each representative Negro must assume the burden of both uplifting and defending the race even at the cost of personal wishes and needs...for Hurston, the race needed no improvement or justification. " This is different from other authors, such as Jessie Fauset, in that Hurston's characters strive to build a family and a world in the African American community.

Jessie Fauset was another dominant Black woman in the Harlem Renaissance. She wrote three novels: *There is Confusion*, published in 1924; *Plum Bun*, published in 1929; and *The Chinaberry Tree*, published in 1931. Fauset said in her own writing:

> "Colored people have been subjects which I have chosen for my novels partly because they are the ones I know best, partly because of all the other separate groups which constitutes the American cosmogony none of them, to me, seems to be naturally endowed with the stuff of which chronicles may be made."

This was her reasoning for writing about her people. In *The Chinaberry Tree*, Faucet discussed her idea that "the colored American who is not being pressed too hard by the Furies of Prejudice, Ignorance and Economic Injustice" is "not so very different from any other American, just distinctive."

In talking about African Americans as having "wholesome respect for family and education and labor and the fruits of labor," she makes this comparison: "The dark American... wears his [or her] joy and rue very much as does the White American. He [or she] may wear it with some differences but it is the same joy and the same rue." Fauset faithfully stuck to this idea of Black Americans throughout her career, but still her work shows "keen awareness of the racism and sexism often beneath the surface in the cultural and literary politics of the 1920s and 1930s." Fauset herself faced racism when she applied to Bryn Mawr. The school was apparently not ready for Black women because it initiated a scholarship for Fauset to attend Cornell.

As for her career during the Harlem Renaissance, she started by contributing to the *Crisis* as early as 1912. In 1919 W. E. B. DuBois promoted her to Literary Editor, a position she held from 1919 to 1926. "Left to pursue her own direction at the magazine, she placed a greater emphasis on poetry and fiction by cultivating the talents of young writers, such as Claude McKay, Jean Toomer, Countee Cullen, George Schuyer, Arna Bontemps, and Langston Hughes, who later recognized her contribution as an enabling force by calling her a 'midwife' to the emerging literary Renaissance in New York." In 1920 and 1921, Fauset worked on an NAACP monthly magazine for children called *The Brownies' Book*. She stated in the magazine's introduction the following: "teach Universal Love and Brotherhood for all the little folks—Black and brown, yellow and White." In 1922, Fauset began writing novels, of which she had four, and all addressed the issue of passing as White and the limitations that African Americans faced in both White society and their own communities as well.

Nella Larsen was a novelist and short story writer who wrote about mulattoes. "Like her heroines, Larsen felt out of place and was in search of a firm foothold in a world that seemed not to understand the inner conflicts associated with mixed ancestry." She was born in Chicago to a West Indian father who died when she was two years of age and a Danish mother who remarried a White man and had a child together. The White stepfather viewed her as an embarrassment. This family life was very uncomfortable for Larsen and she brought these feelings into her writings. She continued being trapped between two worlds, as she attended White prep schools with her half sister, then continued on to all-Black Fisk University in Nashville, Tennessee, before traveling to stay with her mother's side of the family and studying at The University of Copenhagen. Afterwards, she attended

New York City's Lincoln Hospital for nursing. Being not at all comfortable with her family, she married Elmer S. Imes and became a children's librarian from 1921 to 1926, which inspired her to read a lot and eventually led her to write. "As a socialite wife, Larsen became acquainted with a cadre of African American authors in New York City who encouraged her to write, including James Weldon Johnson, Jessie Fauset, Jean Toomer, and Langston Hughes."

Her first novel, *Quicksand*, which was published in 1928, is largely autobiographical in nature. *Passing*, her second novel, came out only 13 months after the "national acclaim" of *Quicksand*. In 1929, "the 38-year-old novelist was hailed as a major New Negro author." *Passing* "centers on women's friendship, women's sexuality, mixed ancestry, and preoccupation with respectability and materiality...*Passing* illustrates that African Americans who pass for White often yearn to be part of the Black community."

In 1930, Nella Larsen became the first African American woman to win a creative writing award from the Guggenheim Foundation. She was later accused of plagiarism, got involved in a messy divorce, and this seemed to be the end of her writing because she went back to nursing. One critic said of Larsen's career: "Larsen made a significant contribution to Black history and culture by capturing in impressive detail and the mannerisms, values, concerns, and emotional conflicts of the Black bourgeoisie, underscoring that even members of this class were victimized by racism.

At a New York Civic Club gathering on March 21, 1924, Gwendolyn Bennett made this dedication: "to all Negro youth known and unknown who have a song to sing, a story to tell or a vision for the sons of the earth." This particular gathering showcased select writers from the Harlem Renaissance and the honorees included Alain Locke, Countee Cullen, Jessie Faucet, Walter White, Helene Johnson, Eric Walrond, and Gwendolyn Bennett.

While attending Girl's High School in Brooklyn, New York, Gwendolyn Bennett became the first African American participant in the literary and drama societies. It was at this point in her life that she first became interested in Harlem and all that it had to offer. "The ambience of Harlem exerted a magnetic pull that drew African American artists to Harlem's cultural centers." In 1921, Bennett entered Columbia University's Teachers College Department of Fine Arts, but "overt racism discouraged her and after two years she transferred to Pratt Institute where she studied art and drama." When she graduated in 1924, she was already being recognized as an artist in Harlem. Because of her reputation as an artist and a poet, she acquired a faculty teaching position at Howard University. Nonetheless, teaching was apparently not her forte. "Teaching limited her, confined her, and stifled her creativity. To add to her gloom, the pretentious Washington, D.C., Black cultural society lacked the closeness, genuineness, and love among peers and colleagues that she had embraced in Harlem." The Delta Sigma Theta sorority gave her a scholarship of $1,000, so Bennett decided to travel to Paris. There she mingled with such writers as Gertrude Stein, Ernest Hemingway, James Joyce, and Konrad Bercovici; but she did not really know that many people so she basically immersed herself in her studies at the Academmie Colarossi, the Academie Julian, the Ecole de Pantheon, and the Sorbonne. Still, she longed for Harlem and traveled back in 1926.

It is at this time that she became the editor of *Opportunity* and wrote a literary gossip column called "ebony Flute." Bennett also served on the editorial board of *Fire!* As well as writing, Bennett also did some illustrating during this time. She illustrated the covers of the December 1923 and March 1924 issues of *Crisis*, as well as the January and July 1926 and December 1930 issues of *Opportunity*. Although she loved Harlem, she was obligated to teaching at Howard and had to return in the fall.

As for her poetry, she will be remembered as one of the most brilliant poets of the era. "Bennett's poetry reflects her love for the literary and the visual, a combination that for her was inseparable ... she was the Renaissance woman of the New Negro movement." Overall, the Harlem Renaissance women were very diverse. While some defined themselves as active protesters and were devoted to the struggle against the most virulent forms of discrimination and racism, others adopted a more contemplative stance.

Dramatic and Literary Activities in the Black Renaissance

The socialist magazine, *The Messenger*, begun by activists A. Phillip Randolph and Chandler Owen in 1917, employed some of the Renaissance writers. The men that comprised this talent included Langston Hughes, Claude McKay, Countee Cullen, Jean Toomer, Walter White, Wallace Thurman, and Arna Bontemps. A majority of the Renaissance writing was not polemical, but the subtle ties that many writers had with established protest organizations were significant in understanding the belief of African American intellectuals that all accomplishments were in a sense political. There was a general belief that individual achievements by any African Americans represented a road to improved conditions for all members of the race.

Langston Hughes, Claude McKay, and Countee Cullen relied on the themes of pride and dignity, atavistic yearnings, and exoticism in their poetry. McKay's "If We Must Die" (1919) is classic in its expression of active resistance:

If we must die-let it not be like hogs
Hunted and penned in an inglorious spot,
While round us bark the mad and hungry dogs,
Making their mock at our accursed lot.
If we must die-oh, let us nobly die...
McKay's "Harlem Dancer" contains exotic imagery
which can be construed as a form of atavistic yearning:
To me she seemed a proudly-swaying palm
Grown lovelier for passing through a storm

. . . .

The wine-flushed, bold-eyed boys, and even the girls,
Devoured her shape with eager, passionate gaze;
But looking at her falsely smiling face,
I knew her true self was not in that strange place.
The image of the palm evokes a tropical African setting,
and the audience "devouring" the dancer seems interested

in the exotic vision, although the place (a Harlem theatre?) was not the dancer's rightful environment.

Cullen explores the question of African descent in his "Heritage" (1925):

> What is Africa to me?
> Copper sun or scarlet sea,
> Jungle star or jungle track,
> Strong bronzed men, or regal black
> Women from whose loins I sprang
> When the birds of Eden sang?
> One three centuries removed
> From the scenes his fathers loved
> Spicy grove, cinnamon tree
> What is Africa to me?

Cullen's answer to his initial question is intricately developed in the long poem, but the idea causes him "no peace." The poem depends heavily on a romanticized concept of Africa, as does most of the writing of the period, and on a use of the exotic and sensual in Cullen's unexplained yearnings to "strip" and "dance" when "the rain begins to fall." However, students must understand that although the African references may be imprecise, it is very important that *for the first time*, African Americans wanted to admit a connection with Africa. Hughes' "Afro-American Fragment," though not published until 1959, also explores African links:

> Subdued and time-lost
> Are the drums—and yet
> Through some vast mist of race
> There comes this song
> I do not understand,
> This song of atavistic land,
> Of bitter yearnings lost
> Without a place—
> So long,
> So far away
> Is Africa's
> Dark face.

For Hughes, the connection with Africa was not distant. According to him, it is "far away," yet it exists in "those songs/Beat back into the blood." Many poems in Hughes' *Weary Blues* exhibit an even subtler tie with African heritage. In the first section of the book, many of the poems are Hughes' famous "Jazz" poems depicting Harlem's nightlife. Yet, the recurring use of the terms "jungle" and "Jazz" together provided a sense that this African American music is born of the jungle beats. For example, this is evident in "Nude Young Dancer":

> What jungle tree have you slept under,
> Midnight dancer of the jazzy hour?
> What great forest has hung its perfume

Like a sweet veil about your
bower?

In "The Negro Speaks of Rivers,"
Hughes reaches back to his African
heritage again:

> I bathed in the Euphrates when
> dawns were young,
> I built my hut near the Congo
> and it lulled me to sleep.
> I looked upon the Nile and
> raised the pyramids about it.
> I heard the singing of the
> Mississippi when Abe Lincoln
> went down to New Orleans,
> and I've seen its muddy
> bosom turn all golden in the
> sunset.
> I've known rivers:
> Ancient, dusky rivers.
> My soul has grown deep like
> the rivers.

Later in the book, Hughes
develops other important themes:
"Songs for a Banjo Dancer" and
"Blues Fantasy" are written in the style
of the Blues, an important folk form
of African Americans; the pain of race
relations, an aspect of the theme of
pride and dignity, are explored in the
second section of the book, as in the
poem, "As I Grew Older":

> I lie down in the shadow.
> No longer the light of my
> dream before me,
> Above me.
> Only the thick wall.

> Only the shadow.
> My hands!
> My dark hands!
> Break through the wall!

The last stanza borders on a kind
of defiance against racial barriers.
Hughes also speaks for the average
Black men and women who have
continued to strive against all odds in
his classic, "Mother to Son," in which
a mother advises her son:

> Don't you fall now—
> For I'se still goin', honey,
> I'se still climbin',
> And life for me ain't been no
> crystal stair.

Arna Bontemps, in his essay, "The
Awakening: A Memoir," sees 1921 as
the beginning of the Harlem
Renaissance. Countee Cullen, soon to
become a noted poet, published his
poem, "I Have a Rendezvous with
Life," in DeWitt Clinton High
School's literary magazine, of which
he was an editor, in January of that
year. In June of the same year, another
young poet, Langston Hughes, just
graduated from high school in
Cleveland and soon to enroll at
Columbia, published his poem, "The
Negro Speaks of Rivers," in the *Crisis.*
At virtually the same time, *Shuffle Along*
became a smash on Broadway.
Hughes recalled coming to Columbia
mostly to see the all-Black musical
(book by Fluornoy Miller and Aubrey
Lyles and lyrics by Eubie Blake and

Noble Sissle), which featured songs that became widely popular, including "I'm Just Wild About Harry." It was a loosely plotted musical about a mayoral election in an all-Black southern town. The dancing and singing were responsible for its great popularity. During the decade, each year saw the opening of new Black musicals inspired by the success of *Shuffle Along.*

Claude McKay's *Home to Harlem* is the tale of Jake, an archetypal folk hero who is successful with women, free to roam in quest of his dreams and, of course, a "man's man." As the novel opens, Jake has returned to Harlem from the World War. He has gone AWOL (i.e. absent without official leave) because he was not pleased with the role he and other Black soldiers had been playing. Throughout the loosely structured episodic novel, the exotic nature of Harlem is viewed in the gay nightlife. Jake himself "took whatever he wanted of whatever he fancied and . . . kept going." Jake operated purely on instinct, pursuing joy in life. His companion, Ray, a would-be writer, is his opposite, and never seems at ease with life partly because he is an "intellectual." Jake, representing the primitive and the "common" Black man, is the positive character. Hence, McKay sought to glorify the working-class "peasant" Negro.

Jean Toomer's *Cane*, in a much more artistic and symbolic way, also seems to extol the virtues of the "primitive" Black peasants. *Cane* is a series of interrelated poems and stories, or sketches, almost mystically evoked and inspired by Toomer's pilgrimage to the South. (Toomer, a very light-skinned African American who later followed the mystic teachings of Gurdjieff, was raised in Washington, D.C.) Although the book was not widely popular at the time of its appearance, it symbolized many qualities and motifs associated with the Renaissance period, notably the desire for atavistic (African) connections and the romanticized concept of strength as located in southern Black peasants, as opposed to fragmentation of northern Black identities.

The strong characters in his book are primarily southern Black women who, however, remain unaware of their own power. For example, the central character in "Fern" is a woman to whom men continue to go, albeit they are ultimately unsatisfied because she never really gives them anything. Afterward, the men feel strangely "bound to her" but, ironically, "nothing ever came to Fern." The collection's later stories are set in the North where Toomer delineates fragmentation of the northern Black personality as in "Box Seat." In the last section, Toomer combines his two themes when the main character in "Kabnis," a northern Negro living in the rural South, is consumed with fear and uncertainty unlike the native southerners who are able to accept their environment and in some senses thrive in it. Much of Toomer's poetry explores African connections, as does "Georgia":

"Race memories of king and caravan,
High-priests, an ostrich, and a juju-man,
Go singing through the footpaths of the swamp."

The last work of Wallace Thurman, *Infants of the Spring*, provides a literary analysis of the Harlem Renaissance. This novel attempts to tell the story of the Renaissance in fictional form. The main character, Raymond Taylor, is a representation of Thurman himself. He is an aspiring author who lives in an experimental house dubbed "Niggeratti Manor" by Taylor. The Manor is a house in Harlem that a concerned Black woman has rented to Negro artists. The tone of the novel is cynical, and most of the characters' stories end in psychological or physical tragedy. After a wild interracial party at the Manor, Ray remarks: "This ... is the Negro Renaissance and this is about all the whole damn thing is going to amount to." Ray also remarks later that "at least the forward of my generation is tired of being patronized and patted on the head by philanthropists and social service workers." Finally, Ray concludes that each Negro artist must be true only to his own sensibilities, not to a movement: "I don't owe anything to

anyone except myself." Langston Hughes' story, "Who's Passing for Who," also takes a satirical look at fictional writers of the Renaissance and the racial games they played.

In 1922, Claude McKay published *Harlem Shadows*, a book of poetry. McKay, a young Jamaican writer, soon became an integral part of the Renaissance. He later contributed three novels, the picaresque *Home To Harlem* (1928), *Banjo* (1929), and *Banana Bottom* (1933), as well as a book on Harlem called *Harlem: Negro Metropolis* (1940), and an autobiography, *A Long Way from Home* (1937). The musicals, *Strut Miss Lizzie* and *Seven-Eleven,* appeared on Broadway in 1922 as well.

In 1923, Charles S. Johnson became editor of the newly born *Opportunity*, Roland Hayes gave his landmark American concert debut in Town Hall, and Jean Toomer published the most remarkable work of the period. His novel, *Cane* (1923), investigates the lower class life of the African American, who in many ways is still connected spiritually and psychologically to slavery, as well as the life of the urbanized "New Negro," who loses sight of his spiritual heritage because he is too intent on pursuing material things. Toomer's novel was one of the first to treat the subject of African American life with dignity, respect, and realism—part of the aesthetic Harlem Renaissance to which writers ascribed.

In 1925, Countee Cullen published a book of poetry entitled *Color*. Langston Hughes also published a book of poetry, *Weary Blues*. Most important, *The New Negro*, edited by Alain Locke, appeared. This work, perhaps more than any other, sought to mark the fact that an "awakening" or "Renaissance" (both terms were actually used in the book and Locke coined the latter) was in progress. The book featured fiction by Rudolph Fisher, Jean Toomer (selections from *Cane*), Zora Neale Hurston, and Eric Waldron, who all became key figures in the movement. Poetry by Cullen, McKay, James W. Johnson, Bontemps, and Langston Hughes was presented along with a play by Willis Richardson, which is one of the few surviving works of the Krigwa Players, a Black repertory group which strove to develop serious Black drama by and for Blacks. The essays explored the basic premises of the period: a new interest in sociology (particularly concerning the migration), an increased interest in the African American past and, most especially, intense affirmation and discovery of the validity of African American folk culture. The collection also featured illustrations by a brilliant young artist, Aaron Douglas, who captured in his Black and White prints the themes featured in the literature. Douglas' work exhibited strong African motifs, another fundamental theme of the Renaissance.

In 1926, Hughes' article, "The Negro Artist and the Racial Mountain," appeared and attempted to define the role of the Black artist: "We younger Negro artists who create now intend to express our individual dark-skinned selves without fear or shame." Hughes, in collaboration with Wallace Thurman, Zora Neale Hurston, Aaron Douglas, John P. Davis, Bruce Nugent, and Gwendolyn Bennett, decided that to express their "dark-skinned" selves, they needed to begin their own magazine. The result was an issue of *Fire*, published in November, which featured works by all the collaborators. Unfortunately, lack of funds ended the project. During this year, too, Carl Van Vechten, the greatest of the wealthy White enthusiasts, published *Nigger Heaven*, his controversial fictional view of contemporary Harlem. This novel enjoyed widespread popularity, but it was sharply criticized by some African Americans (e.g., DuBois) and defended by others (e.g., Hughes). Paul Green's Pulitzer Prizewinning play, *In Abraham's Bosom*, was also produced in 1926.

In 1927, James Weldon Johnson's book of folk poetry, *God's Trombones*, was published. Dubose Heyward, whose *Porgy* had been very popular a few years earlier, wrote and produced a second play, *Mamba's Daughters*. The musical of the year was *Africana*, starring Ethel Waters. In addition, Langston Hughes' second volume of poetry, *Fine Clothes to the Jew*, was published. Rudolph Fisher's novel, *Walls of Jericho*, appeared in 1928, as did McKay's novel, *Home to Harlem*, and Wallace Thurman's *The Blacker the Berry*. McKay's novel was apparently the first fictional work by an African American to reach the best-seller lists. Lyles and Miller tried to recapture their earlier success by producing *Keep Shuffling*, and Bill "Bojangles" Robinson starred in the *Blackbirds* revue of that year. Three other novels published that year were W. E. B. DuBois' *Dark Princess*, Nella Larsen's story of the color line, *Quicksand*, and Jessie Faucet's book on a similar theme, *Plum Bun*.

Due to the stock market crash in 1929, many of the activities of the Renaissance started to decrease; however, many of the authors who became popular during the 1920s published through the 1930s and later. It is interesting that Charles Gilpin, the great Black actor, achieved great fame in *The Emperor Jones* by O'Neill in 1920, the beginning of the Renaissance, and died in 1930. Also in 1930, the Pulitzer Prize-winning musical play by Marc Connelly, *Green Pastures*, became the most successful venture since *Shuffle Along*, and it was also one of the last Black musicals produced until the present period. In addition, Hughes published his first novel, *Not Without Laughter*, Larsen published her second novel, *Passing*, and McKay also published his second novel, *Banjo*.

In 1931, A'lelia Walker died. The heiress to Madame Walker's hair-products fortune, A'lelia had been the great Negro party-giver of the period, using her townhouse in Harlem, her apartment, and her mansion at Irvington-on-the-Hudson to entertain Black and White intellectuals. Her attempt to glorify the Black artists of the period by devoting a floor in her townhouse to walls covered by art and poetry of the period was not wholly successful, but the "Dark Tower," as she called it, was unique. In 1934, two important writers died within a week of each other: Wallace Thurman and Rudolph Fisher. Zora Neale Hurston wrote two novels in the 1930's, *Jonah's Gourd Vine* (1934) and, her best work, *Their Eyes Were Watching God* (1937). Bontemps also published two novels: *God Sends Sunday* (1931) and *Drums at Dusk* (1939). In terms of a literary movement, the period ended with the publication of Richard Wright's *Uncle Tom's Children* in 1938, which marked a sharp difference in style and theme. Wright's naturalistic fiction was a definite departure from the romanticized works of the Renaissance.

Entertainment in the Black Renaissance

The Renaissance brought out the powerful musical talent of singers and musicians who played an important role in the movement. Jazz and Blues were originally played in the South, but it rapidly began spreading to the North. Along with Louis Armstrong, Jelly Roll Morton helped pave the way for Duke Ellington, who was a talented band leader and musician. The leading musicians included Duke Ellington, Jazz band composer; Cab Calloway, Jazz artist; W. C. Handy, "Father of the Blues", Louis Armstrong, "New Orleans"; Jazz trumpeter and singer; Nora Holt, pianist; and Fats Waller, Jazz pianist. The singers included Roland Hayes, tenor singer; Ma Rainey and Bessie Smith, Blues singers; Alberta Hunter and Ivie Anderson, Jazz singers. Josephine Baker, Ethel Waters, and Bill "Bojangles" Robinson were popular dancers.

**Cab Calloway with members
of his orchestra**

African American entertainers often performed before mixed audiences. Harlem's cabarets and clubs attracted both Harlem residents and White New Yorkers seeking out Harlem's nightlife. There were about one dozen of these night clubs in

Harlem—Bamville, Connie's Inn, Baron Wilkins, The Nest, Small's Paradise, The Capitol, The Cotton Club, The Green Cat, The Sugar Cane Club, Happy Rhones, The Hoofers Club, and the Little Savoy. Most of these generally have from two to ten White persons for every Black one. Only The Hoofers, The Little Savoy, and The Sugar Cane Club seemed to cater almost exclusively to African Americans.

Harlem's famous Cotton Club, where Duke Ellington performed, provided entertainment exclusively to White audiences. The Cotton Club helped launch the careers of many brilliant Black musicians like Duke Ellington, yet it was operated by Whites primarily for White audiences. Writes Hughes: "White people began to come in droves. For several years they packed the expensive Cotton Club on Lenox Avenue. But I was never there, because the Cotton Club was a Jim Crow club for gangsters and monied Whites." "Rent" parties (an admission charge helped hosts to pay their rents) and other clubs, including Small's Paradise, were also popular. " At the Bamville and at Small's Paradise.

Wallace Thurman's describes night life in *Negro Life in New York's Harlem*. The Cotton Club and Connie's Inn attempted to provide theatrical performances to "well-to-do folk around town." The Nest and Happy Rhones attracted traveling salesmen, store clerks and commuters from

Jersey and Yonkers. The Green Cat had a large Latin clientele. The Sugar Cane Club on Fifth Avenue near 135th Street, located on the border of the most "low-down" section of Harlem, was visited by few Whites or few "dirty" African Americans. The Sugar Cane Club had a narrow subterranean passageway about 25 feet wide and 125 feet long. Rough wooden tables, surrounded by rough wooden chairs and the orchestra stands, jammed into the right wall center, used up about three-quarters of the space. The remaining rectangular area was sectioned for dancing. It had a capacity for seating about 100 people. Small's Paradise, on Seventh Avenue near 135th Street, was just the opposite of the Sugar Cane Club. It catered almost exclusively to White patrons with just enough African Americans present to give the necessary atmosphere and "difference." Yet even in Small's, with its symphonic orchestra, full-dress appearance and dignified onlookers, there was a great deal of characteristics similar to a Black cabaret. The Glory Hole was hidden in a musty damp basement behind an express and trucking office. It was a social club, commonly called a dive. Such places as the Glory Hole existed all over Harlem. They were not always confined to basement rooms. They could be found in apartment flats, in the rear of barber shops, lunch counters, pool halls, and other such conveniently blind places. Each one

had its regular quota of customers with just enough new patrons introduced from time to time to keep the place alive and prosperous. These intimate, lowdown civic centers were occasionally misjudged. Social service reports criticized them with the phrase "breeding places of vice and crime." They served as good training grounds for prospective pugilists. Fights were staged with regularity and with vigor. The other entertainment places in Harlem were exemplified by the Bamboo Inn, a Chinese-American restaurant that featured Oriental cuisine, a Jazz band and dancing. It was the place for select African American Harlem's night life, the place where debutantes had the coming out parties, where college lads took their co-eds and society sweethearts, and dignified matrons entertained. The Bamboo Inn was the the place to see "high Harlem," just like the Glory Hole was the place to see "low Harlem." When Harlem people wanted to dance, without attending a cabaret, they would go to the Renaissance Casino or to the Savoy, Harlem's two most famous public dance halls. The Savoy was the pioneer in the field of giving dance-loving Harlemites some place to gather nightly. It would open at three in the afternoon and close at three in the morning.

African Americans also provided entertainment in the theater. Two African American comedians, Bob Cole and J. Rosamond Johnson, performed in the first Black musical, *A Trip to Coontown.* They also composed songs and lyrics for such shows as *Shoo Fly Regiment* (1906), *Rufus Rastus* (1905), *Shuffle Along* (1921), and *Chocolate Dandies* (1924). The participants in these plays included Noble Sissle and Eubie Blake; Miller and Lyles, the stars of *Shuffle Along;* and Ernest Hogan, Florence Mills and Ethel Waters. In 1924, Paul Robeson, the brilliant actor and singer, became known to the general public in Eugene O'Neill's play, *All God's Chillun Got Wings,* which played in New York for several weeks. Florence Mills also starred in the musical, *Dixie to Broadway,* which was a tremendous success.

Several African American actors achieved fame for their work in the theater. Charles Gilpin appeared in *Emperor Jones.* For this performance, he won the Spingarn Medal, and the Drama League placed him along the ten people making the greatest stage contribution in 1920. Richard B. Harrison also won the Spingarn Medal for this role of "De Lawd" in *The Green Pastures.* In 1924, Paul Roberson gained recognition in Eugene O'Neill's plays, *All God's Chillun Got Wings* and *The Emperor Jones.* He was noted for his rich baritone voice. Roberson became one of the most popular concert artists of his day. He appeared on the stage in *Black Boy* (1926) and *Porgy* (1928) and in eleven motion pictures. In addition to theater, African

American artists made other significant artistic contributions.

Black Renaissance Artists

The artists of Harlem constantly engaged in the active life of the community. They each brought and shared their own aesthetic values. The leading artists included Henry Ossawa Tanner, Richmond Barthe, Augusta Savage, and Romare Bearden. Among the visual artists who responded to Alain Locke's vision in visual culture during the Harlem Renaissance were mainly four Black artists, each who, like so many others, were actively engaged in the art world of Harlem and the transitional period. These artists were William H. Johnson, Meta Fuller, Palmer Hayden, and Aaron Douglas who produced socially relevant art that was realistically done in the exploration of Black life and artistic themes.

Henry Ossawa Tanner won fame for his religious paintings. The son of an African Methodist Episcopal bishop, he studied art in France and in Palestine. He was recognized as a renowed artist after studying for five years at the Julian Academy in Paris. Tanner's religious paintings include *Resurrection of Lazarus, Christ on the Road to Bethany,* and *Christ at the Home of Mary and Martha.* Richmond Barthe and Augusta Savage were the first African American sculptors to attract attention. Barthe received recognition for his sculptor of Booker T. Washington, his "Head of a Tortured Negro," "West Indian Girl," and "The Boxer." Augusta Savage was noted for her work, "Mother and Child." Romare Bearden's paintings of the African American rural southern experiences were influenced by his experiences in the West Indies, such as his "Pepper Jelly Lady" portrait.

William H. Johnson's art was immense. He interpreted the religious symbols into Black symbols. He cast the northern community in the colors and styles of Carolina. The simple geometric forms and brilliant "Carolina colors" allowed Johnson to beautifully and starkly understate the harshness and beauty of daily life in Harlem. Johnson arrived in Harlem from Florence, South Carolina, in 1918. Upon his arrival in Harlem, he became a student at the National Academy of Design and was invited to assist the painter George Lucas. But like other artists such as Palmer Hayden in the 1920s, Johnson left the United States in 1926 to study art in Europe. Through his travel in London, he came in contact with the art of Vincent van Gogh, Edvard Munch, and Chaim Soutine. He also at this time became very interested in painting Black subjects that emphasized Christian themes. Compositions such as "Descent from the Cross" (c. 1939), "Mount Calvary" (1939), and "Nativity" (1939) show Johnson's presentation of an all-Black cast as the family of Jesus. Johnson

painted subjects that addressed political issues in Harlem. In the painting "Moon over Harlem" (1944), a bloody scene is depicted which shows the police and community citizens in a night brawl. During this period of political dissent, Johnson also included depictions of Black heroes, world leaders, and abolitionist figures in his paintings. These paintings included figures such as George Washington Carver, in his laboratory, accepting awards from various officials and displaying his numerous inventions such as peanuts and sweet potatoes.

Meta Fuller played an early part of this transitional period in Harlem. Her artistic perception and understanding was well ahead of other artists of this time and gained the attention of the leaders of the Harlem Renaissance after she had spent many years working in Paris. As a sculptor in early 1902, Meta Fuller produced many African themes in her art pieces. Her influence of African themes resulted from her marriage to Dr. Solomon Fuller who was from Liberia, West Africa. Through this marriage, she was able to interpret African folktales in her sculptures and bring new insight to the portrayal of neo-African themes in American art. She was the first African American woman to become a professional artist. Other works by Meta Fuller reflect the strong influence of Auguste Rodin, with whom she studied while at the Academie Colarossi in Paris. In 1914,

Fuller created a sculpture that anticipated the spirit and style of the Harlem Renaissance. The artwork entitled *Ethiopia Awakening* symbolizes the emergence of the New Negro and idealizes the conditions of African Americans through a female figure.

Palmer Hayden arrived in Harlem from Virginia after World War I as a self-trained artist who worked as a custodian. However, there are records that indicate that he was a student of Cooper Union in New York and pursued courses at Boothbay Art Colony in Maine as an independent student artist. He also studied and painted in France, where he resided from 1927 until 1932. During his time in Harlem, he became the principal artist who communicated Black folklore from the South through his paintings. He also expressed the native customs of southern Blacks in his works visually. An important element in the paintings of Palmer Hayden includes the people of the community and the fashions and manners that they portrayed. This can be seen in the painting titled "Just Back from Washington." In this painting, there is a young man who is fashionably dressed holding a strolling or walking cane. The figure of the man represents a city dude or city slicker, which is the perennial presence at the nightclubs in Harlem.

Similar to William H. Johnson, Aaron Douglas introduced Black religious subjects into his work in the 1920s. Douglas was a woodcut printer, illustrator, muralist, and was considered the leading painter during the Harlem Renaissance. He arrived in Harlem in 1924 with a certification to teach visual arts. Having been influenced by African American painter Ossawa 0. Tanner, Douglas was very active in New York during the Renaissance. He was one of the first muralists to complete murals in New York during the Renaissance. His first mural was for the New York Ebony Club in 1927. Another completed for Fisk University in 1929 followed this mural. In 1931, Douglas traveled to Paris; and upon his return, he completed yet another mural, *Aspects of Negro Life,* for the Countee Cullen Branch of the Free Public Library in New York. In this mural, Douglas demonstrated the history of African Americans and served as a great signature of work for the Harlem Renaissance.

Douglas explored racial themes in his art and turned to Africa as a source of beauty and artistic inspiration. Through his study of African art, he was able to combine his knowledge of classical art with African art's cubist forms. As a result of his study, he created his own style of painting and modernism. His work became very stylized, elongated with angular figures on the picture plane exhibiting movement. Douglas was familiar with many of the literary writers during the Harlem Renaissance era. He illustrated the works of such figures as DuBois, Countee Cullen, Langston Hughes, and James Weldon Johnson. Some of Aaron Douglas's most notable works include *GOD'S TROMBONES*, a cubist style Black and White rhythmic illustration that was created for James Weldon Johnson's books of poems and sermons in verse. This particular work depicted the Black history and customs of African American people and culture during the time of the Harlem Renaissance. The original series of paintings was completed in 1927 and included the illustrations *JUDGMENT DAY, LET MY PEOPLE GO. GO DOWN DEATH, NOAH'S ARK,* and *THE CRUCIFIXION.* According to Douglas, *THE CRUCIFIXION* had become every Black American's in the 1920s in Harlem. He also created illustrations for Locke, *The New Negro,* published in 1925. Douglas's art appeared frequently in *The Crisis* and *Opportunity* magazines. In these magazines, his work always portrayed some aspect of African American life and experience.

In addition to the arts, African Americans made gains in the arena of sports during the Renaissance Movement. The athletes also helped to elevate the status of African Americans in the midst of artistic, cultural, and social achievements.

Black Athletics

The Black Renaissance era depicted the athletic accomplishments of African Americans in aviation, baseball, and boxing. Bessie Coleman made history in the field of aviation, She was born in 1896 in Texas, the daughter of sharecroppers. About 1916, her family moved to Chicago. Her family came during the "Great Migration." Bessie's interest in aviation was sparked during World War I. However, she was denied entry into flight schools in the U.S. because she was an African American and a woman. Two of Chicago's African American businessmen, Robert Abbott (editor of the *Chicago Defender* newspaper) and Jesse Binga (a banker and philanthropist), encouraged Bessie and financed her aviation schooling in France. In 1921, Bessie became the first American woman to earn an international pilot's license. During the 1920s, Bessie was a barnstormer, parachutist and stunt flyer. She earned international fame. She made appearances throughout the United States, lecturing about opportunities in aviation for African Americans and fighting segregationist laws. Bessie died in 1926, at age thirty, when she was thrown from her plane while performing aerial stunts in Florida.

In baseball, the Negro Leagues came to the forefront. In 1920, an organized league structure was formed under the guidance of Andrew "Rube" Foster, a former player, manager, and owner for the Chicago American Giants. In a meeting held at the Paseo YMCA in Kansas City, Missouri, Foster convinced seven other

Midwestern team owners to join him in forming the Negro National League. Soon, rival leagues formed in eastern and southern states, bringing the thrills and innovative play of Black baseball to major urban centers in the U.S., Canada, and Latin America.

The Negro Leagues maintained a high level of professional skill and became centerpieces for economic development in many African American communities. Satchel Paige was the nearest thing to a legend that ever came out of the Negro Baseball League. His name became synonymous with the barnstorming exhibitions played between traveling Black teams and their White counterparts. Satchel's stories are legion. From "folklore come stories of his pulling outfielders to sit behind the mound while he proceeded to strike out the side with the tying run on base; stories of him intentionally walking the bases loaded so that he could pitch to Josh Gibson, the most dangerous hitter in Negro baseball league." Satchel began his professional career in Negro Baseball League 1926, and soon there after established himself as a star player.

African Americans also gained recognition in boxing. Jack Johnson became the world's first African American heavy weight champion in 1908 in a bout with Tommy Burns. He held the title for seven years. Born in Galveston, Texas, one of seven children, Jack Johnson dropped out of school after the fifth grade and began

to do odd jobs around town. He began training to box after beating up a local bully and by 1897 had become a professional boxer. Jack Johnson trained with people like Joe "the Barbados Demon" Walcott and Joe Choyinski. From 1902 to 1907, he won over 50 matches, some of them against other African American boxers such as Joe Jeannette, Sam Langford, and Sam McVey. Jack Johnson's career was legendary. In 47 years of fighting, he was only knocked out three times, but his life was troubled. There was a campaign of hatred and bigotry waged against him by Whites who wished to regain the heavyweight title and who also resented his interracial relationships with White women.

Johnson fought Bob Fitzsimmons, the ex-heavyweight champion, in 1906 and knocked him out. But, the boxers who succeeded Fitzsimmons refused to fight Johnson because of his color. Instead, another White boxer, Tommy Burns, fought Marvin Hart and won. Burns was then awarded the heavyweight title. He also refused to fight Johnson, but he was pressured until he finally agreed to a fight on Christmas Day in 1908. Like Muhammad Ali, almost 50 years later, Jack Johnson beat Tommy Burns soundly while dancing around the ring taunting him. He became a hero in Harlem. His 1908 championship bout partially financed by Barron Wilkins, a Harlem club owner and philanthropist. Even then, Jack Johnson was not fully accepted as champion, and proponents of White supremacy searched diligently for what they termed a "great White hope" to take the title away from him. They resorted to ex-heavyweight champion James Jeffries to fight Johnson. Their "hope" was defeated in the 15th round in a match surrounded by severe racial tension, in Reno, Nevada, in 1910.

Finally, in 1915, Johnson lost his title to Jess Willard under questionable circumstances. The fight was held in Cuba, and it was rumored that Johnson allowed himself to be knocked out in the 16th round. His marriages to White women, against the law at the time, and his flamboyant lifestyle had brought him a great deal of difficulty. He is said to have intentionally lost the fight in order to avoid further trouble with the authorities. After his career in boxing, Johnson, an amateur cellist and bull-fiddler who was a connoisseur of Harlem night life, eventually opened his own supper club, Club Deluxe, at 142nd Street and Lenox Avenue. He also lectured, sold stocks, and worked as a movie extra. Johnson, who loved to race fancy cars, died as the result of an automobile accident near Raleigh, North Carolina, in June 1946. The play, *The Great White Hope*, by Howard Sackler, which was eventually made into a movie starring James Earl Jones, is based on his life. Johnson was admitted to the Boxing Hall of Fame in 1954.

End of the Renaissance Movement

African Americans made significant accomplishments during the Black Renaissance; however, a number of factors caused it to end by the mid-1930s. The stock market crash of 1929 caused it to decline as the nation ended the Great Depression that increased economic pressure on all sectors of life. Organizations such s the NAACP and the Urban League, which had actively promoted the Renaissance in the 1920s, shifted their interests to economic and social issues in the Black community. Many influential African American writers and literary promoters, including Langston Hughes, James Weldon Johnson, Charles S. Johnson, and W.E.B. DuBois, migrated from Harlem in the early 1930s, most relocating to France. Finally, the Harlem Riot of 1935, set off in part by the growing economic hardship of the Depression and mounting tension between the Black community and the White merchants in Harlem who profited from that community, shattered the notion of Harlem as the Mecca of the New Negro. In spite of these problems, the Renaissance did not disappear overnight. Almost one-third of the books published during the Renaissance appeared after 1929. Lastly, the Harlem Renaissance ended when most of those associated with it left Harlem or stopped performing or writing.

Conclusion

During World War I, the Black Renaissance Movement materialized that reflected the artistic, cultural, and social strivings of African Americans. The participants wrote about race and African Americans' place in America in the 1920s and early 1930s. It is difficult to put an exact date on this period because what was going on during this time was long in developing. This movement was of such great magnitude that this period was renamed the "New Negro Movement" or the "Harlem Renaissance Movement," since Harlem represented the Mecca of urban Black life.

The Harlem Renaissance at the beginning emerged as a social and intellectual uprising in the African American communities. There were many factors or concerns of African Americans that started the groundwork for the movement. These concerns began after The Great Migration, a movement of hundreds of African Americans from the economically depressed rural South to the North. African Americans moved to the North in order to take advantage of the employment opportunities created by World War I. During this time, as more educated individuals arrived in New York's Harlem, it developed into the political and social Mecca of the world.

During the Harlem Renaissance, Black historians and sociologists like Carter G. Woodson and W. E. B. DuBois and Black leader Marcus Garvey advocated for racial equality for African Americans. Alain Locke, W. E. B. DuBois, Walter White, James Weldon Johnson, and others set the stage for literature in Harlem. One of DuBois's most notable books that describe the Black American life is *The Souls of Black Folks* (1903). This particular book presaged the Harlem Renaissance, because DuBois believed that there was a distinct Black aesthetic that should be cultivated.

Alain Locke, a scholar who graduated from Harvard, wrote a book entitled, *The New Negro: An Interpretation* (1925). The book introduced America to what would be the Harlem Renaissance. Most of the writings done by James Weldon Johnson during the time of the Harlem Renaissance described the reality of Black life in America and the struggle for racial identity. African American artists, performers, and writers focused on Black life and race pride. The movement received worldwide acclaim as African Americans continued to make significant achievements until the advent of the Great Depression, leading to economic woes and social problems that caused it to end.

Review Questions

1. What impact did the Great Migration have on the Black Renaissance?

2. How did Marcus Garvey influence the Harlem Renaissance Movement?

3. What literary significance did Jean Toomer's novel, *Cane,* have in terms of the Black Renaissance?

4. Who were the major leaders of the movement, and why were they credited as leaders?

5. What major forms of entertainment existed during the Black Renaissance?

6. What factors might have caused the end of the Black Renaissance?

Chapter 17

Great Depression and New Deal Era

This chapter focuses on the lives of African Americans in the period following the Harlem Renaissance. The Great Depression that ended the movement presented economic and social challenges for African Americans. It marked a time when African Americans became more visible in addressing their needs through government programs instituted to revive the economy. It also witnessed a transition for African Americans in politics. They realized options in party affiliation; therefore, many shifted to the Democratic party, partly due to its social programs that included all Americans as espoused by Franklin D. Roosevelt, a northern Democrat. In 1934, Arthur Mitchell of Illinois, an African American Democrat, replaced Oscar DePriest, an African American Republican, in the House of Representatives, thereby becoming the first African American Democrat in Congress. Two African American lawyers were elected as Democrats to New York City judgeships in 1930.

The Communist Party and the Socialist Party also recruited African American voters. They solicited African American support when they defended the "Scottsboro boys," a group of young African American men who had been unjustly accused of raping two White women in Alabama in 1931. But the vast majority of African Americans merely continued to ignore Communism as a method of achieving their goals. African Americans also participated in the economy as sharecroppers in farming and as laborers in industries.

Onset of the Great Depression

During the terms of Republican Presidents Warren Harding and Calvin Coolidge, the United States enjoyed an unparalleled business boom. The automobile industry grew steadily. The radio rose in popularity. The new rayon manufacturing plants hired thousands of workers. Chain stores came into existence as farming production increased. Wall Street speculators believed that mining and manufacturing formed a firm base for national prosperity. Borrowing on "margin" to finance new business ventures, they watched the inflated dollar become unstable. Some economists issued severe warnings that the boom could not survive without government controls. But they went unheeded. Harding, Coolidge, and Secretary of Commerce Herbert Hoover, who became President in 1929, believed in an unregulated market. Then, on October 29, 1929, came the stock market crash and the Great Depression. Businesses closed. Mines shut down. Banks failed. Workers were without jobs and without cash. The "chicken in every pot" which President Hoover had promised before entering the White House became a grim joke to the hungry millions.

African Americans and the Economic Impact of Great Depression

African Americans, some of whom had participated in the national prosperity of the Roaring Twenties, suffered the hardest from the Great Depression. By 1934, 26 percent were jobless, compared with 17 percent unemployment among Whites. Most attempts to organize labor proved impossible. Asa Philip Randolph and Chandler Owen had formed the National Association of Labor Unionism among Negroes in the twenties, only to see their efforts fail during the Depression's bleak years.

Farmers still suffered from the recession of 1920. The rising cost of manufactured goods worsened their plight, and the masses of African Americans were still employed in farming.

Both in the cities and on the farms, hundreds of thousands of families were reduced to living in crude shanty communities—"Hoovervilles," as the bitter, jobless masses called them. African American owned banks, in particular, met with disaster during the Depression. The Metropolitan Bank and Trust Company (Norfolk, Virginia), the Prudential Bank (Washington, D.C.), the Douglass National Bank (Chicago) all closed after the crash. When this happened, it ensured the failure of other African American financial ventures. The Victory Life Insurance Company, after doing business in 14 states, reorganized but existed for only a short while longer. The National Benefit Life Insurance Company had operations in 28 states. It failed in 1933. Lower wages and unemployment meant that people were not buying insurance. Furthermore, living conditions worsened for African Americans. Many African Americans had to live in crudely built shanties.

African American industrial laborers also suffered major setbacks during the Great Depression. The willingness of White workers to take jobs formerly restricted to African Americans forced many African American laborers onto public relief.

In Chicago, Cleveland and St. Louis —the largest industrial centers, African Americans accounted for up to 50 percent of the jobless totals. At least 75 percent of all African American workers in Birmingham, Alabama, the steel-making center of the South, were out of work. Roughly 80 percent of all African American workers in St. Louis were either unemployed or in jobs far below their abilities. Mechanization, crop reduction and eviction hurt African American sharecroppers and tenant farmers. Overall, the Depression was more severe for African Americans than for Whites. However, the election of Franklin D. Roosevelt, a Democrat, to the presidency changed conditions for African Americans due to reform programs instituted to ameliorate the economy.

Franklin Delano Roosevelt and the Great Depression

African American voters gradually began to shift from the Republican Party to become Democrats as evidenced by the election of 1932, when Franklin Delano Roosevelt, a northern Democrat, won due to their support. Roosevelt faced a dismal economic nation when he took office on March 4, 1933. The American industry in 1932 had operated at less than half its maximum volume of 1929. Total wages paid in 1932 were 60 percent less than in 1929. American

business had run a net loss of more than five billion dollars; well over twelve million Americans were jobless. In towns which relied upon industry, masses of people had no means of survival. But the President came into office with a cheerful resolution. "The only thing we have to fear is fear itself," he had said in his inaugural speech. By the spring of 1933, Roosevelt had begun his series of morale building radio addresses: his "fireside chats." At first, African Americans appeared skeptical of Roosevelt radio broadcasts. Their publications granted him the benefit of doubt when he spoke about justice and equality, in the hope that he was talking, too, to African Americans. He called lynching murder, remarked W. E. B. DuBois, and "these things give us hope." His acknowledgment, through his Secretary of Labor, of the National Urban League's survey of economic conditions among African Americans was, in the words of an *Opportunity* editorial, "an evidence of his deep interest in the African Americans' welfare." By midway through his first term, Roosevelt had captured the admiration and affection of the African American people and, with that, their votes.

During the campaign of 1936, African Americans were outspoken in their support of the Democratic national ticket. Sixteen thousand Harlem residents traveled to Madison Square Garden in September of that year to attend a political rally, and 60 other cities held similar and simultaneous rallies. The New Yorkers mixed a rich fare of music and entertainment with leading New Dealers talking politics, but it was an African Methodist Episcopal Bishop, the Reverend C. Ransome, who symbolized the affair and its meaning by reading a "New Emancipation Proclamation." The vote in November was anticlimactic; the second Roosevelt had swayed African American voters from the Republican Party.

Roosevelt did not publicly associate himself with African American projects or African American leaders before 1935, but his programs and some of his associates were more aggressive. He named Harold L. Ickes, the president of the Chicago NAACP, as secretary of the interior. Speaking to the Federal Council of Churches, Roosevelt recalled Lincoln's phrase, "freedom to the free." Having earlier denounced lynching, the President told the NAACP: "No democracy can long survive which does not accept as fundamental to its very existence the recognition of the rights of its minorities." The President's wife, Eleanor, stood firmly behind her husband in this conviction. Mrs. Roosevelt devoted herself tirelessly to improving welfare and human rights programs.

During 1933 and 1934, the federal government abandoned its former laissez-faire philosophy toward business. Roosevelt embraced the economic theories of England's John Maynard Keynes. They required a planned economy in these hard times, with much more federal deficit spending. Congress created a host of federal agencies during Roosevelt's first months in office. This busy legislative period, known as "the one hundred days," prepared to tackle the massive rebuilding task. Its programs included the Civil Works Administration (CWA), the Public Works Administration (PWA), the Civilian Conservation Corps (CCC), and the Works Projects Administration (WPA). The Roosevelt program, called the New Deal, helped stem the tide of the Depression. Yet even the massive make-work projects under the WPA, which helped millions of families, ultimately failed to bring about a full national recovery, and huge federal debts were incurred to pay for these extensive measures of relief. All these programs were authorized under the National Recovery Act which created the National Recovery Administration (NRA). This agency drafted and acted as overseer for a series of codes to set market prices and limit commerce. When President Roosevelt asked Congress in 1935 to extend the emergency acts for two more years, Congress countered by granting only a ten-month extension. In the meantime, Congress drafted new social-reform laws. It passed the Social Security Act in 1935, two decades after the income tax was adopted. Although critics attacked such measures as "creeping socialism," these policies did help to stabilize the nation in its darkest hour. For more than one million needy African Americans, the Roosevelt crash program was a welcome approach.

African Americans and Farming

The percentage of tenant farmers increased greatly as the Depression dragged on. Yet among African Americans, this shift was barely noticeable by the 1930s. The large proportion of African American tenant farmers remained about the same for most of the period between 1900 and 1935. Prejudice made the poor African American farmers' lot even harder than that of the White southern sharecropper or tenant farmer. Unlike White farmers, African Americans did not have access to credit. Thus, the landlord was expected to furnish seed and fertilizer as well as subsistence credit. In turn, the landlord received a share of the crop. He usually placed a lien upon the crop as security for the credit advanced to the sharecropper. Over the years, the landlord's books invariably showed the tenants' increasing indebtedness. "Even when croppers and share tenants clear anything on the year's farming," one investigator noted, "they usually exhaust their resources within a few months and are destitute again at the beginning of the crop year." Thus, the tenant farmers became virtual serfs in a system similar to medieval feudalism. By 1940, land ownership had risen among African American farmers to 21 percent; sharecropping was reduced by one-fourth. Establishing and maintaining credit remained a problem, even for the middle class farmer. Merchants were the main sources of credit, at prices far above the market rate. Interest rates ran the gamut, sometimes soaring as high as 100 percent.

Severe economic conditions had forced many African Americans back to the White man's fields. African American farmers were severely affected by two factors impacting farm labor. The first was the shift of cotton culture to the Southwest: Texas and New Mexico. African Americans who wanted to follow this path of migration were frustrated by Mexicans and southern Whites who competed against them for the right to work the new plantation land. A second factor was farm mechanization. The use of tractors, the mechanical cotton picker and other farm machinery helped bar unskilled African American labor. Farming with machinery had become skilled work. It was regarded as a White man's job. Just how much displacement occurred as a result of the machine cannot be ascertained, but it has been the basis of much speculation. Farm land had fallen more and more under corporate control. A survey of 46 southern counties in 1934 showed that corporations held one-tenth of the farm land. Other factors slowed the advancement of African American farmers. Some seemed insurmountable: for example, the exhaustion resulting from malnutrition and indifference due to the miserable life on the farm. In addition to the one-crop system, African American workers were victimized by mob law and lynching and the old plagues of southern farming—seasonal labor and the boll weevil.

The farmers received some federal relief during the Depression, but the prospect of aid to African American farmers raised a new issue. Congress had created the Federal Farm Board in 1929, but it had offered little help to African American farms under the Hoover administration. William S. Scarborough, president of Wilberforce University, was among several men appointed to an African American commission established as a branch of the Federal Farm Board. Although these men conducted studies and made local investigations, no help was forthcoming to aid the plight of the African American farmer.

Under the New Deal, two new farm loan agencies were created: the Regional Agricultural Credit Corporation and the Federal Land Banks. But they aided few farmers of either race. However, the agencies did manage to relieve the South's credit system. The Agriculture Department's

county extension workers showed many African American farmers how to improve their crop production as well as how to diversify their crops. Yet these agents, including some 416 African Americans in 1937-38, were far too few to achieve a large-scale solution to the African American farmers' problems.

The Agricultural Adjustment Administration (AAA) introduced federal production restrictions to the farmer. It controlled crop harvests of wheat, corn, cotton, rice and tobacco, as well as livestock and other crops. Farmers were paid cash subsidies to restrict the acreage for their crops or to reduce their livestock. The AAA sought to reduce crop acreage, aimed at providing a controlled harvest at controlled price levels. The farmer was expected to benefit from this planned approach. Yet, the AAA program scarcely helped the African American farmer. Many tenants and farm laborers were made expendable by the acreage reduction. Although federal contracts with employers stated that tenants should not be laid off, evictions and displacements were commonplace. Thousands of African American tenants became jobless. Many could not secure relief checks. Fraud and dishonesty also occurred in payment of parity checks. Tenants reported that they never received their checks. When the government made crop payments directly to farm workers, their status improved. But such justice seldomly prevailed.

Therefore, African Americans sought employment outside farming and focused on jobs in the industries. They encountered problems in securing industrial jobs because many required union affiliation. In this instance, unions at first did not accept African American laborers. Still, African Americans relied on support from the federal government to address their labor concerns. The National Recovery Administration (NRA) assumed responsibility for legislation geared toward the labor force.

African American Laborers and Government Agencies

The NRA, functioning under its Blue Eagle emblem since 1933, attracted criticism from many quarters. Some viewed it as a way for workers to enjoy an easy living without engaging in legitimate work. Others charged that it failed to improve the workers' lot; still others noted the widespread abuse of the NRA's code in the South, where the minimum wage scale was regarded as "too much money for African Americans." NRA relief measures did aid many thousands, but they were of little help in easing racial bigotry. The adoption of codes under the National Recovery Administration promised better times, but they did not appear soon. Attempting a system of equality, the NRA divided the entire nation's work force by jobs and geography. This regional "and occupational quota

system" served unwittingly to remove many southern African American workers from minimum-wage and maximum hour statutes.

The Negro Industrial League proposed a united front of all African American groups in mid-1933. This unit had sought equal treatment of African Americans under the industrial codes. Under John W. Davis, its executive secretary, and Dr. Robert C. Weaver, its director of research, the League had advised the Roosevelt administration in keeping with its aim "to establish a group of fact finders in Washington to study the plans of the federal government for recovery and to seek to integrate the African American into such plans." In response to this request, the Joint Committee on National Recovery was created in the fall of 1933. It represented 22 national "member organizations." The committee studied the announcements, press releases, proposed codes and executive orders which flowed daily from the National Recovery Administration. It appeared publicly before committees of Congress, filed protests and legal briefs, and released federal updates to the African American press. The panel's careful assessments proved beneficial. The White House soon recognized the significance of the NRA's policies for African American workers, as well as the necessity of appointing African American intellectuals to work with branches regulated under the NRA.

Dr. Clark Foreman was named the agency's adviser on African American affairs as a result, and Dr. Weaver became his assistant. An administrative order banned discrimination in the Works Progress Administration "on any ground whatsoever, such as race, religion or political affiliation." Forrester B. Washington of the Atlanta School of Social Work was named WPA adviser for African American affairs. After seven months, Alfred Edgar Smith succeeded him. Under both Washington and Smith, this office dealt mainly with studies. At the time, over 100 African Americans served in jobs at WPA headquarters in the District of Columbia. Other African Americans held supervisory posts on the WPA's field staffs. The Farm Security Administration had already set up an office on race relations headed by Joseph H. B. Evans, to promote racial integration of the federal farm-aid program. By late 1933, the Farm Credit Administration had opened its African American relations section with Henry A. Hunt in charge. Cornelius King, a Louisianan, later succeeded him.

Thus, African American laborers received consideration due to the efforts of African American appointees. However, labor unions hesitated to accept African American workers, despite encouragement from the Roosevelt administration and legislation supporting labor unions in the workforce.

African Americans and Labor Unionism

The Wagner Act of 1935 had set rules for collective bargaining by labor unions, and the Fair Labor Standards Act of 1938 had established wage guidelines. The labor movement regarded both laws as major victories. A new leader, John L. Lewis, had entered the labor scene in the meantime. Lewis, president of the United Mine Workers, had formed the Congress of Industrial Organizations (CIO) in 1935.

The CIO began as a committee of the American Federation of Labor (AFL). But it was an industrial union, not a craft union. It assembled the unskilled and semi-skilled under its wing. When the AFL refused to pursue a more liberal recruiting policy, including seeking more unskilled laborers for unionization, Lewis and his newly formed committee pulled out of the predominantly craft union federation. The union concentrated its activities in areas where no unions existed, or where there were large numbers of unskilled workers who, although unionized, had no national affiliation. From the start, the policies of the CIO were nonrestrictive where African Americans were concerned. The garment workers, composed of two separate unions, had long included African Americans in their midst; and, the longshoremen on the West Coast, headed by Harry Bridges, not only urged African Americans to be unionized but also made certain that no one was discriminated against because of race or color. Only in the South was the African American still forced to remain in all-African American unions under CIO jurisdiction. This was due to the attitude of the southern laborer who refused to fraternize with African Americans in unions. But even in the South, the CIO organizers were eventually successful in breaking down some barriers, and the formation of its Committee to Abolish Racial Discrimination aided the CIO toward that end. When Willard Townsend, president of the newly formed International Brotherhood of Redcaps, received permission for his union to enter the ranks of the CIO, he became the first African American national officer in organized labor. Elected an international vice-president in 1940, Townsend became a motivating force behind complete integration in the labor movement. Townsend's administrative assistant, George L. P. Weaver, went to the CIO national headquarters to become permanent secretary of the Committee to Abolish Racial Discrimination.

The National Labor Relations Board, an outgrowth of the Wagner Act, served further to eliminate discrimination among laborers because it protected the right to form unions in the many industries. Thus, the United Auto Workers, an arm of the CIO, gained jurisdiction over the automobile industry in Detroit and was largely responsible for the inclusion of African Americans in jobs requiring skilled labor. In some instances, however, African Americans were reluctant to join unions for fear of repercussions on their jobs. Many shared a distrust of the national unions based on past experience. The presence of Townsend on the national governing board of the CIO undoubtedly served as an incentive to convince other African Americans to join, as well as provide reassurance that the unions were acting on their behalf.

The initial involvement with the unions on the part of more skeptical members of the African American working class soon convinced them that unionization meant job security and better wages. Furthermore, the open racial policies of the CIO motivated the AFL to place more pressure on some of its affiliates to drop their restrictions or face loss of membership in the national organization. Between 1935 and 1945, African American membership in the CIO increased from 180,000 to 1,250,000. African Americans also joined with Whites in labor blocs like the Southern Tenant Farmers Union. For the first time since the Populist movement of the 1890s, African Americans and Whites joined forces in portions of the rural South, seeking unity for survival. But the Southern Tenant Farmers Union did not succeed in its efforts to force landowners to keep the tenants on the farms where most of the land had been placed in the nonproductive land bank. Instead, as union membership grew, the landowners became more determined to rid themselves of their sharecroppers and tenant farmers. The fact that African Americans had joined forces with poor Whites further annoyed landowners. Therefore, the only advantage for African Americans in this new alliance was the hope of continued unity with their White counterparts. But even this failed when, like the Populists before them, the poor Whites decided that an African American alliance was detrimental to their cause.

African Americans and New Deal Programs

The Roosevelt administration took further steps to address the plight of African American laborers with its New Deal agencies. For the African American, the most significant were the Federal Employment Relief Administration (FERA), the National Recovery Administration (NRA), the Works Progress Administration, later called the Work Projects Administration (WPA), the Agricultural Adjustment Administration (AAA), the Tennessee Valley Authority (TVA), the National Youth Administration (NYA), the Civilian Conservation Corps (CCC), and the public housing efforts of several agencies.

The FERA, the first New Deal agency to work directly to ease the predicament of the needy, tried through locally administered aid and work projects to put more money into circulation. Until the end of 1935, when it was abolished, it administered most of the direct relief and work relief programs which the New Dealers initiated, and it distributed about four billion dollars. Its progress was hindered by racial discrimination, since the design of projects and allocation of funds remained in local hands. In Jacksonville, Florida, African American families on relief outnumbered White families three to one, but the money was divided according to proportions of the total city population. Thus, 15,000 African American families received 45 percent of the funds and 5,000 White families got 55 percent. Along the Mississippi River, from Natchez to New Orleans, African Americans were passed over for skilled jobs and frequently received less than the stipulated minimum wage. When the state of Georgia convinced the FERA administrator to fix hourly wages for African Americans below 30 cents an hour, Urban League's *Opportunity* editorial mournfully questioned: "Does this presage the end of that heralded concern for the Forgotten Man."

There were other agencies which assisted African Americans, as well as Whites, in more specialized ways, such as the Federal Writers' Project and the Office of Education studies, which provided assistance for black education. At its height, the Federal Writers Project employed 5,000 writers on a variety of programs. Most notably, it produced a popular series of state and city guidebooks, each combining history, folklore, and tourism. The 150-volume "Life in America" series included valuable oral histories of former slaves. Work on the Writers Project helped many African American writers to thrive, master their craft, and go on to great achievement and prominence. These included Ralph Ellison, Richard Wright, Margaret Walker, Langston Hughes, and Zora Neale Hurston.

The very number of agencies added credibility to the mounting fact that, for the first time, the federal government had engaged and was grappling with some of the fundamental barriers to race progress. It was one thing to take on and struggle with a problem at the federal level and another thing to implement it at lower levels. Most of the New Deal agency programs ran afoul of local laws and customs, and most of them failed on very practical grounds. As a consequence, African Americans vigorously attacked the inequities, even while they appreciated the limited benefits.

In 1935, the Joint Committee on National Recovery met at Howard University and thereafter decided to create the National Negro Congress. A. Philip Randolph suggested its formation "not only to arouse and fire the brooding masses to action in their own defense, but to attack the forces of reaction that seek to throttle African Americans with increasing Jim Crowism, segregation and discrimination." The following year, the Congress met in Chicago to organize and name local councils. It held its last conference in 1940, when its leaders contemplated on radicalism as a means of achieving racial justice. This radical ideology soon led to the group's demise. The Southern Youth Congress was organized at Richmond in early 1937 and drew a large following. But by 1940, this group had also fallen into leftist hands and had folded. In some areas, other kinds of tactics were used. St. Louis' local Urban League began a Jobs-for-African Americans campaign in 1931 which led to the boycott of a White owned chain store whose trade was almost exclusively African American; however, it did not have any African American employees. Thereafter, White employers in other urban centers were pressured to employ African Americans. Reverend John H. Johnson organized the Citizens League for Fair Play in 1993 to protest the failure of White merchants to hire African American clerks. The league led boycotts, picketed the stores, and led protests. It carried signs with the motto "Don't Buy Where You Can't Work" in front of White stores in African American districts that refused to hire African Americans. The Colored Merchants Association organized by Albon Holsey of the National Negro Business League encouraged African Americans to purchase merchandise cooperatively. The Rev. Adam Clayton Powell, Jr. led a series of such boycotts in Harlem. In 1935, a confrontation between White merchants and landlords in Harlem led to a riot. An African American youth was accused of stealing a knife from one of the stores on 125th Street. A rumor spread that he had been beaten to death. African Americans congregated and accused the police of brutality, and they accused the White merchants of discrimination in hiring. A riot took place, during which three African Americans were killed, 200 store windows smashed, and more than two million dollars worth of damage was done. The city expressed outrage. Mayor LaGuardia appointed a Committee on Conditions in Harlem to investigate the causes of the riot. It was headed by E. Franklin Frazier, a Howard University sociology pro-fessor. Racial incidents such as these convinced African American workers to organize during the period. The National Industrial Recovery Act had a section allowing employees the right to organize and bargain collectively. The National Labor Board enforced provisions of the statute. A majority of African American workers were not protected by the statute.

In the spring of 1935, the Supreme Court ended the National Recovery Act, ruling that it violated the Constitution. Therefore, the National Labor Board was replaced by the National Labor Relations Board (NLRB). It assumed responsibility for establishing rules for collective bargaining. It also set up 22 regional boards to conduct elections in industries to allow employees the right to bargain with the employers. It also handled labor disputes and settled strikes. African American workers used these rights to their advantage whenever possible.

The decision to void the National Recovery Act caused other New Deal agencies to expand their roles. They moved quickly to assume the NRA's program burdens and soon they oversaw such Depression statutes as the Wages and Hours Act. In 1938, Congress passed the Fair Labor Standards Act, better known as the Wages and Hour bill, which established a minimum wage of 25 cents per hour to be increased to 40 cents by 1945, with a maximum work week of 40 hours, and any excess to be paid as overtime. Some African Americans benefited from this act; however, several million did not because it excluded agricultural and domestic workers. Both the Works Progress Administration and the Public Works Administration carried the majority of the former respon-sibilities under the National Recovery Act.

Due to the restructuring of the statute and the expansion of New Deal programs, more than a million African American workers secured employment with the WPA and other agencies. For the first time, thousands of African American women were employed in occupations other than domestic and farm work. African American men, too, acquired different occupations in the job market. They worked in areas ranging from mural painting and stage set design to map-making and plastering. African Americans accounted for 39 percent of all WPA workers in South Carolina and Louisiana, 37 percent in Georgia, and 67 percent in the District of Columbia.

The WPA organized a number of special projects requiring the talents of writers, musicians, artists, teachers and entertainers. The African American Theater Project in New York, for instance, employed 232 theater workers in 1936. The Federal Music Project hired others. The Federal Writers Project gave several hundred African Americans a chance to deve-lop their gifts in literature, history, art, music, drama and education. The Federal Art Project encouraged a number of African American artists whose work was regarded as signi-ficant. Thousands of the Depression's victims also gained access to the projects' health, recreation and social centers.

Another New Deal agency focused on the African American youth. African American staff members sought to develop the special interests of the young. The National Youth Administration (NYA), a WPA subsidiary, through its work program enabled thousands of African American boys and girls to attend high school and college. Many out-of-school youths were aided through community centers, libraries and playgrounds. Two African American educators, Dr. Mordecai W. Johnson, president of Howard University, and Dr. Mary McLeod Bethune, founder of Bethune College, served as mem-bers of the NYA's national advisory committee. Dr. Bethune became director of the division of Negro Youth Affair.

The NYA believed in "learning to do by doing." It planned a vocational guidance and placement program, so that the youth could be aided directly. Scholarships totaling more than $520,000 went to some 113 African American colleges in 1937-38 alone. Roughly 63,000 African American youths (ages 16 to 24) benefited from the program. The NYA's enacting statute required fair distribution of funds without discrimination because of race. It also provided for the creation of an agency to provide training for America's youth. The Civilian Conservation Corps (CCC) trained young African Americans and hired African American educational advisers in its camps. The CCC had segregated camps in the South and in some parts of the North; the great bulk of the integrated camps were in New England. By 1935, its peak year, the CCC had over a half million boys in camp. At first, African Americans were not accepted in CCC camps in as high a proportion as Whites. But as time went on, this situation was largely remedied. The camps reported housing 40,000 African American youths in 1936, as well as 25 medical officers and chaplains, 136 study advisers, 600 business managers and 1,400 chauffeurs. In general, African Americans stayed in CCC camps longer than Whites, were not moved up to administrative posts in camps as readily as Whites, and were restricted to less than 10 percent of the total enrollment. Since the proportion of young African American men in need was substantially higher than this, the quota system was actually inequitable. By 1940, the corps included roughly 300,000 African Americans.

African Americans also secured employment in the federal sector. The number of African Americans listed on the Civil Service Commission roster as federal employees from 1933 to 1938 increased from 50,000 to 82,000. In most cases, prior to 1938, African American workers were assigned to the sub-clerical levels as janitors, porters and messengers. This occurred even under the competitive Civil Service Commission ratings. Certain presidential patronage positions had been lost to them under new rulings, as any one of three top candidates tested could be selected for a job. This became discriminatory when officials exhibited racial prejudice. Some jobs were denied to African Americans by tradition or agreement. Such barriers

worked as "effectively as explicit orders." Professional opportunities opened up in the government, although not at the rate at which African Americans were graduating from college. For the first time, African Americans were employed as architects, lawyers, engineers, economists, statisticians, interviewers, office managers, case aides, and librarians. Nonprofessional white-collar jobs, which had rarely been within reach of the race, now became available to trained stenographers, clerks, and secretaries. While many of these jobs centered around programs for African Americans within the government, such as African American slum clearance projects, African American NYA offices, and the like, they broke down barriers that had excluded African Americans from such positions.

Departmental racial segregation had been sanctioned by some federal officials. The humiliation felt by many African American applicants resulted in a decline of African American workers by 1930. The ratio of African American bureaucrats was usually far below that expected. Many White workers voiced complaints when assigned to work under African American supervisors. This attitude changed slowly with the passage of time.

One method used by the government to bring about the fair treatment of African Americans was to assign African American advisers to federal agencies. This policy first appeared in the 1917 appointment of Dr. Emmett J. Scott as confidential adviser to the secretary of war on matters affecting the interests of African American citizens. Scott had been secretary to Dr. Booker T. Washington at Tuskegee Institute. A second step was taken shortly afterward when Dr. George E. Haynes of Fisk University became director of African American economics in the Department of Labor. The appointments of Drs. Foreman and Weaver were the first under the New Deal, and were the nucleus of a loose coalition of African American advisers who became known as Roosevelt's "Black Cabinet." Never before had African American leaders participated in government affairs as freely and as frequently. The Department of Commerce had E. K. Jones, on leave from the National Urban League; the NYA had Mary Bethune; Interior had Robert Weaver; the Social Security Board had Ira DeA. Reid; Labor had Lawrence W. Oxley; and the Office of Education had Ambrose Caliver, to mention a few. Their appointments attracted attention to issues facing African Americans.

Two other African Americans, James C. Carter of Georgia and Clifton R. Wharton of Massachusetts, served in the Roosevelt administration in the consular and diplomatic service. Lester A. Walton represented the nation as minister to Liberia, and William C. George was the United States vice-consul there. Even so, the number of African American diplomats had declined since Theodore Roosevelt's last term. Eleven African Americans had been foreign service envoys in 1908. By 1938, there were only three.

African American Housing and Resettlement

A handful of other New Deal agencies also aided African Americans in the area of housing. The Home Owners' Loan Corporation loaned funds to forestall mortgage foreclosures. The Federal Housing Authority assisted workers in modernizing their homes. The Reconstruction Finance Corporation granted loans to institutions. The Federal Security Agency also made valuable contributions to the advancement of citizen welfare.

Slums had proliferated in the nation's cities as a result of overcrowding. Low-cost housing projects built by the Public Works Administration relieved these conditions somewhat. The plans for these developments called for African American management staffs and reduced rentals. By 1936, some 35 major cities had opened low-rent housing projects for African Americans at a cost of $130,000,000. The building contracts aided the labor situation by granting jobs to skilled African Americans in proportion to their number in the 1930 census.

African American architects, builders and contractors were hired to plan and construct the housing projects. Dr. Robert C. Weaver helped oversee these policies as special assistant to the administrator of the Federal Housing Authority.

The South grudgingly accepted the federal outlook on hiring African Americans. Several rural resettlement projects were launched at Bricks, North Carolina; Orangeburg, South Carolina; Tuskegee, Alabama; and in Phillips County, Arkansas. They hired qualified African Americans for the work force. Other projects followed these early ones.

By 1937, nine resettlement projects aided roughly 1,000 families at a cost exceeding $7,700,000. When the Tennessee Valley Authority (TVA) opened its model homes for workers at Norris Dam, it stated that African Americans would be barred because "they did not fit into the program." However, African Americans were gradually hired on the project. Investigators later found that the pay scale was proportionately lower for African Americans than for Whites. They also noted the poor conditions under which African Americans worked and the discrimination in housing assignment.

Status of African Americans

Although African American workers made some gains toward employment under the New Deal, many obstacles remained in their way. Private industry's rehiring of African Americans taken off WPA rolls moved very slowly. African Americans were seldom able to find steady work with adequate pay. The National Urban League's annual report for 1936 stated that most African Americans who returned to private firms found work in the basic industries—rubber, packing, iron and steel and the railroads—but seldom did these industries hire more African Americans than had worked for them prior to the Great Depression. As usual, a significant factor in African American unemployment was the substitution of White for African American labor. This trend jeopardized the jobs of African American hotel workers, waiters, elevator operators and bellboys. Racist groups were organized with the sole purpose of driving African Americans from jobs regarded as desirable for White workers. Leaders of the African American Shirts and former members of the Ku Klux Klan made speeches declaring that they loathed African Americans "that held jobs of White men" and "who were usurping the White man's rightful place." Through the years, African American workers found it harder to get jobs as well as to keep them. Discrimination, low wages, the barrier against skilled African American workers and continued joblessness gave rise to the slogan African American labor applied to itself: "Last hired, first fired."

The polls in 1940 showed that African American voters overwhelmingly supported Roosevelt for a third term, and the polls were right. The reason for this support was not difficult to surmise. Outside of what the New Deal Administration had tried to do directly and indirectly, the decade itself was marked with identifiable milestones of progress. In athletics, Jesse Owens won four gold medals at the Olympics in Berlin, Germany; ten other African Americans won 13 medals. African American football players starred on many of the major college teams. In 1937, Joe Louis, "the Brown Bomber," became the first African American heavyweight boxing champion of the world in 22 years when he knocked out his German contender, Max Schmeling, in the first round. The Germans were especially disappointed because Hitler had espoused the doctrine of Aryan supremacy, which claimed the physical and intellectual superiority of all White people, and the German people in particular. On the other hand, Louis' victory symbolized for millions of African Americans the struggle against the racist propaganda of both Hitler and the supporters of Jim Crow in America. In sports, professional baseball still resisted integration, but its time was not far off.

African Americans continued to make progress in other arenas. Zora Neale Hurston produced her most important novels, *Jonah's Gourd Vine* (1934), *Mules and Men* (1935), and *Their Eyes Were Watching God* (1937). Crystal Byrd Fauset of Pennsylvania, in 1938, became the first African American woman elected to a state legislative body. In the following year, actress Hattie McDaniel received an academy award for her role in "Gone With the Wind," thereby becoming the first African American to receive such recognition. In the same year, classical singer Marian Anderson performed at the Lincoln Memorial after the Daughters of the American Revolution (DAR) barred her from performing at Constitution Hall on the basis of her color. In 1940, Richard Wright published his most famous novel, *Native Son*, which addressed race in American society.

In interracial activities, conferences were sponsored on a variety of subjects. College students and adults met to discuss education, religion, economic matters and, of course, civil rights. Even in the South, Mary Bethune organized an interracial conference at the college she founded, and the White University of Florida tentatively sent delegates. In the deep South, interracial conferences were held on a segregated basis; Eleanor Roosevelt is told of attending one in Birmingham and inadvertently sitting in the colored section. "At once the police appeared to remind us of the rules and regulations on segregation. . . . Rather than give in I asked that chairs be placed for us with the speakers facing the whole group." Some White Southerners began to speak up for the African American. They were still a small minority, but the mere fact that a White state supervisor of schools in Georgia would admit to the inequalities of segregated schools, or a White North Carolina legislator would question a decreased appropriation for an African American college, was a sign of change.

Conclusion

The stock market crash of 1929 exposed the economic collapse of the nation. African Americans in cities and rural areas, already in poverty in most areas before the Great Depression, were especially hard hit. The Great Depression and New Deal era presented economic, social, political, and cultural challenges for African Americans. Franklin D. Roosevelt addressed the depression during his presidency by instituting New Deal programs to provide aid and to revive the economy. His "fireside chats" broadcast on radio kept the nation informed on the progress of the nation. African Americans felt included in the reform process.

The New Deal programs provided employment, housing, education, and social service assistance. In many instances, African Americans encountered discrimination in the administration of relief and employment services. In the midst of opposition, they made significant achievements in the workforce. They also made accomplishments in the arts, literature, and sports. They continued to progress as the Great Depression eased. The advent of a world war in Europe helped to end the depression. African Americans faced new obstacles upon the advent of World War II. Thus, in reality, none of the New Deal programs actually ended the Depression. It was the growing war in Europe, the rise of Nazism, American aid to the Allies and, ultimately, U.S. entry into World War II after the bombing of Pearl Harbor that revitalized the nation's economy. Remembering their experiences in World War I, African American soldiers and civilians were increasingly unwilling to quietly accept a segregated military or the discriminatory conditions they had previously endured.

Review Questions

1. Did the New Deal programs benefit African Americans? Explain your answer.

2. How did African American leaders respond to discrimination in hiring as practiced by White merchants in urban centers?

3. What was the "Black Cabinet" in the Roosevelt administration?

4. How did the Great Depression affect African American farmers?

5. Why did African American voters desert the Republican Party during the Great Depression and New Deal era?

6. What accomplishments did African American athletes make during the period, and how did they affect race relations?

Chapter 18

African Americans during World War II

This chapter looks at the activities of African Americans during World War II, with emphasis on their participation in the military and on the home front. African Americans had exhibited concern for the war before America became involved in the conflict when it persisted in Asia and Europe. As Germany and Italy pursued their plans in Europe during the 1930s, Japan attempted to gain control of Asia. Meanwhile, Adolph Hitler's Nazi Party achieved power in Germany in 1933.

Japan's actions caused conflict with the United States, since it threatened America's authority in the Philippines, Guam, Hawaii, and other islands in the Pacific. Germany's capture of Austria and most of Czechoslovakia, and its attack on Poland on September 1, 1939 persuaded Great Britain and France to declare war against the Axis powers that comprised Germany and Italy. America became apprehensive in 1940, when Germany conquered Denmark, Norway, the Netherlands, Luxembourg, and Belgium. President Franklin D. Roosevelt announced that the United States would be neutral;

and shortly thereafter, Congress passed the Neutrality Act of 1939. In June of 1940, Italy, under Benito Mussolini, entered the war on Germany's side; and later that month, France capitulated. With the fall of France, America feared Britain would be next.

In September of 1940, a group of African American leaders, led by Asa Philip Randolph and Walter White, submitted a seven-point program to President Roosevelt that outlined considerations for African Americans in the defense program. They demanded that (a) all available reserve officers be used to train recruits; (b) African American military recruits receive similar training as Whites; (c) existing units of the army accept officers and enlisted men on the basis of ability; (d) specialized personnel such as physicians, dentists, and nurses be integrated; (e) African Americans be appointed to draft boards; (f) discrimination in the Navy and Air Force be abolished; and (g) competent African Americans be appointed as civilian assistants to the Secretaries of War and Navy. The demands for flight training, admission of Black women into the Red Cross and military nursing units, and desegregation of the armed forces were of primary concern. President Roosevelt issued a statement on October 9, 1940 that argued against the latter demand on the basis that it would adversely affect national defense. Even though he promised to ensure the enlistment of African Americans in proportion to their demographic presence, Roosevelt continued policies dating back to WW I. Many African Americans were angered by the White House's erroneous claim that the Black leaders had approved the statement. However, additional political pressure by African Americans and some Republicans convinced Roosevelt to do more. Consequently, Benjamin O. Davis, Sr. was promoted to Brigadier General, flight training for Blacks was planned, more African Americans were drafted, Judge William H. Hastie, Dean of the Howard University Law School, was made a Civilian Aide to the Secretary of War in Matters of Black Rights, and an African American advisor was appointed to the Selective Service Board.

In the spring of 1941, Secretary of State Hull held a conference in Washington with the Japanese ambassador, Kichisaburo Nomura, in an effort to resolve their differences. Hull expressed dissatisfaction with the political and military situation in the Far East. Conditions for Japanese-Americans had worsened steadily after Japan declared war on China in 1937. Hull demanded Japan to withdraw from China and to abstain from attacking Dutch and French colonies in Southeast Asia. How he expected to get Japan to give up its conquest without either making concessions or going to war remained unclear.

By December of 1941, the United States had entered the war. A formal declaration of war could have been avoided had Japan relented. Neither the United States nor Japan wanted war. Roosevelt considered Germany a far more dangerous enemy and appeared disturbed by the possibility of engaging in a two-front war. As relations worsened between the nations, increased tensions finally led to war on December 7, 1941, when the Japanese bombed American warships at Pearl Harbor, Hawaii.

The war had placed tremendous strains on the American economy. About 15 million men and women entered the armed services; they, and in part the millions more in Allied uniforms, had to be fed, clothed, housed, and supplied with equipment ranging from typewriters and paper clips to rifles and grenades, tanks and airplanes. African Americans rallied to America's defense since Black leaders had already expressed interest in the war due to Italy's failed attempt in 1935 to invade Ethiopia.

African Americans on the Home front

African Americans had protested Italy's invasion of Ethiopia in 1935. Due to this incident, the Black community intensified its interest in international affairs. Black leaders in New York met and formed the International Council of Friends of Ethiopia, with Willis N. Huggins as Executive Secretary. Another organization, United Aid to Ethiopia, raised funds for the country. A leading Black newspaper, *The Pittsburgh Courier* sent its historical news analyst, J. A. Rogers, to cover the war. He wrote a booklet, "The Real Facts About Ethiopia," and lectured to Black and White audiences.

African Americans also condemned fascism in Europe and, they detested Hitler's Nazism and Aryan doctrines. Some had read his book, *Mein Kampf*, and resented statements made about Blacks in it. They also remembered when Germany insulted African American Olympic gold medal track stars, Jesse Owens and Ralph Metcalfe.

African Americans also provided tremendous support to the war effort on the home front. They purchased war bonds and signed up for payroll savings plans to purchase bonds. Due to training programs under the National Youth Administration (NYA) and the Works Progress Administration (WPA), thousands of African Americans received jobs in the defense industry and acquired skills in the aircraft industries, shipbuilding, welding, automotive mechanics, electricity, radio and numerous other fields. African Americans became active in preparations to defend the country against possible enemy attack. Crystal Bird Fauset served as a race relations advisor. African Americans served as managers, messengers, auxiliary firefighters and police officers, and they acquired assignments with the Office of Price Administration (OPA) to assist with programs to conserve food and other essential commodities to control prices. They gained employment as attorneys, price analysts, and economists, and they worked as information offices and clerks with local ration boards. African Americans also served in agencies established to build morale. African American women served with the Red Cross as Gray Ladies, as nurse aides, and as drivers in the Motor Corps.

African Americans worked with the United Service Organization (USO), organized in February 1941, to direct the activities of the Young Men Christian Association (YMCA), the Young Women's Christian Association (YWCA), National Catholics Community Services, the Salvation Army, Jewish Welfare Board and the Travelers Aid, into one great effort to boost the morale of service people in the war. More than 300 United Service Oversees (USO) clubs hired African American staff members to perform in

Black USO shows overseas to entertain soldiers in the war zones.

Another activity involving African Americans on a personal level during the war dealt with the government using African American men in a medical scientific study. The Tuskegee Syphilis Experiment was a medical study undertaken in Macon County, Alabama, by the U.S. Public Health Service (PHS), which had been ordered to deny medical attention to 412 African American men suffering from syphilis while pretending to treat them. The study, which received cooperation from the hospital at Tuskegee Institute and the medical community in Alabama, began in 1932. It was designed as a short-term project (six to eight months) whose purpose was to gain a greater scientific understanding of syphilis by studying the untreated progression of the disease. At that time, successful treatment for syphilis that took a year to complete sometimes had serious side affects and was expensive. It was assumed that those African American men with syphilis would remain untreated anyway, since the government did not have a medical program for poor people. They never received information that they had syphilis (they were told they had "bad blood"), never told that their illness could be sexually transmitted to others, and were led to believe that they were, in fact, receiving treatment. In the event that any of them did seek other medical help, area doctors told

them that they could not be treated and, instead, would refer them to the health service program workers. To acquire the cooperation of the Macon County Board of Health, the Public Health Service (PHS) had to agree to provide some treatment; however, they did not provide enough to discover a cure. They also provided the men with aspirin, iron supplements and, beginning in 1935, $50 for burial expenses. The study continued past the first year after acquiring enough scientific information. When the PHS initiated a nationwide venereal disease control program in the late 1930s, it denied treatment to the men in the Tuskegee study. They continued to be denied treatment, even after the discovery of the therapeutic effectiveness of penicillin in the early 1940s. The government finally terminated the study, officially known as the Tuskegee Study of Untreated Syphilis in the Negro Male, in 1972 after it came to the public's attention. By that time, many of the men had died from syphilis, often after going blind or insane from the disease. The approximately 50 survivors received treatment, as well as their surviving wives who had been infected and 20 surviving children who had been born with congenital syphilis. The government also agreed to pay each survivor $37,500 and their heirs $15,000.

In general, African Americans faced many problems on the

homefront because the government refused to intervene to address their concerns. Instead, the government helped to exploit African Americans as exhibited by the Tuskegee Study. Despite their disappointments, African Americans persevered during the war.

African American Soldiers

The War Department in 1940 established a policy to admit African Americans into the military based on the percentage of the African American population, which stood at 11 percent of the national population. The Selective Service Act passed by Congress in 1940 forbade discrimination in the drafting and training of men; thus, it enabled African Americans to become officers in the military. The military upheld segregation as a result of assigning African Americans to separate units. It established senior ROTC units, restricted to African Americans, at West Virginia State College, Hampton, North Carolina Agricultural and Technical College, Prairie View State College, and Tuskegee Institute.

By 1940, nearly 5,000 African Americans had enlisted in the United States army that comprised 230,000 enlisted men and women. Despite such legislation, discrimination still occurred. African American leaders protested unfair treatment toward African Americans in the military and

on the homefront. More than three million Blacks registered for service in the armed forces. The total number of Blacks enlisted in the military was close to one million. The participation of Blacks in the Selective Service reduced discrimination in accepting Blacks into the armed forces. African Americans served in almost every capacity under the Department of Defense Selective Services.

By June of 1940, 4,000 African Americans had joined the Navy. Most served as messmen, with no opportunity to learn trades in the Naval training program. In many instances, African Americans protested discrimination in the Navy. In 1942, the Secretary of the Navy announced that the Navy would accept the enlistment of African Americans for general service and as noncommissioned officers.

At the same time, the Marine Corps announced that African Americans would be accepted into its ranks. Only after the Secretary of War issued a statement to accept African Americans to officer candidate schools without discrimination did they acquire acceptance into the training schools. By the middle of 1942, African American officers had graduated at a rate of approximately 200 per month. They studied and trained with White officers. Only in the Air Corps were commissions given at segregated schools. In 1943, the Navy decided to allow African Americans to enter training programs for officers. The Navy commissioned African Americans as officers beginning in 1944. Before the end of the war, more than 50 Blacks had been commissioned. In the Marines and Coast Guards, African American had become officers.

Approximately half a million African Americans served in the service overseas. By February of 1945, 497,566 had performed in service overseas. In Europe, African Americans comprised almost half of the transportation corps. African Americans made up about one-fifth of the American engineers in Europe. African Americans served overseas in transportation, construction and combat units. Ground operations in Europe included 22 Black combat units. In the Mediterranean, the 92nd Division became a principally Black combat unit. In June of 1944, it served in Africa and later in Italy. In the same year, the U.S. Army integrated African American volunteers with White troops to fight during the "Battle of the Bulge," the Germans' last desperate counteroffensive to break through in the Ardennes forest in Belgium. Over 5,000 African American soldiers in the Army's service units volunteered; 2,500 of them were accepted. After six weeks of training, the African American troops were organized into 37 platoons of 40 men each, which were then attached to White units of 200 men each. Suggested by General John Lee and approved by General Dwight

D. Eisenhower, this was the first and only example of an integrated Army fighting force in WW II. White officers later judged that these Black soldiers had performed "very well" or "fairly well." Although this experiment proved to be quite successful, the Army withheld a favorable survey on the intermixing of its troops because it would supposedly have undermined southern political support for a postwar peacetime draft.

The 761st "Black Panther" Tank Battalion became the first African American armored unit to enter combat during an assault on the French towns of Moyenvic and Vic-sur-Seille. Staff Sergeant Ruben Rivers won a Silver Star for his heroic action in braving direct enemy fire to remove a roadblock that could have seriously delayed the American offensive.

The two major Black combat units overseas were the 99th Pursuit Squadron and the 332nd Fighter Group. The 99th Pursuit Squadron went to Europe, and the 332nd Fight Group went to the Mediterranean. Many African American soldiers participated in various types of fighting over Europe. Black ground crews received training at Chanute Field, Illinois. Approximately 600 African American pilots had received their wings before the end of the war.

African Americans had active roles in the war on both fronts in the Pacific and the Orient. The 93rd Division served as the main Black combat unit. Thousands of African

Americans in the Navy performed numerous technical tasks. High Navy officials complimented the performance of African American sailors. By the fall of 1944, 500 Black seamen had assumed duty on 25 large auxiliary vessels primarily in the Pacific. More than 900 African Americans in the Coast Guard carried out rescue work in the Atlantic. Approximately 24,000 African Americans served in the Merchant Marines where they encountered minimum segregation and discrimination in comparison to those in other branches of the military. They worked as seamen, engineers, and radio operators. The Merchant Marines named 18 ships after African Americans. The Black press and African American leaders portrayed the Merchant Marines as an outstanding example of Blacks and Whites working together for the war effort.

African American soldiers complained that they had not received proper awards for their performance. The military had not awarded the Congressional Medal of Honor to an African American since the Spanish-American War. Many Black units had received the Presidential Distinguished Unit Citation, and individual African American soldiers had received good conduct medals up to the Distinguished Service Cross.

Doris (Dorie) Miller, an African Americans from Waco, Texas, shot down enemy planes to help remove his mortally wounded captain to a place of greater safety. Before the day ended, Miller had destroyed six Japanese planes while manning a machine gun on the water-covered deck of the battleship *West Virginia*. For his heroism, Miller received the Navy Cross. Miller's acts of valor at Pearl Harbor went well beyond the call of duty.

Despite unfair treatment, African Americans made significant achievements. William H. Hastie received an appointment as Civilian Aide to the Secretary of War, and Colonel Campbell Johnson became the executive assistant to the Director of Selective Service.

Tuskegee Airmen

In January of 1941, under the direction of the NAACP, a Howard University student, Yancey Williams, filed a lawsuit against the War Department to gain admission into a pilot training center. Almost immediately following the filing of the suit, the War Department under pressure from northern congressmen, and with an order from President Roosevelt, announced that it would establish an aviation unit near Tuskegee Institute, Alabama, in cooperation with the institute for the training of African American pilots for the Army. The Tuskegee Training Program at the Tuskegee Institute in Alabama had trained by early 1941 approximately 1,000 "Tuskegee Airmen." Although the program's first students graduated three months after the bombing of Pearl Harbor, the army refused to deploy the Tuskegee pilots outside the United States until 1943, when the 99th Squadron came to North Africa. Racial hostility internationally against the military almost led to its recall, but the squadron was saved, thanks to the testimony of its commander, Benjamin O. Davis, Jr., who later became the first African American Air Force General. Tuskegee Institute served as the only training facility for Black pilots until the flying program closed in 1946.

African American Aviators at Tuskegee Army Air Field

The Tuskegee Airmen's accomplishments in the war effort were legendary. The Airmen represented four all-Black World War II squadrons—the 99th, 100th, 301st, and 302nd. In 1944, the 99th merged with the other three Black squadrons to form the 332nd Fighter Group. As a bomber escort group on 200 bomber missions, the 332nd won fame for not

losing a single U.S. bomber to enemy aircraft. In 1,578 combat missions, the Tuskegee Airmen shot down 111 enemy planes, destroyed 150 others on the ground, and sank a German destroyer. The Tuskegee Airmen saw action in Africa, Sicily, Italy, France, Germany, and the Balkans; 66 of them died in action. The members of the 332nd won more than 100 Distinguished Flying Crosses, and the group won three Distinguished Unit Citations.

African American Women in the Military

African American women also served with distinction in various capacities. In January of 1941, the U.S. Army established a quota of 56 African American nurses for admission to the Army Nurse Corps. Through the efforts of the National Association of Colored Graduate Nurses (NACGN), the Army abolished the quota before the end of the war. Frances Payne Bolton, Congresswoman from Ohio, introduced in June 1943 an amendment in Congress that barred racial bias in the Nurse Training Bill. As a result, more than 2,000 African American female students enrolled in the U.S. Cadet Nurse Corps. In 1941, Susan Elizabeth Freeman became one of the first African American women to join the Army Nurse Corps in 1941. On March 9, 1945, Phyllis Mae Daley of New York City became the first

African American female to serve in the Navy's Nurse Corps. Only four African American female nurses, of almost 11,000 Navy nurses, served during the war.

African American nurses served in all Black military hospitals as well as in four general hospitals, the regional hospitals, and at least nine station hospitals. They also served in Africa and in Europe during the war. By late July of 1945, there were 512 in the Army's Nurse Corps, including nine captains and 115 first lieutenants. Of the three units that served overseas, one was a group of 63 African American nurses who worked with the 168th Station Hospital in Manchester, England, caring for wounded German prisoners. This was the first "experiment" in which African American nurses treated White males.

African American women also served in other branches of the military. President Franklin D. Roosevelt created the Women's Auxiliary Army Corps (WACC), converted 14 months later to the Women's Army Corps (WAC) when he signed Public Law 554 on May 4, 1942. The European Theater of Operations was the only theater of operations where African American WACs could serve. More than 4,000 African American women had enlisted into the WAC. African American women served with distinction in various capacities.

The first and only African American WACs assigned to overseas duty were the 800 women of the 6888th Central Postal Directory Battalion, commanded by Major Charity Adams (Earley), the highest-ranking African American woman during the war. The unit served at Birmingham, England before moving to Rouen, France, and later Paris. It facilitated the delivery of mail to all U.S. personnel (military, civilian, and Red Cross) in the European Theater of Operations. After they arrived in France, the women worked three eight-hour shifts daily, seven days a week, handling 65,000 pieces of mail per shift. Viewing this massive effort as a way to improve morale, the women redirected a huge backlog of mail to American men and women serving in Europe.

African American women encountered discrimination and segregation in the military. They were segregated and limited in their assignments in the WAC. With support from activists as well as civil rights groups, African American nurses, led by Mabel Keaton Staupers, pressured the WAC to eliminate racially biased assignments for nurses in January of 1945.

African American women were totally excluded from the Women Accepted for Volunteer Emergency Service in the Navy (WAVES) until 1944. Bessie Garrett became the first African American woman accepted in the WAVES. The first WAVES officer graduates from Smith College included two African American women, Frances Wills and Harriett Ida Pickens. By July of 1945, 72 African American WAVES had been trained in a fully integrated and racially progressive program. On October 20, 1944, the Coast Guard lifted the ban on prohibiting the enlistment of African American women in the Coast Guard. The Coast Guard only admitted five African American women during the war, and among them was Olivia J. Hooker.

The SPARS, the Coast Guard's women auxiliary, began enlisting qualified African American women. Yeoman Second Class Olivia J. Hooker was the first Black woman to enlist. Although the officers training program was closed to civilians by this time, six previously enlisted African American nurses did attend officers candidate school and received their commissions as ensigns before WW II ended.

While enlisted, African American women sometimes encountered abuse from White soldiers. In 1944, a group of African American WACs stationed at Camp Forrest, Tennessee, reported ongoing cases of sexual harassment and assaults from White paratroopers on the base. In a letter, one woman wrote:

> "Two paratroopers came into the barracks last night, downstairs where I sleep.
> When we woke up [one] was between my bed and other girls. He woke her up

> Kissing her. She screamed and I jumped out of bed. The rest of them did the same.
> He and his buddy ran out so fast it was impossible to do anything about it."

In a Kentucky railroad station, White officers brutally assaulted three African American WACs, allegedly because they did not "move along" fast enough when ordered to do so.

Labor and African Americans in Defense Jobs

During the war, African Americans encountered discrimination in employment in the defense industry. Many defense industry plants produced weapons for the war, while the government made efforts to discourage discrimination. The United States Office of Education declared that there should be no discrimination on the account of race, creed, or color. The President spoke out against discrimination. The Office of Production Management established an employment and training branch to facilitate the hiring of African Americans in the defense industry.

In January of 1941, Asa Philip Randolph, President of the Brotherhood of Sleeping Car Porters, proposed a March on Washington of 50–100,000 Blacks to protest discrimination and to demand jobs in defense industries and equality in the armed forces. President Franklin Roosevelt responded and issued, on June 25, 1941, Executive Order 8802 that established the Fair Employment Practices Commission (FEPC) to receive and investigate complaints of discrimination in defense industries and apprenticeship programs. Thus, Roosevelt became the first President to issue an executive order on race relations since the Emancipation Proclamation. However, segregation and blatant discrimination against African Americans in the Armed Forced was not eliminated until Executive Order 9981 was issued several years later by President Harry S. Truman on July 26, 1948.

The Girl Friends for the FEPC presenting check of $500 to Asa Philip Randolph at the office of the Brotherhood of Sleeping Car Porters Union in New York City

The Commission appointed two African Americans, Earl B. Dickerson, a Chicago attorney, and Milton P. Webster, Vice President of Brotherhood of Sleeping Car Porters, and it ordered the United States Employment Services to hire African

Americans in different industries. More than 100,000 African Americans secured employment in the iron and steel industries. African Americans played an important role at labor conventions like the United Automobile Workers, the United Steel Workers, the National Machine Union, and the United Rubber Workers.

African Americans and the Holocaust

African American soldiers were among the advance guard in the liberation of Jewish holocaust survivors in concentration camps like Dachau and Buchenwald (over 100,000 Jews had perished in Buchenwald). "When the survivors of the Buchenwald and Dachau concentration camps were liberated in 1944, the first faces they saw were African Americans" in all Black units like the 371st Tank Battalion.

African Americans on the homefront condemned Hitler's murder of millions of Jews based on the doctrine of "Aryan" superiority. These barbarities compelled millions of African Americans to demand White citizens to reexamine their views about race. If the nation expected African Americans to risk their lives to fight tyranny, how could it continue to treat them as second-class citizens? African American leaders pointed out the inconsistency between fighting for democracy and liberation abroad while ignoring it at home. "We want democracy in Alabama," the NAACP announced, and this argument worked on the conscience of some White Americans.

African American Leaders During the War

Many African American leaders used a dual response to World War II. Known as the "Double V" campaign, they urged African Americans to support the war effort as a way to fight racism abroad, while still criticizing and trying to eliminate segregation and discrimination in the United States. Once again, Black Americans hoped that their military contributions and patriotism would help break down racial barriers and restrictions. With their increased importance as voters, however, African American demands for equal treatment had more impact than ever before. Many African Americans refused to back the war unless they received better treatment.

African American leaders provided guidance and counseling to the Black community as the war continued, and they attempted to convince African Americans that the war posed a special meaning for them, with the anticipation that race relations would improve because of the war. The War Department arranged for leading African Americans to visit the war fronts to raise the morale of service personnel and to inform civilians at home of their activities. Appointed African American members, Lester Granger of the National Urban League and Matthew Bullock of the Massachusetts Parade Board, argued that African Americans were prepared to fight two wars at home and abroad in order to gain better treatment.

The African American leaders during the war included Asa Philip Randolph, civil rights activist and labor union organizer; Mary McLeod Bethune, the National Council of Negro Women; W.E.B. DuBois, civil rights leader; Ralph Bunche, Howard University; Roy Wilkins, NAACP official; Bayard Rusin and James Farmer, Congress of Racial Equality (CORE) leaders. The NAACP campaigned to promote equality and civil rights for African Americans. Its membership increased from 50,600 to over 500,000, with over 1,000 branches. The organization worked through the courts to fight discrimination. It succeeded in having the Supreme Court declare unconstitutional in the case of Smith v. Allwright (1944) a Texas statute that excluded African Americans from democratic primaries in the state. The Urban League also worked to aid the Black community. In 1943, the Congress of Racial Equality (CORE), led by Farmer and Rustin, staged demonstrations to protest segregation and discrimination in public accommodations.

The Black Press and the War

The Black press generally supported the involvement and participation of African Americans in the war effort. For example, the *Afro-American Newspaper* in Baltimore, Maryland, led the way. In an editorial entitled "We Are For War," September 16, 19390, the editors stated the following reasons for supporting the war:

1. The War would stimulate Black migration to the Northern industrial states, a benefit to the race;
2. The War would mean eventual freedom for African Americans; and
3. African Americans were against Hitler because of his hatred of Jews.

The unfair treatment of African American soldiers was of primary concern to the Black press. The Black press was also instrumental in seeking military justice for Black soldiers. As wartime casualties increased, so did the number of complaints about social injustices. African American soldiers stationed in the South experienced the "Jim Crow" segregation laws. The Black press published stories detailing the complaints of the soldiers.

The absence of news about African Americans in the segregated White media inspired the Black press to increase its coverage to keep the Black community informed on the activities of the war. The *Pittsburgh Courier, The Afro-American, Chicago Defender,* and the *Norfolk Journal and Guide* had African American foreign correspondents. Vincent Tubbs of the Baltimore *Afro-American,* one of the most notable foreign correspondents, was the first African American journalist in the Pacific, arriving there in 1943. He reported numerous stories about conditions affecting the Black troops. In November of 1944, Elizabeth B. Murphy Moss (Phillips), became the first African Americn woman certified as a war correspondent during WW II, but she never filed any reports before she became ill and had to return to the United States.

As reporting increased, so did newspaper circulation. Since the primary news of interest to the African Americans appeared in the Black press, it reached its peak circulation during the war years. The *Pittsburgh Courier* had a circulation of 350,000; the Chicago *Defender*, 230,000; the Baltimore *Afro-American*, 170,000; and the Norfolk *Journal and Guide,* 100,000. The Black press continued to increase its readership as African Americans became more involved in the war effort.

Race Relations During the War

It became very difficult to maintain high morale among African Americans in the military. African American soldiers demanded equality. The War

Department acknowledged discrimination against African Americans in its order on July 8, 1944, which forbade racial segregation in recreational and transportation facilities. The government tried to boost Black morale by appointing African American newspapermen as war correspondents. Ted Poston, a veteran Black newspaper-reporter, was appointed as a racial advisor in the Office of the War Information (OWI). In 1943, the OWI distributed two million copies of a pamphlet entitled "Negroes and the War," with numerous pictures of Blacks. Reports from African American correspondents, Ollie Stewart of the *Afro-American* and Lem Graves of the *Journal and Guide*, showed that African American soldiers had experienced unfair treatment and violence.

In 1944, army lieutenant John Roosevelt Robinson, one of the 761st "Black Panther" Tank Battalion's few African American officers, refused orders to sit in the back of a military bus at Fort Hood, Texas. He was subsequently court-martialed, but acquitted because the order was a violation of War Department policy prohibiting racial discrimination in recreational and transportation facilities on all U.S. Army posts. After the war, Jackie Robinson went on to break the "color line" in baseball by being the first Black to play for the Brooklyn Dodgers.

A racial incident had flared up in the closing months of WW II when members of the "Tuskegee Airmen" from the 477th Bombadier Squadron "mutinied" in protest against a discriminatory policy. A total of 104 African American Army Air Corps officers were arrested after they entered the officers club at Freemen Field, Indiana. The men were protesting the violation of an earlier War Department directive prohibiting the segregation in transportation and recreational facilities on all Army installations. The local post commander on April 1, 1945 had issued a letter ordering the separation of officer trainees (all of whom were African American) from base and supervisory officers (all of whom were White), which closed the officers club to African Americans. Second Lieutenant Roger C. Terry and two other African American officers were court marshaled. Terry was convicted of assault for brushing against a superior officer while entering the club. The other 101 men involved in the "mutiny" were given official letters of reprimand for refusing a direct order to sign an endorsement of the discriminatory policy. The U.S. Air Force reviewed the incident years later and, in 1995, set aside Terry's conviction. It also began removing by request the letters of reprimand from the permanent military records of the other airmen involved in the Freemen Field incident.

Grant Reynolds, an African American army chaplain, publicly complained about discriminatory treatment he had faced during the war. As a result of his actions, he received a dishonorable discharge. He did not leave the issue behind him. Instead, by early 1944, he and other African American veterans had organized the Committee Against Jim Crow in Military Service and Training. The Committee dwindled a couple of years after the war, until Reynolds received a phone call from Asa Philip Randolph. He told Reynolds that "I think we ought to get together to talk." They made a surprising but effective team. Randolph, a former socialist, was widely known as one of the most militant leaders in the Black community. Reynolds was a divinity school graduate, a prominent Black Republican, and a member of the New York State Board of Corrections. To gain attention, Reynolds and Randolph established the "Committees of Public Inquiry" in cities across the country. The committees held hearings at which Black veterans told panels of prominent local citizens about their experiences with Jim Crow in the military. Randolph and Reynolds forwarded transcripts of this testimony to Congress and the White House, and demanded that the military prohibits unfair treatment.

African American soldiers continued to demand better treatment, and they protested the Red Cross's policy of separating Black and White blood in blood banks. They pointed out that there would be no blood banks without the work of African American physician, Dr. Charles Drew. At Presbyterian Hospital in New York, Drew pioneered a system for preserving blood plasma, thereby originating the "blood bank." In 1940, the British hired Drew to establish a mass-volume blood plasma project, which became a model for blood banks throughout Great Britain and Europe. In 1941, the United States hired Drew to develop a similar system for American enlisted men. Thereafter, he was appointed to be the first Director of the American Red Cross Blood Bank, which supplied blood to U.S. forces. He resigned from this position, however, to protest the organization's November 1941 decision to exclude Black blood donors. Dr. Drew's research was responsible for saving countless lives during WW II.

Impact of the War in the Black Community

African American civilians also encountered discrimination and segregation as they competed for jobs and housing due to the war. Despite the existence of Executive Order 8802 and the efforts of the Fair Employment Practices Commission, African Americans still encountered a lot of White hostility toward their presence in war plants. During the period, many African Americans traveled to the North and the West for employment in the industries. By 1942, nearly 50,000 new African Americans residents had settled in Detroit. This great influx of African American migrants led to competition for jobs and housing that eventually resulted in conflict between the races. A major riot occurred in the city after labor strikes had disrupted production at a U.S. rubber plant and several former automobile plants where White workers had protested the hiring of Blacks. On June 20, 1942, a race riot marked by looting and bloody fighting broke out. It went on for three days; and by the time federal troops finally restored order, 25 Blacks and nine Whites had been killed. Other race riots erupted in New York and many other cities.

In Los Angeles, attacks occurred against Mexican-born "zoot suiters," gangs whose "uniforms" were broad-brimmed, with fedoras, long coats, and pegged trousers. Wartime employment needs resulted in a reversal of the depression policy of forcing Mexicans out of the Southwest, and many thousands flocked North in search of work. Most had to accept menial jobs, but work was plentiful and they, as well as resident Spanish-speaking Americans, experienced rising living standards. Some of the young Hispanics in the Los Angeles region formed gangs. They had money in their pockets, and their behavior (like their costume) was not always as circumspect as local residents would have preferred. A

grand jury undertook an investigation, and the Los Angeles City Council even debated banning the wearing of zoot suits. In 1943, rioting broke out when White sailors on shore leave, apparently resenting these prosperous-appearing foreign civilians, began roaming the area and attacking anyone they could find wearing a zoot suit. White city residents not only resented the presence of Hispanics, but also African American newcomers. African Americans felt increasingly threatened. Roy Wilkins, head of the NAACP, put it this way in 1942: "No Negro leader with a constituency can face his members today and ask full support for the war in the light of the atmosphere the government has created." Many Black newspaper editors were so critical of the administration to the extent that conservatives attempted to indict them for sedition.

Outcome of the War

World War II formally ended on September 2, 1945, when the Japanese surrendered after the U.S. dropped atomic bomb on its strategic cities—Hiroshima, Kokura, Niigata, and Nagasaki. Franklin D. Roosevelt had died in office after a stroke; therefore, Harry S. Truman made this fateful decision that caused thousands of Japanese civilians to die from radiation exposure. More than 25 million soldiers and civilians died in the war. American losses were smaller—400,000 killed, 800,000 wounded. Nearly one million African American men and women served in the U.S. armed forces during World War II. About 500,000 performed services overseas in Europe, the Mediterranean, and the Pacific.

The War had aroused African Americans' interest in the welfare of Blacks in other countries. To demonstrate their intentions, they focused on the activities of the United Nations that opened in San Francisco in April of 1945. Prominent African Americans present included Mary McLeod Bethune of the National Council of Negro Women, Mordecai W. Johnson of Howard University, and W.E.B. DuBois and Walter White of the NAACP. Ralph Bunche accompanied as a member of the official staff of the United Nations, as Chief of the Division of Dependent Territories (1946) and Chief of the Division of Trusteeship. He also served as Secretary of Palestine Commission to help negotiate Arab-Israeli disputes. He received the Nobel Peace Prize in 1950 for his work as a United Nations Mediator in the dispute. His recognition led to increased interest in the official delegates from developing countries, especially those from India, Liberia, Ethiopia and Haiti, with agencies provided by the United Nations.

African Americans expressed great interest in the United Nations' Economic and Social Counsel that established the Educational Scientific and Cultural Organization (UNESCO), whose responsibility was to develop a worldwide program of fundamental educators. At the first meeting, Charles S. Johnson became a member of the United States National Commission. Later, the establishment of a Commission on Human Rights and the appointment of Eleanor Roosevelt to UNESCO impressed African Americans enough to believe that improvements would be forthcoming.

The Trusteeship Council, under the United Nations, issued a policy to safeguard the interests and welfare of non-self governing people in territories held either under the League of Nations mandates or detached from enemy countries after World War II. African Americans argued that it was unsatisfactory and were elated when African American Ralph Bunche of the State Department's Division of Dependent Territories joined the United Nations to work with the Trusteeship Council.

In 1946, the National Negro Congress filed a petition with the Economic and Social Council on behalf of African Americans and sought aid from the United Nations to eliminate political, economic, and social discrimination in the United States. Charles H. Houston, Dean of Howard University Law School, argued that the national policy of the United Nations had the authority to have jurisdiction over incidents affecting the human rights of African Americans.

African Americans also worked with the United Nations to secure peace. William H. Dean became an economist with the Trusteeship Council, and E. Franklin Frazier served as Chairman of the Department of Applied social Sciences in UNESCO. The United States African American delegation to the General Assembly of the United Nations included Black delegates Edith Sampson, Archibald Cary, Charles H. Mahoney, Marian Anderson, and Jewell Lafontant.

The presence of African American delegates at the United Nations in New York increased African Americans' interest in the international organization with 30 new African states. Many African Americans believed that the United States government had changed its position to improve racial policies in order to win support from African states in the rivalry with the Communist bloc.

Conclusion

During World War II, African Americans served in combat and support units in every branch of the military. Of the more than 2.5 million African Americans registered for the draft, about 909,000 served in the Army. In 1944, the Army established a ten-percent quota system for African Americans and reached its peak enlistment for African Americans with more than 700,000.

Although African Americans were trained for combat on the same basis as other Americans, they saw limited combat action. The majority of the soldiers, 78 percent, served in the service branches which included quartermaster, engineer, and transportation corps. Approximately 75 percent of all drivers on the segregated Red Ball Express in the Motor Transport Service were African Americans. These drivers participated in the transporting of goods and supplies required for American and other Allied forces. Crucial to the defeat of Nazi Germany, this massive supply effort ran until November 16, 1944 and involved over 6,000 trucks and trailers. Red Ball drivers transported 412,193 tons of materiel to American troops as they advanced through France from Normandy to the German border.

Black combat units also distinguished themselves, including the 777th and 999th Field Artillery battalions. The 761st Tank Battalion was the first Black armored unit to go into combat action. The 93rd Division was the only Black division to see service in the Pacific. Although never used in combat, the 555th Parachute Infantry Company was noted for its specialized training. On August 26, 1942, the first contingent of Black Marines began training as the 51st Composite Defense Battalion at Montford Point, North Carolina. The

51st and 52nd Defense Battalions were the only two Black combat units created. In all, some 8,000 Black stevedores and ammunition handlers braved Japanese fire on the Pacific beachheads. The number of African Americans in the Marine Corps during World War II totaled 19,168, equaling 2.5 percent of all Marines.

In March of 1942, the Coast Guard recruited its first group of 150 African American volunteers and sent them to Manhattan Beach in New York for basic training. On February 22, 1943, African American stewards manned a battle station on the USCGC Campbell, which rammed and sank a German submarine. The crew earned medals for their heroic achievement with the highest being a Bronze Star Medal presented to the captain of the Black gun crew. The testimony of Lieutenant Carlton Skinner in June of 1943 proposed assigning a group of Black seamen to a completely integrated operation. This proposal led to the Coast Guard Cutter Seacloud, the first integrated ship in the Armed Forces. Later decommissioned in November of 1944, the Seacloud paved the way for African Americans to serve on ships which were not completely segregated.

A total of more than 5,000 African American Coast guardsmen served during World War II; 965 were petty or warrant officers. The 2.1 percent figure for African Americans in the Coast Guard's wartime population was well below the other services. In 1943, the U.S. Navy began accepting African Americans according to their numbers (10 percent) in the total population. William Baldwin became the first African American recruit for the Navy's general service.

African Americans made significant contributions to the war efforts, despite unfair treatment. At the end of WW II, there were over 695,000 African Americans in the U.S. Army. Throughout the conflict, African American soldiers had been over-represented in the service forces and under-represented in the air corps and ground combat arms. In 1942, about half of all African American troops were assigned to service units; by 1945, this number had climbed to three-quarters. During the war, the soldiers built roads and airports, moved critical supplies, and provided medical services. It was not until the end of World War II that the Armed Forces took action to eliminate racial barriers in the military. African Americans, both male and female, had served in segregated units that prevented them from participating fully in integrated combat units and on battle vessels. Yet, when presented with the challenge, African Americans proved consistently their worth and ability to handle any weapons of war in any situation on land, at sea, or in the air. African Americans at home rallied to support the war effort in every way possible. From jobs in defense factories to the planting of victory gardens, African Americans

demonstrated their commitment to
the allied cause.

Review Questions

1. How did African American women contribute to the war efforts in the military and on the home front?

2. What impact did the war have on the African American community in terms of race relations?

3. How did World War II affect the status of African American workers in the defense industries? What was Asa Philip Randolph's role in relation to labor issues and African Americans?

4. How did African Americans become involved in international affairs that impacted the lives of Blacks in other nations?

5. Identify the Tuskegee Airmen.

6. What was the "Tuskegee Study," and when and why did it occur?

Chapter 19

Post-World War II and the Advent of the Modern Civil Rights Movement

This chapter discusses the experiences of African Americans following the end of World War II up to events depicting the modern Civil Rights Movement. African Americans experienced a new climate in America after the war. This resulted in a new status due to gains made during the war and efforts made to achieve equality for Blacks.

The NAACP and other Black organizations and groups campaigned for equality.The courts addressed racial issues and frequently ruled in favor of equality, as the nation witnessed a transformation in race relations. African Americans appeared more determined to protect their rights. Beginning with President Harry S. Truman's administration, civil rights issues gained precedence during the period.

Truman's Fair Deal and African Americans

President Truman contributed to the gains made by African Americans. He identified with farmers, since he had a rural upbringing. This was evident when he adopted as his election slogan, "Fair Deal," to label his policies and programs. Truman became the first president to publicly and actively promote comprehensive national Civil Rights policies and programs through legislation. In 1946, he appointed a special commission on Civil Rights. In 1948, during the election, Truman's platform included support for anti-lynching, anti poll-tax, desegregation in transportation, and fair employment practices, which led to the establishment of the Fair Employment Practices Commission (FEPC). His actions caused southerners to defect from the Democratic Party to form the Dixiecrat Party, led by South Carolina Congressman Strom Thurman, in opposition to Civil Rights legislation. Despite efforts made by many White southerners to prevent Truman's reelection, he still won. This election was aided by the northern African

American vote. African Americans in the South could not vote due to measures taken by southern governments to keep them from the polls.

Economic and Social Challenges

Religious institutions and organizations played important roles in improving the status of African Americans. African American men faced greater obstacles than African American women in securing employment. Unemployment and homelessness sometimes led to frustration and crime. More African American families became female-headed during the period.

The Black church was also affected by urbanization. Church membership declined during this period. New religious groups and cults competed with older established Black churches. The churches became more involved in numerous secular activities to improve living standards for their members.

Pioneer African American newspapers, such as the *New York Amsterdam News*, *Baltimore Afro-American*, and the *Chicago Defender* lost readers, as they faced competition from White newspapers since they did not offer a daily national circulation. *Jet*, an African American weekly magazine, took on many functions of the African American newspapers. Many local weeklies grew in size and news, and covered news of interest to African Americans.

Savings and loans associations operated by African Americans increased and African American banks multiplied. Insurance companies became the most stable businesses in the African American community. It was difficult for African Americans to engage in large scale manufacturing. Several Black companies in the manufacturing business such as Johnson Products Co. of Chicago, Afro-Sheen, dominated the field of cosmetics and hair grooming products for African Americans. Johnson's company added a whole beauty line called Fashion Fair.

African Americans entered the White business world of banking, manufacturing, high-tech industries, transportation, fast food, and a variety of businesses. The increase in the Black population affected certain types of businesses that performed services for African Americans.

In the midst of such activities during the post-war period, African American music and literature flourished. The leading Blues and Jazz singers included Billie Holiday, Nat "King" Cole, Lena Horne, Wes Montgomery, John Coltrane, Ella Fitzgerald, Dinah Washington, and Miles Davis. In 1949, Davis pioneered a new form of Jazz with his album, "Birth of the Cool."

Paul Robeson, Marian Anderson, and Roland Hayes were the most outstanding classical opera singers. In

1939, Eleanor Roosevelt arranged for Marion to sing at the Lincoln Memorial in Washington, DC, when the Daughters of the American Revolution refused to allow her to sing at Constitution Hall. Marion's performance gained her worldwide recognition. Ella Fitzgerald, Clara Ward, and Thomas Dorsey, among the many outstanding African American Gospel entertainers. Thomas Dorsey popularized gospel music with his song, "Precious Lord, Take My Hand." He became known as the "Father of Gospel Music." The Clara Ward Singers also helped to popularize Gospel Music.

Ward Singers singing Gospels

As in music, so did African Americans excel in literature. In 1947, Ralph Ellison published his famous novel, *The Invisible Man*. Three years later, poet Gwendolyn Brooks won the Pulitzer Prize for poetry for her volume, *Annie Allen*. Writers like Richard Wright, Langston Hughes and Ralph Ellison provided insights into the psychology of American race relations. In *Native Son* (1940) and in *Black Boy*, Wright examined the pressures of racial hatred in both the South and the northern ghetto. Hughes wrote short stories, poetry, and plays during the period. His play, *Mulatto* was performed on Broadway. In 1950, James Baldwin's first novel, *Go Tell It On the Mountain*, was published. Three years later, he wrote *Notes of a Native Son*, a collection of essays.

The post-war era also witnessed serious dramas with African American stars, including Hilda Simms, Ethel Waters, Muriel Smith, Muriel Rahn, Todd Duncan, William Warfield, Kenneth Spencer, and Paul Robeson. Hilda Simms had a leading role in *Anna Lucasta*. In 1940, Ethel Waters headed the cast in the musical titled *Cabin In The Sky*. Muriel Smith and Muriel Rahn performed in Carmen Jones, produced in 1944. Todd Duncan and William Warfield played male leads in Gershwin's *Porgy and Bess*. Kenneth Spencer and Paul Robeson starred in the musical, *Show Boat*, written by Oscar Hammerstein.

In the 1940s, creative dancing had been created by African American Katherine Dunham. Her travels to the Caribbean influenced her dance form. "For my part," states Dunham, "I am satisfied to have been at the base of the awakening of the American Negro to the fact that he had roots somewhere else, and to have presented dark-skinned people in a manner delightful and acceptable to people who have never considered them often even as person." It took important Civil Rights legislation to address the problem of inequality and discrimination African Americans had to tolerate due to their race.

Civil Rights Legislation

President Harry S. Truman's own words perhaps best sum up his opinion of race: "I learned a long time ago that the composition of the human animal is about the same no matter what color the skin is." These personal beliefs did not, however, lead directly to political action towards civil rights for Blacks. While Truman had spoken of equal rights for African Americans as early as 1940, World War II and its aftermath further convinced Truman of the necessity for federal support of civil rights. Furthermore, in light of a foreign policy that saw the U.S. as a "standard-bearer for democracy in a devastated postwar world," Truman saw the need to fight for that democracy at home as well as overseas. Yet the post-war phenomenon that seemed to have the greatest influence on the president was the mistreatment of Black veterans after returning home. Having served in the military during World War I, Truman knew of the great sacrifices made by soldiers, particularly during wartime. One case in particular exemplified for Truman the treatment of Black veterans. Sergeant Isaac

Woodard, discharged from the Army just hours before, was beaten and blinded by the police chief of Batesburg, South Carolina. The day after hearing of the attack from NAACP Executive Director Walter White, the president wrote to Attorney General Tom Clark, requesting that the Department of Justice investigate violence against Black veterans and institute "some sort of policy to prevent such happenings."

On December 5, 1946, less than three months after hearing the story of Isaac Woodard, Truman issued Executive Order 9808, creating the first ever Presidential Civil Rights Commission, which would recommend "more adequate means and procedures for the protection of the civil rights of the people of the United States." Truman requested the committee to make "recommendations with respect to the adoption or establishment, by legislation or otherwise of more adequate and effective means and procedures for the protection of the civil rights of the people of the United States." Truman's commitment to real progress by the committee was evidenced by his decision to make it a sort of "Noah's Ark," with representatives of various interest groups (African Americans, women, labor leaders, etc.) that reflected the diversity of voters in America. While the committee only had investigative and recommendatory powers, Truman ensured that these tasks would be fulfilled by ordering the full cooperation of all segments of the federal government. The committee's report, presented to Truman on October 29, 1947, described the contemporary status of civil rights, outlined the fundamental rights that should be guaranteed to all Americans, and proposed 35 specific actions to be taken to secure those rights. These recommendations included the following:

- the establishment of a Civil Rights Division within the Department of Justice
- a federal anti-lynching law and a federal statue criminalizing police brutality
- an end to poll taxes and comprehensive voting rights legislation
- an end to discrimination in the armed forces
- a federal fair employment practices act
- fair education laws on a state-by-state basis
- outlawing of restrictive covenants in housing
- elimination, by federal and state governments, of segregation in America based on race, color, creed, or national origin

Truman now had a plan for the federal government that would uphold civil rights for all American citizens. Bringing these ideas to reality,

however, proved to be extremely tough.

In both his State of the Union Address in January 1948 and his special message to Congress on civil rights in early February of the same year, President Truman established civil rights as a high priority and advocated action by all three branches of the federal government to ensure those rights. In addition to this general sentiment, he proposed a ten-point legislative program to incorporate several of the recommendations of the Presidential Committee on Civil Rights. In 1948, however, Truman encountered opposition from Congress, which was controlled by Republicans and southern Democrats who supported states' rights above the power of the federal government. They vowed to resist (through means of filibuster) what they viewed as an encroachment of the federal government, particularly when it came to civil rights for Blacks. In this respect, Congress reflected the opinion of most White Americans. A Gallup poll in early 1948 showed that 82% of Americans opposed the president's proposed civil rights program.

Truman refused to yield to the Congressmen's "states' rights" argument. Following the Democratic convention in mid-July of 1948, he summoned the members of Congress back to Washington, D.C. for a special session. While, predictably, no civil rights legislation came out of Congress during the special session, Truman used it as a stage for two dramatic Executive Orders: 9980 and 9981, both issued on July 26th. The first, entitled Regulations Governing Fair Employment Practices Within the Federal Establishment, "mandated the elimination of discrimination based on race, color, religion or national origin," creating a Fair Employment Practices Committee whose mission was to ensure that personnel decisions were made solely on the basis of merit and fitness for the position in question. Passed in 1948, Executive Order 9981 ended segregation in the U.S. military, a controversial decision criticized by military chief of staff Gen. Omar Bradley on the grounds that "the Army is not out to make any social reforms." Accordingly, the Order in establishing the President's Committee on Equality of Treatment and Opportunity in the Armed Services stated:

> Whereas it is essential that there be maintained in the armed services of the United States the highest standards of democracy, with equality of treatment and opportunity for all those who serve in our country's defense:

> Now therefore, by virtue of the authority vested in me as President of the United States, by the Constitution and the statutes of the United States, and as Commander in Chief of

the armed services, it is hereby ordered as follows:

> 1. It is hereby declared to be the policy of the President that there shall be equality of treatment and opportunity for all persons in the armed services without regard to race, color, religion or national origin. This policy shall be put into effect as rapidly as possible, having due regard to the time required to effectuate any necessary changes without impairing efficiency or morale.

> 2. There shall be created in the National Military Establishment an advisory committee to be known as the President's Committee on Equality of Treatment and Opportunity in the Armed Services, which shall be composed of seven members to be designated by the President.

> 3. The Committee is authorized on behalf of the President to examine into the rules, procedures and practices of the armed services in order to determine in what respect such rules, procedures and practices may be altered or improved with a view to carrying out the policy of this order. The Committee shall confer and advise with the Secretary of the

Air Force, and shall make such recommendations to the President and to said Secretaries as in the judgement of the Committee will effectuate the policy hereof.

4. All executive departments and agencies of the Federal Government are authorized and directed to cooperate with the Committee in its work, and to furnish the Committee such information or the services of such persons as the Committee may require in the performance of its duties.

5. When requested by the Committee to do so, persons in the armed services or in any of the executive departments and agencies of the Federal Government shall testify before the Committee and shall make available for the use of the Committee such documents and other information as the Committee may require.

6. The Committee shall continue to exist until such time as the President shall terminate its existence by Executive Order.

Throughout his second presidential term, Truman continued to pursue federal action towards the advancement of civil rights. In the election of 1948, the Democratic Party gained back control of both houses of Congress. Even with members of his own party in control, however, Truman did not gain enough support for the omnibus civil rights bill introduced by Senator J. Howard McGrath of Rhode Island on April 28, 1949; because states' rights Republicans and southern Democrats had joined forces to defeat the bill. Instead, Truman was once again forced to use his executive power to enforce civil rights. His appointment of William H. Hastie to the Third Circuit of Appeals was the first appointment of an African American to the federal bench and set the precedent for more appointments in the 1960s by Presidents Kennedy and Johnson. A few months later, under the direction of President Truman, the Solicitor General announced that the Federal Housing Administration would henceforth refuse funding to projects that discriminated against African Americans. A further step towards desegregating housing occurred when Truman ordered Attorney General Tom C. Clark to file an amicus brief in *Shelley v. Kraemer*, a case considered by the Supreme Court that challenged the constitutionality of restrictive housing covenant agreements. The brief argued that restrictive covenants could "not be reconciled with the spirit of mutual tolerance and respect for the dignity and rights of the individual which give vitality to our democratic way of life."

A unanimous decision, written by Chief Justice Fred Vinson (a Truman appointee to the Supreme Court), found restrictive covenants to be unconstitutional under the equal protection clause of the 14th Amendment. This decision, along with other cases that declared unconstitutional segregation in higher education and interstate travel, began unraveling the potency of *Plessy v. Ferguson*. When *Brown v. Board of Education* definitively dismissed the constitutionality of *Plessy v. Ferguson*, four Truman appointees sat on the Court.

Truman also continued to uphold civil rights by issuing Executive Orders 10210 and 10308, both aimed to enforce non-discriminatory hiring practices in companies that had federal contracts during the mobilization for the Korean War. And in an actual instance of interaction with Congress on a civil rights bill, Truman vetoed H.R. 5411, a bill put forward by southern congressmen that would have implemented segregated schools on military bases in the South. Truman's civil rights efforts were almost always made in defiance of the ruling factions of Congress.

Truman's defiance caused conflict with southerners. In focusing so strongly on civil rights, the president risked losing the support of southern Democrats for funding of the Marshall Plan, designed to revitalize Europe's economy. Some saw the fate of Europe in the early stages of the

Cold War contingent on Truman's willingness to compromise on civil rights with southern Democrats.

Truman's determination *not* to compromise on civil rights came to a head at the Democratic convention of 1948, held in Philadelphia. Outraged at Truman's adoption of the Biemiller civil rights plank which, in detailed terms, advocated congressional legislation guaranteeing "full and equal political participation, equal employment opportunities, personal protection... and integration of the military," southern Democrats defected from the party, forming the States' Rights "Dixiecrat" Party and nominating South Carolina governor Strom Thurmond for the presidency. Deprived of a voting bloc that had consistently voted Democratic since the Civil War, Truman was widely expected to lose in the general election to Thomas Dewey, the Republican governor of New York. With a third Democratic candidate, Henry Wallace, also in the field, Truman's chances appeared dismal. As it turned out, Truman's strong stand for civil rights may have helped him win the election, by winning over African American voters in the key states of California, Illinois, and Ohio. The Civil Rights movement, while by this point several decades old, was still in its infancy compared to the actions that would come out of it during the 1950s and 1960s. Unlike Kennedy and Johnson, Truman did not face substantial pressure from others to provide equal rights to all Americans; his motivetions came from within, from a personal belief that all citizens of the U.S., regardless of race, should be equal under the law. His actions, often unilateral, set the stage for the more dramatic developments of future years; the recommendation of his Civil Rights Committee served as a model for future federal action.

The Korean War and African Americans

The Korean War (1950 to 1953) was the last American conflict involving segregated units in the armed forces. Integration occurred during the Korean War. In 1950, the army had three American infantry divisions— the 25th, the 2nd, and the 3rd—that contained Black combat units. Between May and August of 1951, integration jumped from 9% to 30% of troops in the field.

The African American involvement began right at the onset of hostilities. Just 17 days after Soviet-armed Communist soldiers invaded the Korean peninsula, the men of the 24th (all-Black) infantry reached Korea from Japan and immediately began a dramatic series of blows that caused North Korea to suffer from one strategic defeat after another. Then on July 22, 1950, world headlines proclaimed the historic news that the all-Black 24th infantry in the battle of Yech'o made the first major victory against Korea .

Approximately 3,100 African Americans died in the conflict. Private first class William H. Thompson was awarded the first Congressional Medal of Honor for heroic action on August 6, 1950, for single handedly manning a machine gun against the enemy that enabled his comrades to retreat to safety, whereas he lost his life to save his comrades.

During the war and post-war period, increased employment opportunities materialized for African Americans in the aircraft, electronics, automotive and chemical industries. The unions, especially the Congress of Industrial Organizations (CIO), undertook efforts to increase job opportunities for African Americans in various fields. Labor unions gradually increased their membership by allowing African Americans to join. The American Federation of Labor (AFL) and the Congress of Industrial Organizations (CIO) merged in 1955 and elected as Vice President two African Americans, Asa Phillip Randolph and Willard Townsend. As a result of acquiring jobs in the industries, the Black middle class increased. African Americans also began to focus more on international issues that involved America. African American leaders undertook efforts to keep the Black community informed about domestic and international affairs. The most renowned African Americans in the forefront of international affairs and politics included Dr. Ralph Bunche and Congressman Adam Clayton Powell, Jr.

International Affairs and African Americans: Ralph Bunche

Ralph Bunche graduated from the University of California at Los Angeles in 1927, where he had excelled both in and outside the classroom. He wrote for the school newspaper, won oratorical contests, was sports editor of the yearbook, played guard for three years on the basketball team, and became Phi Beta Kappa. He then entered Harvard University, where in 1934 he became the first African American to earn a Ph.D. in Government and International Relations. While completing his doctoral studies, Bunche joined the faculty at Howard University, where he established and chaired the Political Science Department and served as Special Assistant to Howard's President. He organized the Joint Committee on National Recovery to lobby Congress for Black participation in New Deal programs and to fight against racial discrimination in New Deal agencies. He also helped form the National Negro Congress in an effort to arouse Blacks to work for social and economic progress and to unite Black and White workers.

According to Bunche, the so-called Black problem in America was "rooted more in economic and class conflict than in racial antagonism." He was one of Gunnar Myrdal's six staff members for the study on race relations that resulted in the monumental two-volume, *An American Dilemma*, in 1944. Bunche wrote extensive memoranda on Black politics, organizations, leadership, and ideology for the study. After the United States entered World War II, Bunche took a leave of absence from Howard and joined the Office of Strategic Services as a senior social scientist for research on Africa and other colonial areas. Given his doctoral research on colonial administration, he was the foremost American authority on colonialism in Africa. In 1944, he moved to the State Department, where he gave advice on dependent territories to U.S. representtatives at the Dumbarton Oaks Conference that established the United Nations.

Ralph Bunche, African American Diplomatic leader and scholar.

Bunche helped draft the trusteeship provisions of the U.N. Charter and assisted in organizing the Division of Trusteeship at the United

Nations, becoming its director in 1947. That same year, he became Secretary to the U.N. Special Committee on Palestine and Acting Mediator in 1948 after the assassination of the first Mediator, Count Folke Bernadotte of Sweden. Bunche earned high praise for his skillful handling of the armistice negotiations that ended the Arab-Israeli conflict in 1949, for which he won the Nobel Peace Prize. He became the U.N. Under Secretary General in 1955 and directed U.N. peacekeeping missions in the Suez in 1956, in the Congo in 1960, and in Cyprus in 1964. An indefatigable advocate of human rights at home and peace abroad, Bunche received the NAACP's Spingarn Medal, its highest honor, in 1949. He served on the NAACP's board of directors for 22 years. In 1937, he walked his first picket line for civil rights in Washington, DC; he later participated in the 1963 March on Washington and in the 1965 Selma to Montgomery march for voting rights. In 1953, the American Political Science Association elected him President in recognition of his scholarship and mediation of international conflict; and, in 1963, President John F. Kennedy bestowed upon him the nation's highest civilian award, the Medal of Freedom.

Northern Black Political Leader: Adam Clayton Powell, Jr.

Voters from Harlem elected Powell as their representative nearly two dozen times. With long service in Congress comes seniority, and ultimately, the chance to head one of the powerful committees that draft bills on which the full House and Senate eventually must vote. In 1941, Powell won a city council seat as an independent. He continued to challenge discrimination, particularly in New York's public schools, occasionally irritating even reformist mayor Fiorello LaGuardia. In 1943, a new congressional district was established in Harlem that would almost certainly produce the state's first Black congressperson. Powell undertook an ambitious campaign for the seat, winning the support of Democrats (on whose ticket he ran), Republicans, and Communists. In 1945, he became the second of two Black Congress members; the other was William Dawson of Chicago. In his first year, Powell denounced First Lady Bess Truman for her affiliation with the Daughters of the American Revolution that discriminated against Marian Anderson by not allowing her to perform at Constitution Hall. Furthermore, the organization had racially discriminatory policies. His actions infuriated President Harry S. Truman.

While in Congress, Powell criticized Congress for allowing the lynching of African American men to continue. He rallied against the unconstitutional southern practice of charging potential African American voters "poll taxes." Even Democratic presidents Roosevelt and Truman, who owed African Americans for having voted for them, were forced into issuing executive orders ending discrimination in military bases and war factories. If his colleagues ignored him and voted down his proposals, and if Truman, Eisenhower, Kennedy, or Johnson wouldn't grant him a personal session to discuss civil rights or helping the poor, Powell made vicious public statements or sent embarrassing "open" telegrams to the press describing their insensitivity. He perfected his role as an agitator. According to Powell, "Whenever a person keeps prodding, keeps them squirming...it serves a purpose. It may not in contemporary history look so good, but...future historians will say, 'They served a purpose.'"

Powell ended segregation in congressional service facilities and challenged congresspersons who spoke against African Americans. He also repeatedly tried to pass what became known as the Powell Amendment, which would have denied funding to institutions that practiced racial discrimination. This meant, for example, that even school districts in the deepest South had to open their doors to African American teachers and students or risk losing funds set aside for them.

In the 1956 presidential election, Powell infuriated his party by supporting Republican Dwight D. Eisenhower, whom he saw as mildly progressive on civil rights. However, in 1960, Powell campaigned ardently for Democrat John F. Kennedy, bringing with him many of the Black votes that had gone to Eisenhower in 1956. Kennedy's narrow victory coincided with Powell's rise to the position of chairman of the House Committee on Education and Labor—the first time an African American chaired such a powerful committee.

At the same time that Powell's power was growing, his support was being drained by accusations and scandals. The most serious of these emerged in the early 1950s, when several of Powell's aides were convicted of income tax evasion and rumors circulated that they had also given him kickbacks from their salaries. Powell was indicted for tax evasion in 1958, but his trial resulted in a hung jury and the Department of Justice declined to retry him. In 1960, Powell was again embroiled in a scandal when he accused a constituent of being a "bag woman," someone who transported payoffs to police from illegal gambling rackets. The constituent sued for libel and won a large judgment against Powell, who refused to honor the court's decision and its warrants. The case dragged on for years before Powell agreed to settle. Powell also received negative publicity for his many absences from Congress and for his personal extravagances. Despite criticism of Powell's personal actions, he was instrumental in passing much of the progressive legislation enacted in the 1960s, including increases to the minimum wage, protection of civil rights, and the creation of Medicare, Medicaid, and Head Start. A version of the Powell Amendment was finally codified in the landmark Civil Rights Act of 1964. The effective leadership of Powell helped pave the foundation to address race issues affecting African Americans. He used politics to campaign for the rights of African Americans. Of course, it was necessary to have other means to reach the goal of equality for African Americans. Thus, organizations were created to address problems facing African Americans due to race.

Race and Issues in the African American Community

Groups like American Friends Service Committee and the American Association addressed race problems in the African American communities, set up programs on race relations, and published reports and studies on race. The National Council of Churches carried out similar efforts. While the churches had integrated, many priests and bishops spoke out against discrimination and segregation. The change in the status of African Americans appeared most dramatic in cities such as Washington, D.C., where desegregation occurred throughout the city in federal facilities, public parks, and schools.

White supremacist supporters intensified their efforts to suppress improvements in the status of African Americans. New groups such as the National Association for the Advancement of White People and the White Citizens Council represented newly established White supremacist chapters in the South. White southern leaders fought the school desegregation decision Brown vs. the Board of Education (1954) and Brown II (1955). Southern members of Congress denounced the desegregation decision. In March of 1956, more than 90 southerners led by Senator Walter George, presented to Congress the "Southern Manifesto" that condemned the decision.

White southerners attacked the NAACP and criticized its mission to fight desegregation. In 1956, several southern states increased their operations to support southern resistance to integration. This resulted in violence against African Americans. Near Greenwood, Mississippi, Emmett Till was murdered. White opponents against integration and equality killed several other African Americans in Mississippi and other southern states during the same year. Such violence caused African Americans to leave the South to escape persecution and hard times.

Upon their migration to urban centers, African Americans encountered new problems such as housing, unemployment, crime, and juvenile delinquency.

African American Urban Migration

The migration of African Americans complicated not only the problem of housing, but that of employment as well, as discrimination in employment persisted. Some states set up fair employment committees. However, many Black migrants to the cities failed to secure employment.

Of the fifteen million Blacks in the United States in 1950, about 52% lived in metropolitan areas. The African American urban population increased from 6.1 million in 1950 to 15.3 million in 1980. During these years, Whites left the urban cities to move to the suburbs. As they left, African Americans moved into the cities to improve their lifestyles. In many ways, they were soon disappointed because they had to cope with extreme unemployment, discrimination in jobs, lack of or poor housing, and Black-on-Black crime. Conditions, however, did improve for many African Americans who had moved to industrial centers. They believed that it would have been difficult to have made the same accomplishments in the South where discrimination and segregation persisted. At the same time, African Americans became aware of the Civil Rights Movement that focused on civil

rights, equality, and suffrage. As early as the 1940s, the Civil Rights Movement had gained momentum due to the efforts of African American leaders who may have migrated North, but remained dedicated to uplifting African Americans regardless of whether they lived in the North or South.

Conclusion

The end of WWII presented new challenges for African Americans. Their involvement in the war made them more determined to demand equality and justice. President Truman undertook efforts to address civil rights by desegregating the military during the Korean War and by establishing a commission on civil rights. He continued to support civil rights legislation throughout his administration.

African American leaders Randolph, Bunche, and Powell campaigned against discrimination and segregation. Their efforts helped to support the drive for equality and justice. Randolph's threat to carry out a march on Washington in 1941 demonstrated his determination to protest unfair treatment toward African Americans. Ralph Bunch became a champion of international affairs and justice, which included rights for African Americans. Adam Clayton Powell used politics to oppose violence against African Americans and to support equal rights for them. Due to the efforts of these Black leaders and others, African Americans were prepared to carry out a Civil Rights movement to demand equality. Although many African Americans may have moved North to secure better opportunities, they still supported the movement due to encountering similar mistreatment as in the South. Thus, the modern Civil Rights Movement leading into the 1950s involved African Americans throughout America.

Review Questions

1. What major legislation did President Harry S. Truman pass to address civil rights in America?

2. What accomplishments did Ralph Bunche make in the area of international affairs?

3. How did Adam Clayton Powell contribute to the struggle for equality for African Americans?

4. How were African American soldiers involved in the Korean War?

5. What achievements did African Americans make during the period in the areas of entertainment and literature?

Chapter 20

Modern Civil Rights Movement

This chapter explores the modern Civil Rights Movement, with emphasis on the African American community, race relations, and African American leadership. African Americans faced many challenges to their civil and human rights. They used diverse techniques to cope with race issues, which enabled them to persevere amidst formidable obstacles. African Americans developed a variety of grassroots organizations to challenge discrimination and segregation in the South, and formed organizations to transform local and regional allies to promote social change. African Americans suffered from Jim Crow restrictions and White violence.

The modern Civil Rights Movement started in the 1940s when Asa Philip Randolph threatened to carry out a march on Washington with 100,000 demonstrators. President Franklin D. Roosevelt responded to this threat by passing Executive Order 8802 that led to the creation of the Fair Employment Practices Commission responsible for investigating allegations of discrimination in defense programs. To further demonstrate his intentions to address race issues, Roosevelt worked with African American leader to improve relations between the races. Six months before the Japanese attack on Pearl Harbor, as defense plants geared up for anticipated U.S. involvement in World War II, African American leaders saw an opportunity to associate equality for African Americans with the fight for democracy abroad. President Harry S. Truman fulfilled Roosevelt's goal to eliminate discrimination in the

Southern Congressmen with their grievances against President Truman's civil rights programs

armed forces. Despite opposition from southern congressmen, Truman orchestrated the passage of major civil rights legislation that ended segregation in the armed forces. His actions heightened the civil rights debate leading into the 1950s, a very intense period in the movement's history.

The 1950s marked a period of prosperity for White Americans with few gains for African Americans who continued to demand desegregation and voting rights. Civil rights for African Americans became a major national political issue in the 1950s and early 1960s. Thousands of Americans, White and Black, demonstrated across the South to end segregation in stores, restaurants, hotels, libraries, and all other public places. Fair housing and equal employment opportunities became major issues that divided the nation. A step toward change came in 1954 when the Supreme Court ruled on segregation in Brown v. Board of Education, Topeka, Kansas.

Brown v. Board of Education, 1954

The Brown case had started four years earlier, when Oliver Brown sued to allow his daughter to attend a nearby White school rather than the Black school across town. The Kansas courts rejected his lawsuit, pointing out that the availability of a school for African Americans fulfilled the Supreme Court's separate but equal ruling. The NAACP appealed. In addressing the Supreme Court, Thurgood Marshall, an African American civil rights lawyer who years

later became the first African American on the Supreme Court in 1967, held that the basic concept of "separate but equal" was inherently unequal. He used statistics to show that Black schools were separate and unequal when it came to finances, quality and number of teachers, and physical and educational resources. He further stressed that segregated educational facilities, even if physically similar, could never yield equal results.

Thurgood Marshall, civil rights lawyer in the Brown v. Board of Education case.

On May 17, 1954, the Supreme Court overturned Plessy v. Ferguson—the "separate but equal" decision passed in 1896—in a stunning 9-0 decision written by Chief Justice Earl Warren who stated that racial segregation had a "detrimental effect" on African American children by making them feel inferior to Whites. "In the field of public education the doctrine of 'separate but equal' has no place," he stated. "Separate educational facilities are inherently unequal." White Southern reaction was intense. Moderates urged caution and respect for the law. Others, however, preached open resistance and hate. Violence flared across the South. The Ku Klux Klan mobilized to protest the decision, and new groups like the White Citizens' Council evolved to defend segregation and the "Southern way of life."

The Brown v. Board of Education Supreme Court decision built the New Civil Rights Movement

In 1955, in a second Brown decision, the Court provided enforcement guidelines. The high Court did not expect segregated schools to change overnight but wanted school districts to begin the process of integration and to proceed with "all deliberate speed." The Court's decision led to angry protests by White southerners, who vowed to resist segregation by all means possible. Virginia passed a law to close all integrated schools. Southern Congressmen led by Strom Thurman, in what was called the Southern Manifesto, proudly pledged to oppose the Brown ruling. Southern White

reactions to the Brown case confirmed to African Americans that efforts to undo existing social traditions and controls would be met with strong opposition, even violence. The Jackson *Daily News* openly declared in an editorial: "YES, WE DEFY THE LAW." Throughout the summer of 1955, coinciding with African Americans increased political boldness in the wake of the Supreme Court's Brown II ruling, violent acts and even murders committed by Whites against African Americans increased at an alarming rate. The murder of Emmett Till in 1955 showed how far some White southerners would go to protect the southern "tradition" of White supremacy.

Death of Emmett Till

On August, 20, 1955, Emmett Till (14 years of age), along with his cousin Curtis Jones, (17 years of age), boarded a southbound train in Chicago, Illinois, to visit relatives (Curtis Jones' grandfather and Emmett Till's granduncle, Mose Wright) in Money, Mississippi, a tiny town located in the Delta. Prior to his journey, Emmett's mother, Mamie Till Bradley, had cautioned him to "mind his manners" with White people.

While staying with Moses Wright, Curtis Jones' grandfather (a preacher), Emmett Till and his cousin drove Wright's 1941 Ford into Money to buy candy at Bryant's Grocery and Meat

Market. Emmett made friends with some local boys his age hanging around the store and showed them a picture of a White girl, claiming that the girl in the picture was his "sweetheart." One of the local boys then dared Emmett Till to speak to the White woman (Carolyn Bryant) in the store. According to Curtis Jones, Emmett went back inside the store and bought more candy, saying "Bye, baby" to the White woman as he left. Curtis Jones, Emmett Till and the other boys jumped in their car as Carolyn Bryant came out the swinging screen doors, and then they drove out of town. News of the incident quickly spread among the local African American youth, and Emmett and Curtis were warned to leave town before the woman's husband found out. But a week passed without the threatened retribution. Then, in the "wee hours of the morning" of August 28, 1955, Mose Wright was awakened by a knock on his door. Upon opening, two White men (later identified as J. W. Milam and his half-brother, Roy Bryant) asked him for the "nigger here from Chicago," the boy "that did all the talking." Emmett Till then was abducted at gunpoint. Mr. Wright tried to defend him, but he was struck in the head with the side of a shotgun. First, they made him carry a 75 pound cotton gin fan to the riverbank. They then ordered him to strip, beat him severely and then gouged out his eyes. Bryant then shot Emmett through the back of his head

and again through the body, and afterwards, wrapped his body in barbed wire and connected it to the cotton gin fan, which was then thrown in the river. Four days later, Emmett's mutilated body, with a 75-pound cotton gin fan tied around his neck with barbed wire, was found at the bottom of the Tallahatchie river.

The police recovered the body on Wednesday, August 31. It was so badly beaten that Emmett could only be identified by a ring on his finger. The authorities attempted to immediately have the body buried and forgotten. But, this did not happen, because Emmett's mother insisted that the body be returned to Chicago where she decided to have an open casket funeral. This would allow the whole world to see what White racists had done to her son.

Two weeks after the funeral, Roy Bryant and his brother-in-law J. W. Milam went to trial for the murder. Mose Wright bravely identified the two men who had kidnapped Emmett. Despite this, the jury returned a verdict of not guilty after an hour deliberation, claiming that the state failed to prove the identity of the body.

The world reacted with amazement and disgust, and condemned Mississippi in the newspapers as a city that approved of the murder of Black children. The murder really upset African Americans throughout the United States. The death of Emmett Till, although senseless and horrible, did serve a purpose. It became a rallying point and a wake up call for a generation of young African American southerners who, a decade later, would become the moving force behind the civil rights movement. Students became primary in the movement by carrying out demonstrations, sit-ins, and protest movements.

Students in the Crusade for Civil Rights

Elementary school student, Margaret Givner Brown, participated in the movement for civil rights. According to Margaret, her parents were very active, and they approved of their children's involvement. She stated: "my sister told me she wanted to participate and that she was not afraid. I told her that dogs would be there and she still was not scared. She was older than I was, and I said 'well if you go, I want to go.' Her confidence and lack of fear made me brave and I wanted to participate too. I was eight years old and when we were arrested, the police asked my name. Just as I had been instructed to do, I simply said, 'no comment.'"

Mrs. Flora W. Smith was 54 years old, attended the mass meetings, but was hesitant to demonstrate. She said: "I would pray every night that the Lord would send some marchers, but I wasn't about to go myself." Reverend Shuttlesworth made his appeal by saying that "Mordecai told

Esther don't you think that because you are in the King's palace that you will not be destroyed along with the rest of us." The next morning, Mrs. Smith woke up singing movement songs and decided she would be arrested that day. She stated: "I am going to be somebody's mother today, in jail. I packed my little bag with my Bible and my toothpaste and got arrested."

Jessie Shepherd was a 15-year-old high school student when she was arrested for demonstrating. She spoke of her experience as follows: "Well I remember being very scared and we all cried a lot because we wanted to go home. And we were told that we could not go home, that we had to stay until the Movement got the funds to get us out.... The first day wasn't too bad, but as the days progressed, it got worse and worse...."

Many other students demonstrated across the nation. They not only participated in sit-ins, but they did sit-ins as well. On February 1, 1960, one of the first major sit-ins by students materialized at the lunch counter of a Woolworth's in Greensboro, North Carolina, when Joseph McNeill, an African American college student, returned the next day with three classmates—David Richmond, Franklin McCain, and Izell Blair—to sit at the counter until they were served. They were not served. The four students returned to the lunch counter each day. When an article in the *New York Times* drew attention to the students' protest, more students, both Black and White, joined them and, thereafter, students across the nation launched similar protests. "In a span of two weeks, sit-ins demonstrations had occurred in eleven cities".

Despite beatings, being doused with ammonia, heavy court fines, arrest and imprisonment, students went to lunch counters across the South to continue the sit-ins through February and March. "By late March, the police had orders not to arrest the demonstrators because of the national publicity the sit-ins were attracting." Senator John F. Kennedy, one of the candidates in the presidential election that year, sent a statement to the sit-in students in Atlanta expressing the sentiment that "they have shown that the new way for Americans to stand up for their rights is to sit down." This represented one of the few times that either presidential candidate addressed a civil rights issue during the campaign.

Despite the violence, demonstrators known as "Freedom Riders," led by James Farmer, decided to force the South to desegregate interstate transportation. A group of Nashville sit-in students decided to go to Birmingham to participate in the Freedom Ride. Diane Nash, who helped organize the group, later explained: "If the Freedom Riders had been stopped as a result of violence, I strongly felt that the future of the movement was going to be cut short. The impression would

have been that whenever a movement starts, all [you have to do] is attack it with massive violence and the Blacks [will] stop."

The Nashville students traveled to Birmingham and asked the bus company to let them use their buses. Attorney general Kennedy also contacted the bus company and the Birmingham police. Kennedy was determined to enforce the Supreme Court's decision that called for integration of interstate travel, and he expressed concern that violence might occur if the Nashville students remained in Birmingham much longer. On May 17, the Birmingham police arrested the Nashville Freedom Riders and placed them in protective custody. At 2:00 a.m. on Friday, the police drove the Riders back to Tennessee and dropped them off by the side of the highway at the state line. After they got a ride back to Nashville, 100 miles away, they went right back to Birmingham to continue their protests. The Freedom Rides continued throughout Alabama, Mississippi, and Georgia. Due to the efforts of the Freedom Riders, the Interstate Commerce Commission, in 1961, declared illegal segregation in all interstate transportation facilities.

Students and religious leaders in both the South and the North played key roles in every phase of the civil rights movement—from bus boycotts to sit-ins to freedom rides to social movements. The student movement involved such celebrated figures as

John Lewis, the single-minded activist who "kept on" despite many beatings and harassments; James Lawson, the revered "guru" of nonviolent theory and tactics; Diane Nash, an articulate and intrepid public champion of justice; Bob Moses, a pioneer of voting registration in the most rural—and most dangerous—part of the South; and James Bevel, a fiery preacher and charismatic organizer and facilator. Other prominent student activists included Charles McDew, Bernard Lafayette, Charles Jones, Lonnie King, Julian Bond, (associated with Atlanta University), Hosea Williams (associated with Brown Chapel), and Stokely Carmichael, who later changed his name to Kwame Toure.

The students received support from African American women involved in boycotts, demonstrations, and protests. The Civil Rights movement always possessed a strong female presence. From Rosa Parks in Montgomery and Daisy Bates in Little Rock to Ella Baker of the Student Nonviolent Coordinating Committee and Fannie Lou Hamer of the Mississippi Freedom Democratic party, African American women played a prominent role in the struggle for equality. The success of the civil rights movement of the 1950s and 1960s occurred in large part due to the crucial role they played in propelling and sustaining mass action. Throughout the south, African American women acted as activists, leaders, members, and organizers within the movement.

African American Women in the Civil Rights Movement

The actions of Rosa Parks, a seamstress in Montgomery, Alabama, sparked off the bus boycott in the movement. Rosa Parks' active involvement in the NAACP actually led to her arrest on December 1, 1955. At 42, Mrs. Parks, a high school graduate who earned $23 a week as a seamstress, had not boarded the with the intention of disobeying the law, although she strongly opposed the bus company's policy and had been involved in efforts to fight it. Seated in a colored seat on the bus, Rosa was absorbed in her thoughts about preparing for an upcoming NAACP Youth Council conference. She was not aware that the White section of the bus had filled up and the bus driver was yelling at her to stand up. Aroused from her thoughts by a bullying bus driver, Rosa decided she was tired of the treatment she and other African Americans received every day of their lives. Quietly and respectfully, when the bus driver asked her if she were going to stand up, Mrs. Parks just responded: "No." The bus driver said: "Well, I'm going to have you arrested." She answered: "You may do that." Those were the only words exchanged.

Mrs. Parks' quiet strength and dignity launched a boycott of the Montgomery buses for 381 days. The soft-spoken, mild-mannered, hard-working lady became the symbol that the Montgomery NAACP and the Women's Political Council needed to challenge the law. Rosa continued to work behind the scenes for the NAACP and the newly formed Montgomery Improvement Association under the leadership of Dr. Martin Luther King, Jr. Rosa Parks' act of defiance that sparked the national civil rights movement probably would not have been as successful without the behind-the-scenes work of Jo Ann Gibson Robinson, Mary Fair Burks, and the Montgomery Women's Political Council.

Robinson led the campaign for the boycott. An English teacher at an all-Black Alabama State College, she served as president of the Womens' Political Council (WPC), an organization of African American professional women, mostly teachers, founded in 1946, shortly after dozens of African Americans had been arrested on the buses for violating the segregation law in public transportation. The WPC initially focused on voter registration and citizenship education with the intent of mobilizing African Americans to protest segregation. The WPC had in fact met with the city officials about the bus situation almost two years earlier. Following Parks' arrest, the newly formed Montgomery Improve-

ment Association (MIA) organized a year-long bus boycott. The WPC communicated the strategy and tactics essential for mass mobilization.

By February 1, 1956, downtown merchants in Montgomery had claimed losses over $1 million. The bus company estimated it had lost 65 percent of its income. By late April, Montgomery City Lines announced it would no longer enforce segregation. The city countered with a threat to arrest bus drivers who did not abide by Jim Crow laws and followed through with a court order restraining the company from desegregating its buses.

In June, the U.S. District Court ruled for the Montgomery Improvement Association in its suit against bus segregation. The city of Montgomery immediately appealed to the U.S. Supreme Court. In mid-November, the Supreme Court reaffirmed the district court's decision and declared segregation on Alabama's buses unconstitutional. Meanwhile, the city had obtained a state court injunction against the car pools. People no longer had a choice. They had to walk until the Supreme Court decision took effect. That happened on December 20, 1956.

Arkansas emerged at the center of the school desegregation campaign in the wake of the Brown decision. Under the leadership of Daisy Bates, president of the Arkansas NAACP, African Americans in Little Rock, Arkansas, urged the city to move swiftly to integrate its schools, particularly Central High School. By the fall of 1956, the city had developed a plan to integrate its schools, but the state's Supreme Court rejected the plan and blocked the admission of African American students to previously all-White facilities. Governor Orval E. Faubus defied the court order requiring integration and sent the Arkansas National Guard to Central High School to block the enrollment of nine African American students. President Eisenhower sent units of the U.S. Army to Little Rock to enforce the order. Arkansas officials eventually closed Little Rock public schools for two years before they were reopened on an integrated basis.

Ella Baker worked with students, and she organized sit-ins and protest demonstrations. Baker had also worked with groups of people teaching them how to buy in bulk and share the goods. Co-ops (cooperatives) were formed with Baker's help and guidance. Baker also worked for the Works Progress Administration and then for the NAACP. She was involved in many aspects of social change. She helped to organize the Southern Christian Leadership Conference and paved the way for the creation of the Student Nonviolent Coordinating Committee (SNCC), as well as the Mississippi Freedom Democratic Party, organized in 1964 to serve as a political voice for disenfranchised voters. Baker believed

that "strong people do not need strong leaders that do not allow for all to participate." From its inception, Baker influenced African American women who held key leadership positions within SNCC—Ruby Doris Smith Robinson, a Spelman College student from Atlanta, and Diane Nash of Fisk University. White college students were equally influenced by Baker; they included SNCC members Mary King, Casey Hayden, Jane Stembridge, and Dorothy Dawson.

Similar to Baker, Fannie Lou Hamer worked as a delegate with the Mississippi Freedom Democratic Party (MFDP). Her role and political influence within the party proved critical for the effectiveness of the organization from the outset. In 1963, Hamer had suffered from a brutal beating in a Winona, Mississippi, jail cell after attending a voter registration workshop. At the 1964 democratic National Convention in Atlantic City, New Jersey, MFDP party delegates sought to unseat the all-White Mississippi delegation. The MFDP attracted nationwide attention when Fannie Lou Hamer gave a compelling televised testimony that exposed violence and poverty suffered by African Americans in Mississippi. The MFDP ultimately succeeded in unseating the regular Mississippi delegates. In a political maneuver orchestrated by the Democratic Party, the MFDP received an offer to have two at-large seats, which they refused to accept. Mrs. Hamer eloquently captured the party's commitment to full equality, which, on principle, they refused to relinquish. She remarked: "We didn't come all this way for no two seats."

Stokely Carmichael at a Student Nonviolent Coordinating Committee rally

Parks, Robinson, Bates, Baker, and Hamer were among many African American women who contributed to the civil rights movement. Women in Black communities worked with African American men in the movement to make it successful. They helped them to organize and to protest the discriminatory treatment of Blacks in America. African American male leaders prominent in the movement included not only Dr. Martin Luther King Jr., but also Medgar Evers, Bayard Rustin, Malcolm X, Stokely Carmichael and many others.

Southern Civil Rights Movement and Black Leaders

Medgar Evers (1925-1963) served as field secretary in Mississippi for the NAACP. The Mississippi where Medgar Evers lived was a place of blatant discrimination and where African Americans feared to even speak of civil rights, much less actively campaign for them. Evers, a thoughtful and committed member of the NAACP, wanted to change his native state.

Medgar Evers, Mississippi NAACP official and civil rights leader

In his dealings with Whites and Blacks alike, Evers spoke constantly of the need to overcome hatred, to promote understanding and equality between the races. It was not a message that everyone in Mississippi wanted to hear. Evers was shot in the Back on June 12, 1963 after returning late from a meeting. He was 37 years old. Still in his early thirties, he was one of the most vocal and recognizable NAACP members in his state. He paid for his convictions with his life, becoming the first major civil rights leader to be assassinated in the 1960s. His death prompted President John Kennedy to ask Congress for a comprehensive civil-rights bill, which President Lyndon Johnson signed into law the following year.

Leadership of Dr. Martin Luther King, Jr.

Dr. Martin Luther King, Jr. was one of the most influential leaders in the Civil Rights movement. He was elected president of the Montgomery Improvement Association, the organization responsible for the successful Montgomery Bus Boycott from 1955 to 1956 (381 days). He was arrested 30 times for his participation in civil rights activities.

In 1957, King helped found the Southern Christian Leadership Conference (SCLC), an organization of Black churches and ministers that aimed to challenge racial segregation. As SCLC's president from 1957 to 1968, King became the organization's dominant personality and its primary intellectual influence. He was responsible for much of the organization's fund raising, which he frequently conducted in conjunction with preaching engagements in Northern churches.

King also served as vice president of the National Sunday School and Baptist Teaching Union Congress of the National Baptist Convention, as well as a member of several national and local boards of directors. He also served on the boards of trustees of several institutions and agencies.

King made strategic alliances with Northern Whites that helped to augment his success in gaining support for civil rights in the United States. Through Bayard Rustin, an African American civil rights and peace activist, King forged connections with older radical activists, many of them Jewish, who provided money and advice about strategy. King's closest adviser at times was Stanley Levison, a Jewish activist and former member of the American Communist Party. King also developed strong ties with prominent White protestant ministers in the North.

In 1959, King visited India and studied *Satyagraha*, Gandhi's principle of nonviolent persuasion. Thereafter, King decided to use Gandhi's teachings as his main instrument of social protest. The next year, he gave up his pastorate in Montgomery to become co-pastor (with his father) of the Ebenezer Baptist Church in Atlanta. In May of 1963, King and his SCLC staff escalated anti-segregation marches in Birmingham by encouraging teenagers and school children to join. Hundreds of singing children filled the streets of downtown Birmingham, angering Sheriff Bull Connor, who sent police officers with attack dogs and firefighters with high-pressure water hoses against the marchers. Scenes of young protesters being attacked by dogs and pinned against buildings by torrents of water from fire hoses were shown in newspapers and on televisions around the world. During the demonstrations, King was arrested and sent to jail. He wrote a letter from his jail cell to local clergymen who had criticized him for creating disorder in the city. His "Letter from Birmingham City Jail," which argued that individuals had the moral right and responsibility to disobey unjust laws, was widely read at the time, and it added to King's standing as a moral leader. National reaction to the Birmingham violence built support for the struggle for Black civil rights. The demonstrations forced White leaders to negotiate a solution to end segregation in Birmingham. Even more important, the protests encouraged many Americans to support national legislation against segregation.

To further promote the movement, King and other Black leaders organized, on August 28, the 1963 March on Washington, a massive protest in Washington, D.C. for jobs and civil rights. King delivered the keynote address to an audience of more than 200,000 civil rights supporters. His "I Have A Dream" speech expressed the hopes of the Civil Rights Movement in oratory as moving as any in American history: "I have a dream that one day this nation will rise up and live out the true meaning of its creed: 'We hold these truths to be self-evident, that all men

are created equal.' ... I have a dream that my four little children will one day live in a nation where they will not be judged by the color of their skin but by the content of their character."

The speech and the March evolved from the Birmingham demonstrations and created the political momentum that resulted in the Civil Rights Act of 1964, which prohibited segregation in public accommodations, as well as discrimination in education and employment. As a result of King's effectiveness as a leader of the Civil Rights Movement and his highly visible moral stance, he was awarded the 1964 Nobel Prize for peace.

Black Organizations in the Civil Rights Movement

Dr. Martin Luther King's SCLC, the NAACP, SNCC and CORE endorsed peaceful methods and believed that change could be effective by working around the established system; other groups such as the Black Panthers, the Nation of Islam, and the Black Nationalist Movement advocated retaliatory violence and a separation of the races. Numerous marches, rallies, strikes, riots, and violent confrontations with the police occurred within the movement. Since its founding, the NAACP had established a history on litigation, legislation, and education to achieve racial equality in America. In 1967, the NAACP boasted a membership of over

400,000, but it was often criticized by other Black organizations for not being more radical in its efforts for equality.

In April of 1960, the SNCC was established in Raleigh, North Carolina, to help organize and guide the student sit-in movement. King encouraged SNCC's creation, but the most important early advisor to the students was Ella Baker, who had worked for both the NAACP and SCLC. She believed that SNCC should not be part of SCLC, but a separate, independent organization led by the students. She also believed that civil rights activities should be based in individual Black communities. SNCC adopted Baker's approach and focused on making changes in the local Black communities, rather than striving for national change. This goal differed from that of SCLC, which worked to change national laws. During the civil rights movement, tensions occasionally arose between SCLC and SNCC because of their different methods.

SCLC's greatest contribution to the civil rights movement was a series of highly publicized protest campaigns in southern cities during the early 1960s. The protests intended to create such public disorder until local. White officials and business leaders would be compelled to end segregation in order to restore normal business activity. The demonstrations required the mobilization of hundreds, even thousands, of protesters who were willing to participate in protest

marches as long as necessary to achieve their goal and who were also willing to be arrested and sent to jail. The first SCLC direct-action campaign began in 1961 in Albany, Georgia, and continued thereafter, throughout the South until desegregation ended.

The Congress of Racial Equality (CORE) was founded in 1942 as the Committee of Racial Equality by an interracial group of students in Chicago. Many of the students were members of the Chicago branch of the Fellowship of Reconciliation (FOR), a pacifist organization seeking to change racist attitudes. Similar to Dr. Martin Luther King, Jr., the founders of CORE were deeply influenced by Mahatma Gandhi's teachings of nonviolent resistance. CORE had started as a nonhierarchical, decentralized organization funded entirely by voluntary contributions from its members. The organization was initially co-led by White University of Chicago student George Houser and Black student James Farmer. In 1942, CORE began protests against segregation in public accommodations by organizing sit-ins. In the same year, CORE expanded nationally. James Farmer traveled the country with Bayard Rustin, a field secretary with FOR, and recruited activists at FOR meetings. CORE's early growth consisted almost entirely of White middle-class college students from the Midwest. CORE pioneered the strategy of nonviolent direct action, especially the tactics of sit-ins, jail-ins, and freedom rides. Other mainstream organizations involved in the civil rights movement included the Council of Federated Organizations (COFO), an umbrella organization composed of various civil rights groups working independently in Mississippi; Deacons for Defense and Justice, a Black organization established to protect civil rights workers against the Ku Klux Klan; and the Tuskegee Civic Association, a group of African Americans dedicated to civil rights, voter education, and community welfare in Alabama. Formed in 1941, the Tuskegee Civic Association grew out of a group of men who had been meeting since 1910 as The Men's Meeting and, later, as The Tuskegee Men's Club. Its members worked on several fronts to improve the lives of African Americans in Tuskegee, Alabama, and its surrounding area, Macon County. The activities of these groups helped lead to the passage of major civil rights legislation.

Civil Rights Legislation

During the civil rights movement, the most prominent civil rights legislation since reconstruction was passed: the Civil Rights Act of 1964. It was the most significant civil rights legislation since the Reconstruction Era. The decisions of the Supreme Court at the time limited Congressional enforcement of the 14th Amendment to state action. Since 1964, the Supreme Court

has expanded the scope of the 14th Amendment in some situations to individuals discriminating on their own. Therefore, in order to reach the actions of individuals, Congress used its power to regulate interstate commerce enacted under the Civil Rights Act of 1964. According to the act, "discrimination based on race, color, religion, or national origin in public establishments that had a connection to interstate commerce or was supported by the state is prohibited." Public establishments included places of public accommodation (e.g., hotels, motels, trailer parks), restaurants, gas stations, bars, taverns, and places of entertainment in general. The Civil Rights Act of 1964 and subsequent legislation also declared a strong legislative policy against discrimination in public schools and colleges which aided in desegregation. Title VI of the civil rights act prohibits discrimination in federally funded programs. Title VII of the Civil Rights Act prohibits employment discrimination where the employer is engaged in interstate commerce. Subsequently, Congress has passed numerous other laws dealing with employment discrimination.

The Voting Rights Act of 1965 also addressed discrimination. The act suspended literacy tests and other voter tests, and authorized federal supervision of voter registration in states and individual voting districts where such tests existed. African

Americans who had been barred from registering to vote finally had an alternative to the courts. If voting discrimination occurred, the 1965 Act authorized the Attorney general to send federal examiners to replace local registrars. In the midst of such important legislation passed during President Lyndon B. Johnson's administration, African American leaders Malcolm X and King continued their crusade for equality and justice. Both leaders faced formidable opposition that resulted in deadly violence.

Leadership of Malcolm X

Malcolm X (1925-1965), later known also by the religious name El-Hajj Malik El-Shabazz, served as one of the most important African American leaders in the civil rights movement. His militant views that Western nations were inherently racist and that Black people must join together to build their own society and value system had an important influence on Black nationalist and separatist movements of the 1950s and 1960s. During the decade between 1955 and 1965, while most Black leaders worked in the civil rights movement to integrate African Americans into mainstream American life, Malcolm X preached the opposite.

Malcolm X was born Malcolm Little in Omaha, Nebraska. He was the son of Earl Little, a Baptist preacher, and his wife, Louise. The family moved to Lansing, Michigan, shortly after Malcolm's birth. Earl Little was an outspoken promoter of social and economic independence for Blacks and a supporter of the "Back to Africa" movement of Black nationalist leader Marcus Garvey. In 1931, Earl Little was murdered, probably by White terrorists because of his political and social activism.

His father's death had a disastrous effect on Malcolm and his family. His mother suffered a nervous breakdown, and the welfare department took the eight little children away from her. Malcolm was placed in a foster home and then in reform school. In 1941, he went to live with his half-sister in Boston. While there, he soon entered the fringes of the underworld; and at the age of 17, he moved to Harlem in New York City. Known as Detroit Red, Malcolm turned to a life of crime, including drug dealing and armed robbery. When he was 20, Malcolm received a sentence of ten years in prison for burglary.

While in prison, Malcolm read widely and developed an interest in the Nation of Islam, a Black nationalist religious movement whose members are known as Black Muslims. Malcolm studied the teachings of the leader of the Black Muslims, Elijah Muhammad, who advocated an independent Black state. The Nation of Islam was based on a theology adapted from several models: traditional Islamic teachings, Marcus

Garvey's principles of Black nationalism, and economic self-help programs that addressed the needs of African Americans living in urban ghettoes.

Unlike traditional Islam, which rejects all forms of racism, the Nation of Islam declared that Whites were the "devil by nature," and that God was Black. Also, the Black Muslims predicted that in the near future a great war would take place in which Whites would be destroyed and Black people would rule the world through the benevolence of Allah, their creator. To prepare for this new order, the Nation of Islam stressed personal self-restraint, opposed the use of drugs and alcohol, and organized economic self-help enterprises that eventually included farms, food stores, restaurants, and small businesses. The Black Muslims recruited heavily among the poorest of urban Blacks and in prisons, where Malcolm Little was converted to the faith.

When Malcolm left prison in 1952, he went to Detroit, Michigan, and joined the Nation of Islam temple in that city. He dropped his last name—considered a "slave name" by Black Muslims—and became Malcolm X. In 1958, he married Betty Sanders, later known as Betty Shabazz, and they eventually had six daughters.

Malcolm X rose rapidly in the Nation of Islam organization as a minister and recruiter of new members. Elijah Muhammad appointed him as the chief minister of Harlem's main temple in June of 1954. Malcolm X also helped to establish the movement's main information and propaganda newspaper, *Muhammad Speaks*. Within five years, Malcolm X had become a more prominent spokesperson for the Nation of Islam than Elijah Muhammad. His fiery style and natural speaking ability made him a popular public speaker, but his growing reputation caused tension with Elijah Muhammad and other Black Muslim leaders. While Muhammad strenuously tried to maintain the Nation of Islam as a religious self-help movement, Malcolm was increasingly moving towards a political response to racism. He called for a "Black Revolution," which he declared would be "bloody" and would renounce any sort of "compromise" with Whites. In this way, Malcolm X rejected the conservative values of the Nation of Islam in favor of a more radical, revolutionary approach to social change.

In 1963, Elijah Muhammad silenced Malcolm X for his statement that the assassination of U.S. president John F. Kennedy had represented "the chickens coming home to roost"—a repayment for America's continuing failure to end racial cruelty and hatred. This comment, often taken out of context, was not meant to be disrespectful to the late president, although, in fact, Malcolm X had little respect or admiration for any White political leader. Rather, he was trying to make the point that the violent treatment of Blacks had now come back to the "roost" with violence against a White president. However, the insensitive nature of the statement reflected poorly on the Black Muslims and led Muhammad to silence Malcolm X. In essence, Muhammad told his most prominent follower that he could not speak in public and remain within the Black Muslim organization.

Rather than accept this silencing, Malcolm X publicly broke with the Nation of Islam on March 8, 1964 and formed his own movement, the Muslim Mosque, Inc. Even before the split, however, Malcolm X had already begun to part ways with the Black Muslims because he felt stifled by the authoritarian organization of the Nation of Islam. He was ready to be his own leader rather than to follow the dictates of Muhammad or anyone else.

In 1964, shortly after his break with Elijah Muhammad, Malcolm X made a pilgrimage to Mecca, the holy Muslim city in Saudi Arabia that is the birthplace of the founder of Islam. He also visited several other African and Arab nations. While on this trip, he wrote a highly publicized letter expressing his own faith as a follower of traditional Islam and renouncing the Black Muslim teaching that all White men are evil. He became an orthodox Sunni Muslim (Sunni Islam). He also adopted a religious name, El-Hajj Malik El-Shabazz, meaning the Malcolm (or Malik) who is from the tribe or family of Shabazz and has made the Hajj, or pilgrimage, to Mecca. However, most people in the United States continued to call him Malcolm X, a name he did not reject.

When Malcolm X returned to America, he held the first rally for a Black nationalist group he had founded, the Organization of Afro-American Unity (OAAU). This group, which had no direct religious ties, advocated racial solidarity and strove to unify all Black organizations fighting White racism. At the same time, Malcolm X renounced his previous racism against Whites, declaring that in Mecca he had realized that people of all colors were children of Allah. In contrast to his earlier views, he encouraged Blacks to vote, to participate in the political system, and to work with one another and with sympathetic Whites and Hispanics for an end to racial discrimination. As he told a group of African leaders, the problem of race was "not a Negro problem, nor an American problem. This is a world problem, a problem of humanity."

On February 21, 1965 Malcolm X was assassinated while addressing an OAAU rally in New York City. At least two of the three men later convicted of the crime were connected with the Nation of Islam. Many scholars and supporters of Malcolm X have speculated that leaders or individuals within the Nation of Islam,—including Elijah Muhammad, —considered him a danger to their own movement and could not forgive him for rejecting their authority and organizing a rival movement. These observers believe that the Nation of Islam leadership may have ordered the assassination of Malcolm X because he had spoken gainst some of the teachings of the Nation of Islam, including Elijah Muhammad's theory that the White race was created by a dissident "mad scientist." His beliefs gained a broader audience through *The Autobiography of Malcolm X* (1965), published after his assassination. A few years later, one of the most prominent African American leaders of the civil rights movement would also be assassinated.

The Death of Martin Luther King, Jr.

In the late 1960s, Dr. King had joined a nationwide campaign to help the poor; at the same time, he had insisted that nonviolence must remain the central tactic of the civil-rights movement. He decided to go to Memphis to help lead sanitation workers in a protest against low wages and intolerable conditions. On April 4, 1968, King was shot by James Earl Ray while standing on the balcony of the Lorraine Motel in Memphis, Tennessee. He was only 39 at the time of his death.

In the accepted version of the assassination—one which no credible historian, or federal or state investigation has disputed—James Earl Ray, a career criminal and open racist, murdered Martin Luther King on April 4, 1968. An escaped convict, Ray rented a room in Memphis across from the Lorraine Motel where King was staying while mediating a sanitation workers' strike. Using a rifle with a sniper scope, he shot King from his bathroom window as King stood on the balcony of the motel. The single bullet severed King's spinal cord and killed him. Witnesses reported seeing Ray fleeing from his rooming house moments later. Ray's fingerprints were found on a pair of binoculars and the rifle, which records show he had purchased six days before the shooting. Following a two-month-long manhunt, Ray was arrested at Heathrow Airport after he had robbed a London bank. As he told his first attorney, Percy Foreman, "I thought I could get to [South] Africa and serve two or three years in one of them mercenary armies and those folks over there wouldn't send me back."

To escape facing the possibility of execution, Ray pleaded guilty in March 1969. As a result, a trial was waived and Ray was given a 99-year prison sentence. Even though he had told the judge he understood that a guilty plea could not be appealed, he recanted his confession three days later. Despite many appeals, none of Ray's numerous lawyers ever produced evidence convincing a court of law to reopen the case. A federal investigation in 1977–1978 by the House Select Committee on Assassinations concluded that although "there is a likelihood" that Ray did not act alone in planning the assassination, he alone pulled the trigger. While in his death bed, Ray stated that he did not pull the trigger. King's death had occurred during a period marked by riots and violence.

Urban Riots and Violence

On August 11, 1965, five days after President Lyndon Johnson signed the Voting Rights Act, the arrest of a 21-year-old for drunk driving ignited a riot in Watts, a predominantly Black section of Los Angeles. The violence lasted five days and resulted in 34 deaths, 3,900 arrests, and the destruction of over 744 buildings and 200 businesses in a 20-square-mile area.

Over the next four summers, the nation's inner cities experienced a wave of violence and rioting. The worst violence occurred during the summer of 1967, when riots occurred in 127 cities. In Newark, 26 persons lost their lives, over 1,500 were injured, and 1,397 were arrested. In Detroit, 43 people died, $500 million in property was destroyed, and 14 square miles gutted by fire. The last major wave occurred following the assassination of Martin Luther King, Jr. in Memphis, Tennessee, on April 4, 1968. Violence erupted in 168 cities,

leaving 46 dead, 3,500 injured, and $40 million worth of damage. In Washington, D.C., fires burned within three blocks of the White House.

In 1968, President Johnson appointed a commission to examine the causes of the race riots of the preceding three summers. Led by Illinois Governor Otto Kerner, the commission attributed racial violence to "White racism" and its heritage of discrimination and exclusion. Joblessness, poverty, lack of political power, decaying and dilapidated housing, police brutality, and poor schools bred a sense of frustration and rage that had exploded into violence. The commission warned that unless major steps were taken, the United States would inevitably become "two societies: one Black, one White—separate and unequal."

Resistance to racial equality in the Deep South came not only from extremist groups like the Ku Klux Klan and "White citizens' councils," it also occurred at all levels of government and society—from federal judges to state governors to county sheriffs to local citizens serving on juries. Governors Ross Barnett of Mississippi and George Wallace of Alabama physically blocked school doorways at their respective states' universities. E.H. Hurst, a Mississippi state representative, stalked and killed a Black farmer for attending voter registration classes. Laurie Pritchett, Albany, Georgia's police chief, thwarted student efforts to integrate public places in the city. Sheriff Jim Clark of Dallas County, Alabama, let loose his deputies on "Bloody Sunday" marchers and personally menaced other protestors. Police all across the South arrested civil rights activists on trumped-up charges. All-White juries in several states acquitted known killers of local African Americans. Most importantly, resistance to equality for African Americans continued in the South as well as in the North.

Black Athletes and Desegregation of Sports

African American athletes had a history of facing discrimination in team sports prior to and during the civil rights movement. The most violent reaction to African American participation in sports had taken place in boxing. After the controversial African American boxer Jack Johnson defeated White boxer Jim Jeffries for the world heavyweight title in 1910, Whites rioted and lynched African American men throughout the country. Between 1919 and the 1930s, White boxers refused to fight African Americans for the heavyweight title. Only in 1937 was African American boxer Joe Louis officially recognized as the world heavyweight champion.

As the dominant heavyweight boxer of the 1960s and 1970s, Muhammad Ali won an Olympic gold medal, captured the professional world heavyweight championship on three separate occasions, and successfully defended his title 19 times. Ali's extroverted, colorful style, both in and out of the ring, heralded a new mode of media-conscious athletic celebrity. Through his bold assertions of Black pride, his conversion to the Muslim faith, and his outspoken opposition to the Vietnam War (1959-1975), Ali became a highly controversial figure during the civil rights movement. At the height of his fame, Ali was described as "the most recognizable human being on earth." Returning triumphantly to Louisville from the Olympic games of 1960, Muhammad Ali was bitterly disappointed that he was not welcomed as an American hero in his segregated hometown. According to one story, Muhammad Ali threw the Olympic medal into the Ohio River after being refused service at a Louisville diner while wearing the medal around his neck.

Integration provided greater opportunities to individual Black players, but Black teams, such as the Harlem Globetrotters and Negro League teams, were excluded from the new system. As talented athletes joined the ranks of the National Basketball Association and major league baseball, the quality of play and fan support waned in the segregated leagues. The Harlem Globetrotters became a traveling entertainment act, while the Negro League teams simply disappeared. On the other hand,

African American athletics had a significant role in promoting the ideals of the civil rights movement.

Conclusion

The civil rights movement marked a period of unprecedented energy against the second class-citizenship accorded to African Americans in the South. Discrimination and segregation against African Americans in the North also persisted; however, segregation in the North was somewhat less oppressive than in the South. In many ways, northern African Americans had greater freedom than southern African Americans: segregation in the North was by custom rather than by law. However, since segregation laws did not exist in the North, it was sometimes more difficult to recognize civil rights violations.

Resistance to racial segregation and discrimination with strategies such as civil disobedience, nonviolent resistance, marches, protests, boycotts, "freedom rides," and rallies received national attention, as newspaper, radio, and television reporters and cameramen documented the struggle to end racial inequality. Continued efforts by African Americans leaders and major civil rights organizations challenged discrimination and segregation throughout the period. Their efforts resulted in the Brown decision in 1954, the Civil Rights Act of 1964, and the Voting Rights Act in 1965 that helped bring about the demise of the entangling web of legislation that restricted African Americans to second-class citizenship. The Black struggle for civil rights also inspired other liberation movements, including those of Native Americans, Latinos, and women, and African American support of the liberation struggle in Africa.

Review Questions

1. What event led to the Montgomery Bus Boycott during the civil rights movement?

2. Identify and discuss three major civil rights organizations that were prominent in the movement.

3. Compare and contrast African American female civil rights activists Ella Baker and Fannie Lou Hamer.

4. What contributions did Dr. Martin Luther King, Jr. make to the civil rights movement?

5. Who was Malcolm X, and what philosophy did he use to address race relations?

6. How were students in the South involved in the civil rights movement?

7. What were the major legislative successes, and how did they end discrimination and segregation in American society?

8. Describe the Brown decision and its significance in terms of segregation.

Chapter 21

African American Activist Black Pride Movement

This chapter discuses the rise of the Black pride movement during the modern civil rights era. Black Power became a symbol of African American unity in the 1960s, stressing group strength, independent action, and racial pride. In local communities, African American activists lobbied school boards to add African American history and culture to the curriculum. On college campuses, African American students pressured administrators to speed up minority recruitment, especially in Black Studies programs, and provide separate living quarters. In the political arena, Carl Stokes of Cleveland and Richard Hatcher of Gary, Indiana, became the first African American mayors of northern cities. Across the nation, African Americans wore African clothing, took on African names, and wore their hair un-straightened in an "Afro" style. "Black is Beautiful" became a powerful slogan during this period, as did "Say it Loud, I'm Black and I'm Proud" by soul singer James Brown. To militants within the move-ment, Black Power meant a political separation of the races. The separatist impulse had deep roots in the African American community. Its renewed strength in the 1960s occurred, in large part, due to a Black nationalist movement that appealed to young people in urban America. Further-more, the doctrine of Black nation-alism, self-help, and racial separation appealed to thousands of African Americans oppressed by inequalities and injustices.

Rise of the Black Power Movement

Black Power was a political movement which arose in the mid-1960s that endeavored to express a new racial consciousness among African Americans in the United States. Robert Williams, who revived the Monroe, North Carolina chapter of the NAACP and later was exiled in Cuba and China, was the first to put the actual term to effective use in the late 1950s. Williams, who was also the first to publish the poetry of Ray Durem, used the phrase "Black Power" in the American political context. The movement stemmed from the earlier civil rights movements, but its meaning was vigorously debated. To some African Americans, Black Power represented racial dignity and self-reliance (i.e. freedom from White authority in both economic and political arenas). To others, it was economic in orientation.

**Stokely Carmichael's
"Black Power" speech at Berkeley**

Led in many ways by Malcolm X, who supplied the rhetoric, style, and attitude, the Black Power Movement encouraged African Americans to focus on the improvement of African American communities, rather than the fight for complete integration. The Black Panther Party for Self-Defense represented the vanguard of the Black Power Movement. In addition to Robert Williams, Stokely Carmichael played a key role in the formation of the ideas of Black Power. Carmichael made Black Power more popular, largely through his use of the term while reorganizing the Student Non-

violent Coordinating Committee (SNCC) so that Whites would no longer control leadership in American society.

Some African Americans sought cultural heritage and history and the true roots of Black identity as their part of the Black Pride movement. This was thought of as the "consciousness" aspect of the Black Power Movement. The classic phrases belonged to the musicians: "Free your mind . . ." (George Clinton/ Funkadelic) and "Say it loud, I'm Black and I'm proud" (James Brown). The movement also recognized that standards of beauty and self-esteem were integral to power relations. Other interpreters of the Black Power Movement included Harold Cruse and Amiri Baraka who dealt with the cultural-nationalist perspective of Black Power as related to the artistic realm. In his essay, "The Black Arts Movement," Larry Neal explains the effects of the Black Power Movement on the Black Arts Movement. He writes that "the political values inherent in the Black Power Concept are now finding concrete expression in the aesthetics of Afro-American dramatists, poets, choreographers, musicians and novelists." Like those who emphasized "consciousness," the artists of Black Power likewise emphasized the central importance of self-representation and productive autonomy.

One main point of the Black Power concept was the necessity for African Americans to define the world in their own terms. At times, this included a request for a revolutionary political struggle to reject racism and imperialism in the United States. As the Black Power concept began to grow, it also began to build resistance and criticism from Whites and from several African American organizations, including the NAACP, because of the anti-White message associated (often unfairly) with Black Power.

The Black Panther Party, evolving in the late 1960s, became the largest African American organization advocating Black Power. Eventually because of the continuous condemnation of the theory of Black Power as a separatist and anti-White movement, along with the destruction of the Black Panthers in the early 1970s, the Black Power concept seemed to disappear. Yet, scholars of African American art and politics still see the idea of Black Power as a strong effect on the consciousness of Black America today, although its institutions have been destroyed and the radical politics largely discredited and defused. In essence, the focus on cultural autonomy and self-esteem of the Black Power Movement has survived and, not surprisingly, grown in strength.

Government "COINTELPRO" Program

In the midst of the Black Power Movement, the federal government undertook efforts to suppress the activities of groups associated with the movement, most notably the Black Panther Party and its supporters. The Federal Bureau of Investigation (FBI), under J. Edgar Hoover, created a program called COINTELPRO (counterintelligence program) to break up the spreading unity of revolutionary groups that had been inspired and influenced by the Black Panthers. The FBI initiated covert investigations designed to destroy the party, by killing leading members of the party such as Fred Hampton they knew could not be otherwise subverted. A series of arrests followed these mass killings, and afterwards, a program of psychological warfare was launched to divide the party both politically and morally through the use of espionage and provocatures.

It was through COINTELPRO that the public image of African Americans identified with Black Power was distorted to legitimize their arrest and imprisonment, and to scapegoat them as the cause for the nation's problems. The FBI and police instigated violence and fabricated false reports of horrible actions. The nonconformists were deliberately "criminalized" through false charges, frame-ups, and offensive, bogus leaflets and other materials published in their name. COINTELPRO enabled the FBI and police to exacerbate the movement's internal stresses until beleaguered activists turned on one another. Whites were pitted against African Americans, African Americans against Chicanos and Puerto Ricans, students against workers, workers against people on welfare, men against women, religious activists against atheists, Christians against Jews, Jews against Muslims. Money was repeatedly stolen and equipment sabotaged to intensify pressure and cause suspicion and mistrust. Otherwise manageable disagreements were instigated by COINTELPRO until they exploded into hostile rifts that destroyed alliances, split groups apart, and drove dedicated activists out of the movement.

Government documents implicated the FBI and police in the hostile disintegration of such key groups as the Black Panther Party and the Liberation News Service, and in the collapse of repeated efforts to form long-term coalitions across racial, class, and regional lines. While genuine political issues were often involved in these disputes, the outcome could have been different if government agencies had not covertly intervened to sabotage alliances by promoting enmity and rivalry.

COINTELPRO enabled the FBI and police to eliminate the leaders of mass movements without undermining the image of the United States as a democracy, complete with free speech and the rule of law. Charismatic orators and dynamic organizers were covertly attacked and "neutralized" before their skills could be transferred to others and stable structures established to carry on their work. Malcolm X was killed in a "factional dispute" which the FBI took credit for having "developed" in the Nation of Islam. Martin Luther King, Jr. was the target of an elaborate FBI plot to drive him to suicide and replace him "in his role of the leadership of the Negro people." Many believed that King's assassination, as well as Malcolm's, was a domestic covert operation carried out by the federal government.

To help bring down a major target, the FBI often combined these approaches in strategic sequence. Take the case of the "underground press," a network of some 400 radical weeklies and several national news services, which once boasted a combined readership of close to 30 million. In the late 1960s, government agents raided the offices of alternative newspapers across the country in purported pursuit of drugs and fugitives. In the process, they destroyed typewriters, cameras, printing presses, layout equipment, business records, and research files, and roughed up and jailed staffers on bogus charges. Meanwhile, the FBI persuaded record companies to withdraw lucrative advertising contracts and to arrange for printers, suppliers, and distributors to drop underground press accounts. With their already shaky operations in disarray, the papers and news services were easy targets for a final phase of COINTELPRO disruption. Forged correspondence, anonymous accusations, and infiltrators' manipulation provoked a flurry of ridiculous charges and counter-charges that played a major role in destroying the leaders as well as the foundations of the organizations.

What proved most devastating in all of this was the effective manipulation of the victims of COINTELPRO into blaming themselves. Since the FBI and police operated covertly, the injustices they made up appeared to originate from within the movements. The activists lost trust in one another and their collective power was subverted; thus, the hopes of a generation died, leaving a legacy of cynicism and despair. The Black Panther Party became a major victim of COINTELPRO.

The Black Panther Party

The Black Panther Party for Self-Defense was founded in October of 1966, in Oakland California, by Huey Newton and Bobby Seale, with Hubert (H. "Rap") Brown, and Eldridge Cleaver as Minister of Information. The Panthers practiced militant self-defense of minority communities against the U.S. government and fought to establish revolutionary socialism through mass organizing and community based programs. The party was one of the first organizations in U.S. history to militantly struggle for ethnic minority and working class emancipation—a party whose agenda was the revolutionary establishment of *real* economic, social, and political equality across gender and color lines. The practices of the late Malcolm X were deeply rooted in the theoretical foundations of the Black Panther Party. Malcolm had represented both a militant revolutionary, with the dignity and self-respect to stand up and fight to win equality for all oppressed minorities; while also being an outstanding role model, he was someone who sought to bring about positive social services; something the Black Panthers would take to new heights. The Panthers accepted Malcolm's belief of supporting international working classes across the spectrum of color and gender; thus, it united with various minority and White revolutionary groups. From the tenets of Maoism, they set the role of their Party as the vanguard of the revolution and worked to establish a united front, while from Marxism they addressed the capitalist economic system, embraced the theory of dialectical materialism, and represented the need for all workers to "forcefully take over the means of production."

Stokely Carmichael, the former chairman of the Student Nonviolent

Coordinating Committee (SNCC) and a nationally known proponent of Black Power, was recruited into the party through this struggle, and he soon became the party's Prime Minister in February of 1968. Carmichael was adamant against allowing Whites into the Black liberation movement, arguing that Whites could not relate to the Black experience and that they would have an intimidating effect on Blacks, a position that caused opposition within the Panthers.

Eldridge Cleaver, Minister of Information for the Black Panther Party

African American Black Power supporters assumed significant roles within the Black Panther Party from 1967 to the early 1980s. They "held party leadership positions at local levels as well as well as national levels, delivered speeches at rallies, and participated in the organization's community survival programs (free food, clothing, and health services, among other necessities)." Kathleen Neal Cleaver, Elaine Brown, and Ericka Huggins were the most prominent female members. Kathleen Cleaver was the first woman to hold a national leadership position; she was the communications secretary from 1967 to 1971. Elaine Brown became the first and only female chairperson of the party from 1974 to 1977. Ericka Huggins directed the organization's Oakland Community School from 1973 to 1981. The women supported the programs provided by the Party. It provided free breakfast for schoolchildren, free medical care, free transportation to visit relatives in prison and for senior citizens, free shoes and clothing, political education classes, voter registration, petition campaigns for community control of police, and legal aid and counseling, among other programs.

The pressures that female members of the Black Panther Party faced sometimes caused them to rescind their membership. Since police surveillance and harassment were equally problematic for women and men, female members faced both internal and external pressures.

By the beginning of the 1980s, attacks on the party and internal degradation and divisions caused it to fall apart. The intensity of undercover FBI involvement and local police harassment helped to weaken and curtail public interest in the party's activities and members' involvement. The leadership of the party had been absolutely destroyed, and its rank and file were constantly terrorized by the police. Many remaining Panthers were hunted down and killed in the following years, imprisoned on trumped charges (Mumia Abu-Jamal, Sundiata Acoli, among many others), or forced to leave the United States (Assata Shakur and others).

Black Power in Sports (Muhammad Ali)

One of the most celebrated figures linked to the Black Power Movement, Muhammad Ali, born Cassius Clay, in January of 1942, to a poor working-class family in Louisville, Kentucky, became probably the greatest heavy-weight boxer of all times. Clay took the name Muhammad Ali when he joined the Black nationalist Nation of Islam in 1964. Thereafter, Ali was forced to take on the world, not just as a champion boxer, but as part of the struggle for Black rights. Despite a close friendship that had grown between Malcolm X and Muhammad Ali, before Ali faced Sonny Liston for the world championship in 1964, the political split within the Nation separated Malcolm and Ali, whose political inclinations were closer to Elijah. Ali, having embraced the religion and at the same time conquered the boxing world, now became the most famous member of the Nation of Islam. He also became the centre of a power struggle within the Nation itself and, at the same time, a major cause of discussion in the civil

rights movement. Two men publicly congratulated him on his victory over Liston: Malcolm X and Dr Martin Luther King. Jackie Robinson meanwhile commented that Ali's conversion meant 'nothing' to the civil rights movement. Robinson also warned that "if Negroes ever turn to the Black Muslim movement in any numbers… It will be because White America has refused to recognize the responsible leadership of the Negro people and to grant us the same rights that any other citizen enjoys in this land." Despite criticism, Ali's successes became a powerful symbol of defiance and pride for African Americans and oppressed people around the world. At this time of the movement, emphasis was also placed on the arts and Black expression.

Black Arts Movement

The Black Arts Movement within the Black Power Movement represented a loose network of Black Nationalist African American artists and intellectuals from the mid-1960s to the mid-1970s. In many respects, the Black Arts Movement was the cultural wing of the Black Power Movement. Like the Black Power Movement, its participants held a variety of political beliefs, ranging from revolutionary Marxism to versions of what was understood as the cultures and ideologies of traditional pre-colonial Africa. Despite this range of often conflicting beliefs, there was a generally shared concept of African American liberation and the right of African Americans to determine their own destiny. There was also usually some common notion of the development or recovery of an authentic national Black culture that was linked to an existing African American folk or popular culture.

It is difficult to date the beginning of the Black Arts Movement exactly. One possibility is 1965, when Amiri Baraka and other Black cultural activists founded the Black Arts Repertory Theatre/School (BARTS) in Harlem, New York. However, a number of important forerunners to BARTS helped make the larger movement possible. For example, Umbra, a semi nationalist group of African American writers in the Lower Eastside of New York City in the early 1960s, provided a training ground for a number of influential Black Arts activists, including Ishmael Reed, Lorenzo Thomas, David Henderson, Calvin Hernton, and Askia Muhammad Toure. The influence of the Nation of Islam on many African American jazz musicians in the 1950s and early 1960s also helped prepare the way for a Black Nationalist arts movement. The journals, *The Liberator* and *Negro Digest* (later *Black World*), offered important outlets and encouragement for emerging literary and artistic nationalists in the early 1960s. Baraka's pre-BARTS drama, particularly *Dutchman* (1964) and *The Slave* (1964), were crucial in shaping the form and direction that African American nationalist drama would take in the late 1960s and early 1970s.

After 1965, however, the Black Arts Movement took on a more cohesive presence. Although there often existed sharp conflict about politics and aesthetics between participants in the movement, there was enough common ground to produce national conferences, journals (such as *Black Dialogue*, *Journal of Black Poetry*, and *Black World*), organizations, and widely read anthologies (such as Baraka and Larry Neal's seminal *Black Fire* [1968]).

Unlike earlier groupings of African American artistic production, the Black Arts Movement flourished in a wide range of locations. Virtually every sizable African American community, and many college campuses saw the rise of new Black theaters and organizations of nationalist-minded visual artists, writers, dancers, and musicians. The Association for the Advancement of Creative Music, the Organization of Black American Culture, and the African Commune of Bad Relevant Artists, all in Chicago, Illinois; Spirit House in Newark, New Jersey; the Black Arts Group in St. Louis, Missouri; the Watts Writer's Workshop in Los Angeles, California; and Broadside Press in Detroit, Michigan, were among the leading organizations and institutions associated with the Movement.

Artistic, Cultural, and Intellectual Developments

Due to the emphasis on civil rights and Black Power, the 1960s in the United States was a decade marred by social unrest, civil rights injustice, and violence both home and abroad. These were some of the factors that led to a cultural revolution. The revolution attempted to diverge the fabric of American society. Teenagers were living dangerously and breaking away from the ideals that their parents held. In the process, they created their own society. Their leaders had lofty goals as well. Dr. Martin Luther King, Jr. had dreams of a truly equal America. John F. Kennedy dreamed of a young vigorous nation that would put a man on the moon. The youth wanted to live in a state of love, peace, and freedom. Through the stormy decade of the 1960s, it seemed that popular music was at the eye of every storm.

During this time, musicians reacted to what they saw and often the youth of the Sixties were living out lyrics and popular songs of the day. For every headline, there was a song by artists such as Bob Dylan, James Brown, Aretha Franklin, The Jefferson Airplane, and The Beatles. Some remember the decade's music as a representation of the moral decline and the representation of the inappropriate ideal of the youth. The youth movement became the counterculture and its members

became hippies, who preached mysticism, honesty, joy, and nonviolence. Music played an intricate part in the hippie lifestyle. The music reflected the sentiment of the youth. It became an outlet for teenagers to express themselves and voice their concerns about society. Folk music was the musical choice of the youth in the early Sixties. Bob Dylan and Joan Baez were the most popular folk singers of the day.

In the early Sixties, the union of the civil rights movements and folk music on campuses led to the rise of folk songs called "message songs." Songs like "Blowin in the wind" by Bob Dylan began opening up the minds of the youth to the social problems facing America such as the civil rights movement. The Rascals' "People Everywhere Just want to be Free," Joan Baez's "We shall overcome," and Dylan's "The times they are a changin'" were message songs that helped start the firestorm of politically charged music that fueled a revolution and a generation. Songs of the decade reached for the poetic, symbolic, and the mystical to better pinpoint the mood of the times. With the assassination of President John F. Kennedy, folk music movement began to fraction. The disillusionment and shock caused by the assassination had an especially strong effect on the youth. Drug abuse became a trademark of the hippie movement. The use of drugs was glorified in many ways by bands like The Jefferson

Airplane, The Grateful Dead, Jimi Hendrix, and Pink Floyd. This music became known as "acid rock." The music fashioned the ideas of peace and love along with it a dark trend. San Francisco was bursting with rock activity and it became the center for the hippie culture. The heart of the hippie activity was the Haight-Ashbury district. Thousands of middle class, college educated youths flocked to San Francisco to demonstrate their counter cultural beliefs. These summers began to be known as "Summers of love." They lived on the streets, did drugs, and sat in groups strumming their guitars. They wore flowers in their hair, leading to the nickname "flower children" and phrase "flower power." Songs like White Rabbit by the Jefferson Airplane told the stories of their mind-altering experiences: "one pill makes you larger, and one pill makes you small, and the ones that mother gives don't do anything at all...remember what the doorknob said, feed your head."

The Civil Rights movement may have been the most emotionally charged movement of the Sixties. The music reflected this feeling. Soul music and Motown became the driving music by African American artists who fought for equality. Songs by Aretha Franklin, Curtis Mayfield and James Brown expressed the sentiments of the times. When morale was down, songs like Curtis Mayfield's "We are winners" and James Brown's

"Say it loud, I'm Black and I'm proud" provided support to the downtrodden Black youth. Aretha Franklin's song, "Freedom," was written after the assassination of Martin Luther King, Jr. in 1968. It inspired the world to "think about what you are trying to do to me, think, let your mind go and let yourself be free, oh freedom, freedom, I said freedom." Within 48 hours after the assassination of Martin Luther King, Jr., 130 cities had major riots. However, in Boston, James Brown in a televised concert pleaded for a stop to the violence. He said "we are Black, now are we together or are we aint," and no rioting took place in Boston that night.

**Police arresting a rioter
in the urban unrest**

Motown music was a great supporter for Black pride within the Civil Rights Movement. Motown was the first African American owned label. The founder, Berry Gordy, supported peaceful integration, and recorded speeches by Martin Luther King, Jr. Folk music had its share of freedom songs. Dylan's "Blowin in the wind" asks "How many roads must a man walk down before you call him a man…how many times can a man turn his head pretending he just doesn't see…the answer my friend is blowin in the wind, the answer is blowin in the wind." Rock music was building a bridge across the racial division; African American guitarist Jimi Hendrix was a star of the times and the main attraction at the Woodstock music festival.

The feminist movement was also surged by African American singers during the1960s. Inspired by singers like the Supremes, Aretha Franklin, Grace Slick of the Jefferson Airplane, and Janis Joplin, women all over the United States began to fight for equality. Franklin's song "Respect," which simply asks for a little respect, is an example of how the women felt. Janis Joplin made a political statement every time she went on stage. She held nothing back during her performances. Her stage presence was just as strong if not stronger than the male stars of the day. Protests and demonstrations were the order of the day. Musicians often attended the protest and their songs illustrate this. The Rolling Stones song, "Street fighting man," was inspired by the protests taking place in London that Stones singer Mick Jagger had attended. "Every where I go I hear the sound of marching charging feet," Jagger said. True to his words, protests were held all over the world, from Paris to Mexico City. The Beatles

song, "Helter Skelter," also reflected on the madness that could and usually occurred when the demonstrations turned violent and deadly. Smokey Robinson also felt that the demonstrations were a strong force of change; in his song, "Get Ready," it says "people get ready for the trains are coming." The Chambers Brothers drew the line in the sand and summed up the protest movement by saying "The time has come today, young hearts must go their way, can't put it off another day." In 1968, the Beatles released a double album called the White album. On that album, there is a song called "Revolution." John Lennon wrote the song not as a call to arms but as a personal statement to the demonstrators saying "so you say you want a revolution, well you know, we all want to change the world…when you talk about destructtion brother you can count me out…you better free your mind instead."

Blaxploitation films

During the 1960s, with the full flowering of the Black Power Movement, such films began to take on a harsher, more politically demanding edge. At first from abroad, later from sources outside the major studios, they challenged the simplistic optimism of Sidney Poitier as portrayed in his movies. Costa-Gavras's *The Battle of Algiers* (1966) seemed to some African American militants a textbook for direct action, while Amiri Baraka spoke of the movie version of his short play, *Dutchman* (1967), as a "revolutionary revelation." Even the Hollywood movies hardened: Robert Mulligan's film version of Harper Lee's novel, *To Kill a Mockingbird* (1962), ended with the death of its African American protagonist, and Sidney Lumet's *The Pawnbroker* (1965) is set in a harsh Harlem dominated by a coldly ominous drug dealer (played by Brock Peters). By contrast, more pastoral films such as Martin Ritt's *Sounder* (1972) and Gordon Parks's autobiographical, *The Learning Tree* (1969), deviated from the coming wave of angry films. The catalysts for this turn toward rage was attributed to the cities of the late 1960s when they burst into riots of despair upon the assassination of Martin Luther King, Jr. Thousands of African American youths influenced by this new wave of films identified with the Civil Rights Movement.

In the 1970s, African American directors produced a number of urban crime dramas with African American actors. The prototype of the new genre, soon dubbed "blaxploitation" films by the trade paper *Variety*, was Melvin Van Peeble's *Sweet Sweetback's Baadasssss Song* (1971). More than any other movie, Sweetback defined the era. "Jangling in its lighting and music track, and heady with contempt for the White social order and its cops," the film's success all but invited Hollywood's major studios to rush forward in pursuit of the new audience. MGM's *Shaft* (1971), for example, played to the crowd by featuring a mouthy, streetwise hero who, in reality, was not an outlaw in Sweetback's mold but merely a plainclothes cop. From the outset, the Hollywood studio version of this Black, urban, outlaw culture cynically followed familiar pattern. *Cool Breeze* (1972) was remade from The Asphalt Jungle, *The Lost Man* (1969) from Carol Reed's *Odd Man Out, and Up Tight* (1968) from John Ford's film of an Irish rebellion, The Informer. The Hollywood studios even plundered genres like horror movies in films such as *Blacula* (1972) and Blackenstein (1972).

Anti-war Protests

The Anti-war movement was the most recognized aspect of the Sixties during the Civil Rights Movement when Black pride was at the forefront. African Americans also identified with the anti-war movement. African Americans identified with this generation that preached against the war and coined the phrase "make love not war." All men ages 18-25 were forced to register for the draft. The Vietnam War was like nothing America had seen before, with 90 percent of the troops ages 19-23. The anti-war sentiment was strong both at home and in

Vietnam, and music was at the heart of the movement. The soldiers would listen to anti-war and protest songs while they were fighting in the conflict. The feeling among the youth was that America was murdering innocent people for an unknown reason. Country Joe and the Fish's song, "I feel like I am fixing to die rag," captured the attitude: "Come on all you big strong men, Uncle Sam needs your help again, got himself in a terrible jam, way down yonder in Vietnam, put down your books pick up a gun, whoopee we're gonna have a whole lot of fun, and its one, two, three what are we fighting for?, don't ask me I don't give a damn, next stop is Vietnam, whoopee we are all gonna die." Dylan's song, "The times they are a changing," has lyrics that "gave a warning to authority that America was experiencing a new consciousness, and that the establishment (government) have to face the opposition of much of the population, especially the young."

Many songs implied what life was like in Vietnam, like African American Jimi Hendix's "Purple Haze"song, which symbolized the illusion that appeared in the landing zones for helicopters in Vietnam. Along with the rebellion at home, the soldiers staged their own form of rebellion. A statistic from 1967 stated that more "American troops were arrested for smoking marijuana than for any other major crime." The soldiers even had their own bandit radio stations. This

was because the Armed Forces Vietnam Network was heavily censored and screened out the anti-war songs. On the rebel radio stations, soldiers on the front lines could talk to men like "midnight Jack" and have songs played to them.

The war was also racially biased, as many artists expressed in their songs. Jimi Hendrix's released a song titled "If 6 was 9" that described his oppression. It stated "White collared conservative flashing down the street, pointing their finger at me, they're hoping soon my kind will drop and die...go on Mr. Buisniness man, you can't dress like me." John Foggerty also sang about his days in the army. In his song, "Fortunate son," he talked about the racial division along with the division among the rich Whites and poor Whites. He said that "some folks inherit star spangled eyes, and they will send you down to war; and when you ask them how much should we give, they only answer more, more, more." Music provided a support during the turbulent times of the Sixties. It stood firmly while the smoke from the devastation in Vietnam caused protest marches all over the country from 1965 through 1972. Draft card burning begun in Boston, and protest marches in 1964, gained national prominence by 1967 as popular forms of protests. In 1965, there were 380 prosecutions for draft resisters. By 1968, the number reached 3,305.

The Chicano Moratorium, the largest anti-war protest in southern California, reflected a growing involvement of ethnic minorities, influenced by the Civil Rights Movement, to protest the war. The Black Panthers had a large membership of returning Black Vietnam Veterans, who were angry at having fought for Vietnamese civil rights while being denied their own back home. Additionally, they knew that a disproportionate number of their Black brothers were being drafted and to possibly die in an unjust war.

The Vietnam War helped split the civil rights coalition. White liberals once active in civil rights became preoccupied with the war, and White student activists, part of the civil rights struggle since the 1961 Freedom Rides, were overwhelmingly drawn to antiwar protests. The war had also divided the Black leadership. Moderates such as Rev. Martin Luther King, Jr., Bayard Rustin, and Whitney Young were reluctant to speak out against the war. The earliest protests came from radicals such as Malcolm X, who in 1964 linked the war to racial discrimination at home. In January of 1966 the leadership of the Student Nonviolent Coordinating Committee (SNCC) condemned the draft; a year later, heavyweight boxing champion Muhammad Ali refused to be drafted. Ali insisted that he would not "murder and kill and burn other people simply to help continue the domination of the White slave masters over the dark people of the world."

Martin Luther King, Jr., in his "Beyond Vietnam" speech at New York's Riverside Church on April 4, 1967, for the first time, "linked the civil rights movement to the anti-war movement and Johnson's war on poverty to his war against Vietnam," according to Marilyn Young in *The Vietnam Wars 1945-1990*. The war had a profound effect on King. He denounced the war, lamenting that "the Great Society has been shot down on the battlefields of Vietnam." The war revolutionized King's thinking, helping him place the Civil Rights Movement in a world context.

In 1968, the morale of American troops collapsed due to the communist Tet Offensive, and racial hostilities sharpened considerably following King's assassination. African American opinion turned steadily against the war. A 1971 Gallup poll found a higher level of dissatisfaction with the war among African Americans (83 percent) than among Whites (67 percent). Yet Vietnam remained a place of much interracial cooperation. Combat troops realized that they had to count on one another regardless of race. In the midst of the war, social and economic issues were tackled by the government in the form of social welfare.

Social Welfare Campaigns

The Movement concerned jobs as much as equality—indeed, the two were seen as inextricably linked. Martin Luther King, Jr. was defending the rights of striking sanitation workers in Memphis and planning a "Poor Peoples' Campaign" march to Washington to promote the linkage between civil rights and economic opportunity at the time of his assassination in 1968. Dr. King and others, including President Lyndon Johnson, knew that there was a close connection between those denied civil rights and those mired in what seemed to be intractable poverty.

The National Welfare Rights Movement emerged in a political climate of social protest. The Kennedy administration of the early 1960s displayed a commitment towards equality and improved race relations that led to the desegregation of public facilities. Kennedy's successor, Lyndon Johnson, supported the passage of the Civil Rights Bill and the Voting Rights Act in 1964 and 1965, respectively. Whitney M. Young, Jr. (1921-1971) was one of the African American leaders who advised President Johnson on the landmark Civil Rights Act of 1964. Young served on numerous private and federal commissions related to social welfare. Elements of his "domestic Marshall Plan" were incorporated into the federal antipoverty program during the 1960s.

In 1965, President Lyndon Johnson began his "War on Poverty," a series of programs to provide job training, housing, education, health care and other social benefits for the poor. Johnson's "The Great Society" programs encompassed both those elements in a host of legislative and other initiatives that came to be known as the War on Poverty. In recent decades, however, some critics have not only declared Johnson's War on Poverty a failure, they have also blamed it as the cause of contemporary economic woes. Some have even used the very phrase "Great Society" as to denounce nearly all government programs aimed at helping the working poor and others in or near poverty. Generally, however, those who use the phrase in a derogatory manner are often uncertain as to what constituted either the "Great Society" or the War on Poverty. As a result, a number of myths and misconceptions have developed around both phrases.

First and foremost among the misconceptions is that the major federal welfare program (Aid to Families with Dependent Children, or AFDC) was a Great Society program. In fact, AFDC was created by President Franklin D. Roosevelt in 1935 as part of the Social Security bill. Moreover, no substantive changes in the AFDC program were made during the Johnson era.

Between 1964 and 1968, the Great Society programs promoted by the Johnson administration turned national attention to poverty issues. Johnson's pledge to improve economic conditions for the nation's poor led to increased government funding for urban projects dedicated to serving this population. This economic and political support was vital to the emergence of a national welfare rights organization.

Most of Johnson's "War on Poverty" was carried out by the Office of Economic Opportunity. The "War on Poverty" was, Paul E. Peterson has written, "little more than a call for citizen participation combined with a hodgepodge of hastily designed educational, job training and neighborhood service programs that had little internal coherence and only limited financial backing." It was more important as a "vehicle for involving African Americans and other minorities in local political processes than as a mechanism for redistributing wealth." In addition to economic progress, many African Americans desired improvements in education, employment, and politics.

Legacy of Affirmative Action Legislation Due to the Civil Rights Movement

Many civil rights leaders sought to achieve greater direct political power through political office, and they sought to achieve more substantive economic and educational gains through affirmative-action programs

that compensated for past discrimination in job hiring and college admissions. African Americans made impressive gains in education, employment and, to a lesser degree, in housing. Nevertheless, historic patterns of hiring and promotion left African Americans economically vulnerable, especially in a weak national economy.

One of the more controversial issues the Supreme Court dealt with concerned affirmative action. The depth of the Court's ambivalence on this issue was illustrated by the 1978 *Bakke* case, in which the Court ruled against the use of racial quotas. In 1986, the Court supported the limited use of affirmative action to help minority groups compensate for past job discrimination; and in 1987, the Court upheld the right of employers to extend preferential treatment to minorities and women in order to achieve a better balanced work force. In 1987, in *Johnson* v. *Transportation Agency, Santa Clara County,* the Court upheld the use of affirmative action programs.

In several close rulings in 1989, however, the Court's conservative majority moved towards reversing this direction by making it even more difficult for women and minorities to use the courts to remedy discrimination in hiring practices or on the job. President Ronald Reagan's administration slowed down enforcement of certain civil rights laws and opposed government-enforced quotas and "goals and timetables." In addition, President George Bush signed the Civil Rights Act of 1991, which limited affirmative action.

Conclusion

The Civil Rights Movement had many events that helped African Americans achieve some rights. Federal legislation was passed to protect the civil and voting rights for African Americans. The Civil Rights Act declared discrimination in all public places on the basis of race illegal. After the Civil Rights Act was passed, more African Americans entered the work force. Prior to President Lyndon B. Johnson signing the Voting Rights Act in 1965, African Americans had to pass a literacy test, pay poll taxes, and qualify under the grandfather clause just to vote. A small number of African Americans registered to vote in those days because they could not read, answer absurd questions, or pay the tax. However, after passage of the Act, more African Americans registered to vote. African Americans were elected to public offices as mayors and state and congressional representatives. Voter eligibility was now based on age, residency, and citizenship. There were many leaders who helped contribute to the success of the Civil Rights Movement.

Many people believed that Martin Luther King, Jr.'s death marked the end of the Civil Rights Movement in terms of nonviolence and in some ways it did. The Black Power Movement marked a continuation of the Civil Rights Movement to the 1980s, as well as a deviation from "nonviolence" as it became more radicalized due to events beginning in the 1960s. As African Americans attempted to embrace their rights, they encountered new challenges. Many organizations were established during the period that reflected an awareness of rights to be protected by the government. The Black Panther Party emerged with emphasis on Black Power, Black nationalism, self-defense, and protection of civil and human rights. The young African American leaders of the movement were determined to fight for their rights by "any means necessary." At the same time, they used Black pride to exhibit a new attitude, as reflected in the media, politics, and other arenas.

Review Questions

1. How were African American women involved in the Black Panther Party?

2. What factors caused the rise of the Black Power Movement?

3. How did African Americans react to the Vietnam conflict?

4. How did President Lyndon B. Johnson's "Great Society" social programs benefit African Americans?

5. How did the FBI's "COINTELPRO" program affect African Americans in the Black Power movement?

6. What were "blaxploitation films," and how did they impact the period?

Chapter 22

Blacks in Politics

Events in the 1960s led to significant transformations for African Americans entering into the new decade up to the 1980s. In politics, they exhibited political independence and maturity. This chapter focuses on the involvement of African Americans in politics on local, state, and national levels, as well as on other activities involving African Americans that captured the nation's attention. The fact that African Americans became dominant in politics helped to enhance their accomplishments in other areas.

In the economic realm, Black businesses increased from 231,203 in 1977 to 339, 239 in 1982. They often encountered problems attributed to competition from White companies, lack of funds, and capital formation. On the other hand, unemployment caused major problems in the Black community because it became difficult to secure employment in clerical, technical, and service professions. Thus, households headed by African American females rose from 20.6% in 1960 to 44.1% in 1980. The number of African American professionals increased in the fields of education, law, and medicine. African American farmers declined due to discrimination in securing land and financial support. It was extremely difficult for them to get credit. By 1984, America had only 148,000 African American farmers out of a population of 28 million African Americans.

African Americans also encountered other problems such as economic discrimination and lack of housing. In spite of such disparities, they expressed renewed race pride while addressing these problems, refuted theories of Black inferiority, and criticized racial stereotypes. African Americans had a determined attitude due to accomplishments made in diverse fields.

In athletics, African Americans captured the nation's attention. In football, O.J. Simpson played for the Buffalo Bills and later for the San Francisco 49ers. Karem Abdul Jabbar (formerly Lew Alcindor), and Julius Irving starred in basketball. African Americans dominated boxing with champions such as George Forman and Sugar Ray Leonard.

African Americans also helped to reform education in the midst of politics. Due to their efforts, African American Studies departments and programs were instilled in the curriculum in higher education. Students at colleges and universities across the nation expressed interest in Black history, as well as oral history. African Americans researched the past by participating in genealogy studies. In 1977, the Afro-American Historical and Genealogical Society was founded in Washington, DC. In the same year, the Association of Black Women Historians was also established in Washington, DC.

The period marked a time when African Americans expressed mounting interest in the creative and visual arts, drama, and literature. Due to the growing interest in Africa among African Americans, the novel, *Roots,* by Alex Haley, became a national bestseller. It sensationalized slavery by portraying the life of a slave named Kunta Kinta through generations of slavery in America. Furthermore, it helped to increase interest in Black Studies. Historian Robert Weisbord labeled it "Afro-America's African Renaissance." African American artists and writers exposed a variety of taste in the arts, literature, and music. Many well-known African American artists were still living at the time; these artists included as, Romare Bearden, Jacob Lawrence, Lois Mailou Jones, and Elizabeth Catlett-Mora. African

American dance was also influential due to the accomplishments of Alvin Ailey, founder of the American Dance Theater, and Arthur Mitchell of the Dance Theater of Harlem. African Americans Leontyne Price, opera singer, and Charlie Pride, country and western singer, were also recognized for their musical talents.

African American Voters in Washington, DC

In reality, the participation of African Americans in all facets of politics in America helped to elevate their status in society. Politics gave them visibility, which in turn enabled progress in other venues. Thus, the accomplishments made during the Civil Rights movement and the Black Power movement laid the foundation for African Americans to have a voice in governing the nation. As a result of the migration of African Americans to urban centers during the periods, their population increased to the extent that they became powerful enough to influence politics on all levels. African Americans registered to vote throughout America.

Black Urbanization and Politics

The increasing urbanization of African Americans, coupled with problems of an increased crime rate, increased racial tensions; and integrated schools, which in every measured case led to a fall in educational standards, created in the 1970s the phenomenon called "White flight." Entire neighborhoods of Whites started moving, lock stock and barrel, out of the major American cities into outlying suburbs. In this way, many city centers became almost overnight African American-only areas; and this, combined with the dropping of any type of voter qualification, meant that by the mid-1970s, a number of these major cities had elected African American mayors and city councils for the first time.

The movement for elective office took place at a series of Black Power conferences between 1967 and 1974 designed to mobilize African American electorates to take control of major cities through conventional means. The first meeting convened in Newark, New Jersey, and the last one was held in Little Rock, Arkansas; but the most significant one met in Gary, Indiana, in 1972. It had emerged from the collaborative efforts of African American elected officials and leading African American nationalists. The 3,000 delegates and 5,000 observers at the convention reflected the political diversity within the Black communities. It was dominated by educated African American professionals, businessmen, and public officials. Detroit Congressman Charles Diggs; Richard Hatcher, mayor of Gary, Indiana; and writer Amiri Baraka of Newark, New Jersey, served as co-chairs of the convention. Howard University political scientist, Ronald Walters, helped coordinate the convention. According to Walters, "It was this body of people who really were contending for the national leadership of the Black community in the early seventies. And in the seventies this new group of Black elected officials joined the civil rights leaders and became a new leadership class...." The discussions motivated many African Americans to run for political office. They made profound advancements by gaining seats in Congress, becoming Mayors of major cities, and officials in state governments. As the number of African American officials increased, the Congressional Black Caucus became increasingly important in guiding African American politics at the national level.

Congressional Black Caucus

In January of 1969, newly elected African American representatives of the 77th Congress joined incumbents to form the "Democratic Select Committee." The Committee was renamed the Congressional Black Caucus (CBC), and this was born in 1971. The 13 founding members were Representatives Shirley Chisholm,

William Clay, George Collins, John Conyers, Ronald Dellums, Charles Diggs, Augustus Hawkins, Ralph Metcalfe, Parren Mitchell, Robert Nix, Charles Rangel, Louis Stokes, and Washington, DC Delegate Walter Fauntroy. Their goals were to positively influence the course of events pertinent to African Americans and others of similar experience and situation and to achieve greater equality for persons of African descent in the design and content of domestic and international programs and services. While the CBC primarily focused on the concerns of African Americans, it stood at the forefront of legislative campaigns for human and civil rights for all citizens.

In 1976, the CBC established the Congressional Black Caucus Foundation, Inc. (CBCF) as a non-partisan, non-profit, public policy, research and educational institute. As envisioned by its founders, the CBCF's established in its mission major goals to educate future leaders and to promote collaboration among legislators, business leaders, minority-focused organizational leaders, and organized labor to effect positive and sustainable change in the African American community.

Due to the activities of the Congressional Black Caucus, African Americans became less apathetic toward politics, and some former civil rights activitists like Andrew Young and Walter Fauntroy of the Student Nonviolent Coordinating Committee

managed to transform themselves into successful politicians. In 1973, Black Panther Party founder Bobby Seale ran unsuccessfully for mayor of Oakland, California, and 20 years later Bobby Rush, a former Black Panther leader in Illinois, won a congressional seat. Former African American activists made the greatest political gains on the local level as a result of becoming mayors of cities formerly dominated by White politicians.

Founding Members of the Congressional Black Caucus

Rep. Parren Mitchell, Maryland
Rep. Charles Diggs, Michigan
Rep. Robert Nix, Pennsylvania
Rep. John Conyers, Michigan
Rep. Gus Hawkins, California
Rep. Walter Fauntroy, Washington D.C.
Rep. Charles Rangel, New York
Rep. Ronald Dellums, California
Rep. William Clay, Missouri
Rep. Shirley Chisholm, New York
Rep. George Collins, Illinois
Rep. Ralph Metcalf, Illinois
Rep. Louis Stokes, Ohio

Black Mayors in Urban Areas

The rise of Black mayors indicated progress in politics made by African Americans. According to David Colburn, "Black mayors opened up the American political process in ways that nobody ever imagined, not only for Black citizens but for other minorities as well." On November 7, 1967, the voters of Cleveland, Ohio, and Gary, Indiana, elected the nation's first African American mayors to govern their cities. The number of American Black mayors grew from two in 1968—Carl Stokes in Cleveland, Ohio, and Richard Hatcher in Gary, Indiana—to 48 in 1973 and 316 in 1990. Between 1971 and 1975, the number of African American mayors increased from eight to 135, and the National Conference of Black Mayors was founded in 1974. In 1973, Coleman Young in Detroit and Thomas Bradley of Los Angeles became the first African American mayors of cities of more than a million citizens. The first Black mayors were extremely well educated, Colburn said. All but one of those elected prior to 1976—Detroit Mayor Coleman Young—were college graduates, and a large percentage had advanced degrees, often doctorates or law degrees, he said. "In the early days of the post-civil rights movement, it really did take an extraordinary Black candidate to get elected, and particularly to get any kind of White support," he said. Cities across the country became governed by African Americans strongly oriented to integrating police and municipal offices and carrying out policies aimed at helping the poor. Their success encouraged many other Black candidates to seek mayoral office.

According to Colburn, "between 1973 and 1990, there was a huge increase in the election of Black mayors from the smallest cities in the nation to the largest." "At one time or another, Black mayors were elected to all of the largest cities in the U.S., from New York to Los Angeles and Atlanta to Seattle." In 1983, Harold Washington became the first African American mayor in Chicago, Illinois. By 1993, 67 major urban centers, most with majority-White populations, were headed by African Americans. Mayors profiled include Carl B. Stokes (Cleveland), Richard G. Hatcher (Gary), "Dutch" Morial (New Orleans), Harold Washington (Chicago), Tom Bradley (Los Angeles), Marion Barry (Washington, D.C.), David Dinkins (New York City), Coleman Young (Detroit), and a succession of Black mayors in Atlanta (Maynard Jackson, Andrew Young, and Bill Campbell).

"By the '90s, there was much less pressure on Black candidates to show they were better educated than their White opponents. Getting out a large Black vote and attracting liberal White support was the key to Black mayors' election," Colburn said. In predominantly White communities such as

Dallas and Denver, it was important for Blacks to portray themselves as mainstream candidates, he said. This was not easy because some issues that appealed to Black residents did not appeal to Whites, Colburn said. For example, Black community support for government spending to provide jobs faced opposition from Whites who feared an increase in property taxes, he said. One popular strategy of Black candidates to turn out the White vote—first used by Willington Webb in Denver—was speaking to neighborhood residents in the homes of liberal Whites who were sympathetic to civil rights changes, he said. In cities with large Hispanic populations, Black candidates followed the lead of Jesse Jackson in building a rainbow coalition and reached out for Hispanic support, he said. Once in office, Black mayors generally pushed very traditional political agendas that included sponsoring urban renewal projects, lowering the tax base to attract businesses, and urging greater support for police departments to fight crime, he said. "A key difference was that Black mayors spoke out very strongly and forcefully for the needs of the downtrodden in the community," Colburn said. Interestingly, much of the strongest opposition they faced was from poor Whites. But their proposals were aimed at helping all people, particularly the poor. African Americans mayors in major cities by 2000 included the following:

John Street - Philadelphia, PA (1,517,550 43.2% Black)

Kwame Kilpatrick - Detroit, MI (951,270 81.6 % Black)

Michael Coleman - Columbus, OH (711,470 24.5% Black)

Willie W. Herenton - Memphis, TN (650100 61.4% Black)

Anthony A. Williams - Washington, DC (572,059 60.0 % Black)

C. Ray Nagin - New Orleans, LA (484,674 67.3% Black

Shirley Franklin - Atlanta, GA (416,474 61.4% Black)

Jack Ford - Toledo, OH (313,619 23.5 % Black)

Sharpe James - Newark, NJ (273,546 53.5% Black)

Bernard Kincaid - Birmingham, AL (242,820 73.5% Black)

Glenn D. Cunningham - Jersey City, NJ (240,055 28.3 % Black)

William A. Johnson, Jr. - Rochester, NY (219,773 38.5% Black)

William E. Ward - Chesapeake, VA (199,184 28.5% Black)

Rudolph C. McCollum Jr. - Richmond, VA (197,790 57.2 % Black)

William V. Bell - Durham, NC (187,035 43.8% Black)

Harvey Johnson, Jr. - Jackson, MS (184,256 70.6% Black)

Colburn further states that the "challenges Black mayors face in the 21st Century include meeting the needs of senior citizens as urban populations age and those of immigrants from far corners of the globe as cities become polyglots." Furthermore, he argues, "despite the successes of Black mayors throughout this period—1968 to 1996—we don't see as many being elected today." It is possible that some highly qualified candidates may be thriving in the new economy or fear being vilified if they run for public office. It is believed that racial inequality "continues to hang over American society, despite the gains and contributions of these Black mayors." Colburn concludes that "what is needed is more leadership positions being held by Black Americans. When that happens, race won't stand out as an issue. We'll just see the person, not the race or ethnicity."

African American Elected Officials on Federal, Local, and State Levels

The concentrations of urban African Americans provided political bases for an increasing number of Black officeholders in local, state and federal politics. On the federal level, beginning with the election of Oscar DePriest from Chicago's Black Belt in 1928 and continuing with the elevation of Chicago's William L. Dawson, New York's Adam Clayton Powell, Jr., and Detroit's Charles Diggs, Jr. in the 1940s and 1950s, a growing post-Reconstruction African American presence was reestablished in the Congress of the United States. Edward Brooke III became the first African American in the 20th Century elected to the U.S. Senate. Brooke was born in Washington, D.C. on October 26, 1919. His father, Edward William Brooke, Jr., was an attorney for the Veterans Administration for more than 50 years; and his mother, Helen, later worked on all of Brooke's political campaigns. Brooke entered Howard University at the age of 16, and earned his B.S. in Sociology in 1941. After graduation, Brooke entered the Army and was sent overseas. A decorated captain in the all-Black 366th Combat Infantry Regiment, Brooke defended men in military tribunals. During the Italian campaign, Brooke crossed enemy lines to fight with the Italian Partisans and defeat Nazi and Fascist troops. Returning from the war and experienced in legal proceedings, Brooke enrolled in Boston University School of Law, earning an LL.B. in 1948 and an LL.M. a year later, as well as serving as editor of the school's Law Review. While practicing law in Boston, Brooke began seeking political office. Despite good showings in several races between 1950 and 1960, he failed to win. However, in 1960, he was appointed chairman of the Boston Finance Commission, where he exposed corruption in many city departments. His popularity high from his work there, Brooke was elected to the office of Massachusetts Attorney General, becoming the first African American to hold that post in the nation. He remained in office for two terms; in 1967, he won election to the U.S. Senate, where he was the first African American to be elected by popular vote, the first to be seated since Reconstruction, and later the only to be re-elected.

During his first term in the Senate, Brooke spent a great deal of time on the issue of Vietnam, traveling to Asia on fact-finding missions. Upon his return, he requested that the United States cease bombing and using napalm. He also began calling for an end to trade with South Africa because of its apartheid policies. In 1967, President Lyndon B. Johnson appointed him to the President's Commission on Civil Disorders, which made recommendations that ultimately took shape as the 1968 Civil Rights Act. Brooke later challenged

Richard Nixon's Supreme Court nominees Hainsworth and Carswell, even though he had supported Nixon's bid for the presidency. Brooke later became the first senator to call for Nixon's resignation. Leaving Congress in 1979, Brooke spent another six years in private practice before retiring.

In addition to Brooks, at the time of Richard M. Nixon's ascendancy to President of the U.S. in 1968, 13 African Americans, all male except for one woman, had been elected to the United States Congress. This number was the highest number of African American representatives in Congress since the days of Reconstruction, which ended almost one hundred years earlier. This change was due to a number of factors. A few of them were the 1965 Voting Rights Act which enabled millions of African Americans to vote for the first time. Prior to 1968, Congress—except for literally a few exceptions—had been an all-White institution that was unresponsive to the many social and legislative needs of the country's African American population. By 1968, the combinations of voting empowerment and public outrage resulted in some congressional districts to be redrawn, which was a necessity if the country's previously ignored African American population was to be more adequately represented. Since 1968, the number of Black congresspersons has increased with each congressional election.

African American women also became more visible in politics. The National Black Women's Organization (NBWO) was founded in 1972. Shirley Chisholm made history by becoming the first African American woman elected to the U.S. House of Representatives in Congress. In 1972, she ran for president of the United States, thereby becoming the first woman presidential candidate. She campaigned under the slogan "Unbrought and Unbossed." She voiced support for racial and gender equity. In addition to Chisholm, three other African American women won seats in Congress in 1976: Yvonne Braithwaite Burke (California), Cardiss Collins (Illinois), and Barbara Jordan (Texas). Years later, Carol Moseley-Braun made history in 1992, when she was elected to the U.S. Senate, becoming the first African American woman to do so. She upset two-term incumbent Alan Dixon in the Democratic primary and went on to defeat Republican candidate Richard Williamson. A Chicago native and lifelong resident, Moseley-Braun graduated from the University of Illinois at Chicago in 1969 and earned a law degree from the University of Chicago in 1972. She was an assistant U.S. attorney from 1972 to 1978, when she was elected to the Illinois House of Representatives. She served in the statehouse for 10 years, making education reform her priority. From

1988 to 1992, she was Cook County Recorder of Deeds. As a Senator, she sponsored several progressive education bills and championed strong gun control laws. She served on the judiciary, banking, housing and urban affairs, and small business committees. Her career suffered when it was revealed that she used campaign money to cover personal expenses, helped to loosen legal restrictions to facilitate the sale of two broadcasting companies, and promoted legislation that favored a corporate donor. She lost her 1998 reelection bid. In 1999, she was confirmed as ambassador to New Zealand. In September of 2003, she announced her candidacy for U.S. president but pulled out in January of 2004, giving her endorsement to Howard Dean

African American men and women continued to make gains in politics during the administrations of U.S. presidents from the Black Power era to the current Bush administration. In the midst of politics, they had to address economic and social issues that affected the nation. Nixon's presidency in the 1970s was very controversial, and it was at the same time a period when African Americans associated economics with equal rights and politics.

At the local level, African Americans gained greater access to municipal services and employment opportunities. In Gary, Indiana, during the Hatcher administration, the city constructed over 1,000 low income housing units. African Americans also secured city government jobs. While Maynard Jackson served as mayor in Atlanta, employment for African Americans in the city's workforce increased from about 40 percent in 1972 to about 50 percent near the end of his first term.

On the state level, the greatest indication of progress for African Americans in politics was exemplified by Lawrence Douglas Wilder, the grandson of slaves and a graduate of Howard University Law School. Wilder became the first African American elected Governor in U.S. history. As a Democrat, his political career began when he was elected a state senator in 1969, becoming the first African American to serve in the Virginia legislature since Reconstruction. Wilder was subsequently Virginia's lieutenant governor (1986–1990) and then governor (1990–1994). During his term in office, he held the line on taxes, balanced the state budget, and succeeded in passing controversial bond issues and a handgun control measure. The outspoken and often combative Wilder was briefly an unsuccessful aspirant for the Democratic presidential nomination in 1992 and just as briefly an independent candidate for the U.S. Senate from Virginia in 1994. In 2004, however, he made a political comeback when he was elected mayor of Richmond, Virginia.

Nixon, Ford, Carter, and Reagan Administrations

During Richard Nixon's presidency, the concept of "equal rights" was broadened from desegregation to include school busing, affirmative action in hiring, women, the elderly, the physically disabled, and an expanding and overlapping list of other groups. Nixon steered a middle course in domestic affairs and did not attempt to dismantle Lyndon B. Johnson's civil rights or domestic programs but attempted to make them more efficient. Robert J. Brown was an African American member of Nixon's White House staff who served as a liaison to the Black community. He dealt with issues related to civil rights legislation, funding for jobs, Black colleges and inner-city housing. The Nixon administration addressed the underlying problems of bigotry and economic empowerment by putting teeth into anti-discriminatory laws, boosting the budget of civil rights enforcement, and sponsoring minority business initiatives. Brown recalled that one of his priorities as a Nixon staffer was to promote Black colleges. He arranged a series of meetings between Nixon and Black college presidents, "knowing that the president saw education as a great equalizer." President Nixon doubled aid to Black colleges and issued an executive order denying tax deductions for contributions to segregated schools.

John Calhoun, an African American special assistant to President Ford, would continue this concern for the status and funding of Black colleges. He strongly supported the Ford administration's efforts to renew the Voting Rights Act and to improve the funding and research capabilities of Black colleges. President Ford backed Calhoun's efforts to reach out and to work with African American members and staffers on Capitol Hill. Calhoun held monthly luncheon meetings to address issues in the Black community. This outreach program and Calhoun's access to the president was significant in influencing decisions concerning busing, school desegregation and voting rights. Also, in Ford's administration, William T. Coleman Jr., the first African American to serve as a clerk in the U.S. Supreme Court in 1948, was appointed Secretary of Transportation.

Jimmy Carter, elected president in 1976, appointed more African Americans to influential positions in the federal government than any president before him, and he seemed to have a deep personal commitment to racial equality. Patricia Roberts Harris, former Dean of Howard University's Law School, was appointed Secretary of Housing and Urban Development by Carter in 1976, making her the first African American woman appointed to a cabinet position. Eleanor Holmes

Norton, a former Student Nonviolent Coordinating Committee (SNCC) worker and one of the founders of the National Black Feminist Organization, became chair of the Equal Employment Opportunity Commission. Former SNCC chair John Lewis became Associate Director of Action, the federal volunteer agency. Andrew Young of Georgia became U.S. Ambassador to the United Nations, thereby becoming the first African American to serve in this high position. Clifford Alexander, Jr. was appointed Secretary of the Army. He held this position from 1977-1980. Ernest Green, who had been one of the "Little Rock Nine" students to desegregate Little Rock's Central High School, was appointed Assistant Secretary of the Department of Labor. Wade McCree was appointed Solicitor General in the Justice Department. Drew Days III served as Assistant Attorney General for Civil Rights. Carter also appointed Historian and civil rights activist Mary Frances Berry as Assistant Secretary for Education.

Although Carter elevated African Americans to cabinet appointments throughout his administration, the economic situation deteriorated under his presidency. The Congressional Black Caucus labeled Carter's federal budget favoring military spending over domestic funding for social relief programs "an unmitigated disaster" for Black people. Black unemployment had remained in double digits since the mid-1970s, twice the rate for Whites.

The appointment of African Americans declined during Ronald Reagan's presidency in the 1980s. Reagan ignored opposition from civil rights groups and appointed African American conservatives to administrative positions. William Bell replaced Eleanor Holmes Norton as Chair of the Equal Employment Commission (EEOC). In appointing Bell, Reagan attempted to reverse progress made in civil rights. He appointed African American conservative Samuel R. Pierce Jr. to a cabinet position, as Secretary of (HUD) Housing and Urban Development. Clarence Thomas, who strongly opposed affirmative action, later replaced Bell to head the Equal Employment Opportunity Commission (EEOC). Thomas was chosen because of his conservative views on Affirmative Action. Despite such appointments, many African Americans opposed Reagan because he failed to support civil rights or equality for African Americans and did not promote legislation to benefit the African American community. Furthermore, the African Americans appointed by Reagan did not support affirmative action or programs that would have benefited African Americans. Reagan also cut the affirmative action enforcement powers of the Office of Federal Contract Compliance (OFCC) and the Equal Employment Opportunity Commission (EEOC)

and reduced expenditures for social welfare services.

In 1983, in opposition to Reagan, many, but not all, African American political leaders endorsed the idea of an African American presidential candi-ate to create a "people's" platform, increase voter registration and have a power base from which there could be greater input into the political process. As a result of Reagan's conservation policies that hindered progress for African Americans, his presidency was to be challenged by Jesse Jackson with support from African American voters.

Jesse Jackson's Presidential Campaigns in the 1980s

Jesse Jackson in the 1980s ran twice for the Democratic nomination for the presidency of the United States. His 1984 campaign was launched under the aegis of the National Rainbow Coalition, Inc., an umbrella organization of minority groups. African American support was divided, however, between Jackson and former Vice President Walter Mondale. In the Democratic primary of 1984, Jackson received 3.5 million popular votes. Four years later, the 1988 campaign of Jackson showed enormous personal and political growth; his candidacy was no longer a symbolic gesture but was a real and compelling demonstration of his effectiveness as a candidate. He took up the cause of the victims of "economic violence," including indebted farmers who had their lands seized by creditors and women who received less pay than men doing similar work. He also gave the nation a vivid description of the problems caused by drug abuse and the drug trade. Jackson focused on new and expanded programs to help people improve their lives and proposed financing these efforts by reductions in military spending and higher taxes on wealthy people.

Jackson won 15 primaries and caucuses with the support of almost all Blacks who voted as well as one-eighth of White Democrats. He received seven million votes in all, one-third of the total Democratic vote, and more than one-fourth of the Democratic convention delegates. He became the party's second most popular choice for president. Jackson electrified the national Democratic Convention with an impassioned speech in which he used the refrain "Keep Hope Alive." This speech and his success in the primaries forced other Democratic leaders to recognize the power of his coalition and to acknowledge him as its spokesman. By the time the Democratic convention rolled around, media pundits were seriously discussing the likelihood of Jackson's nomination as the Democratic presidential candidate, and "what to do about Jesse" became the focus of the entire Democratic

leadership. At the end of the primary campaign, Jackson had finished a strong second to Massachusetts Governor Michael Dukakis and changed forever the notion that an African American President in America was inconceivable. Jackson took his defeat in stride and continued to campaign for the Democratic ticket until the November election.

Jackson's efforts and campaigns helped African American candidates to break racial barriers that had kept them from higher political offices. By 1988, more than 6,800 African Americans served in elected positions at the local, state and federal levels, and African American mayors governed at least four of the ten largest U.S. cities. Leading into the 1990s, African Americans continued to gain appointments to higher offices.

African Americans in the George H.W. Bush Administration

Prominent African American appointees in George H.W. Bush's administration included Colin Powell, Condeleeza Rice, and Clarence Thomas. At 52, General Colin Powell became the youngest and first African American Chairman of the Joint Chiefs of Staff, America's highest-ranking soldier. He served as Chairman from October 1, 1989 until September 30, 1993, serving under both Président George H.W. Bush and President Bill Clinton.

Colin Powell was born in New York City on April 5, 1937 and raised in the South Bronx. His parents, Luther and Maud Powell, immigrated to the United States from Jamaica. Secretary Powell was educated in the New York City public schools, graduating from the City College of New York (CCNY), where he earned a bachelor's degree in Geology. He also participated in ROTC at CCNY and received a commission as an Army second lieutenant upon graduation in June of 1958. His further academic achievements include a Master of Business Administration degree from George Washington University. Powell was a professional soldier for 35 years, during which time he held myriad command and staff positions and rose to the rank of Four-Star General. He was Assistant to the President for National Security Affairs from December of 1987 to January of 1989. His last assignment, from October 1, 1989 to September 30, 1993, was as the 12th Chairman of the Joint Chiefs of Staff, the highest military position in the Department of Defense. During this time, he oversaw 28 crises, including Operation Desert Storm in the victorious 1991 Persian Gulf War.

Another high profile Bush appointee, Condolezza Rice, was in government service from 1989 through March of 1991, the period of German reunification and the final days of the Soviet Union, when she served in the Bush Administration as Director, and then Senior Director, of Soviet and East European Affairs in the National Security Council, and as Special Assistant to the President for National Security Affairs. In this position, she helped formulate the strategy of President Bush and Secretary James A. Baker III in favor of German reunification and "helped bring democratic reforms to Poland, and played a vital role in crafting many of the Bush administration's policies with the former Soviet Union."

On July 1, 1991, George Bush quickly nominated Clarence Thomas to replace Thurgood Marshall, the first African American justice of the Supreme Court. Thomas had been chairman of the Equal Employment Opportunity Commission (EEOC) during the Reagan administration, and in 1990 Bush had successfully appointed him to the U.S. Court of Appeals. Many civil rights groups, notably the NAACP and the Congressional Black Caucus, refused to support Thomas because of his opposition to the traditional civil rights agenda. His endorsement by African American conservatives caused increased attention, however, on the diversity of African American politics. In succeeding to the seat of civil rights justice Thurgood Marshall, Thomas contributed to the conservative character of the nation's highest court during the 1990s.

By the early 1990s, William Jefferson Clinton entered the presidential race to challenge and defeat

George Bush. In doing so, he elevated African Americans to high level positions unprecedented in history. Thus, his African American appointments far exceeded the previous presidents in many ways.

African Americans in the Clinton Administration

In 1992, William Jefferson Clinton won the presidency with overwhelming support from African American voters, winning 78 percent of the Black vote. He became the first Democratic president since Jimmy Carter. Clinton established close ties with Black leaders such as former Urban League Director Vernon Jordan, and he reached out to the Black community. He gave his first pre-inaugural speech at Howard University.

Clinton appointed many African Americans to high positions on the federal level. Members of his transition team included his longtime friend and supporter, Vernon E. Jordan, as chairman of his transition team; and Barbara Jordan, William Gray III, and Marian Wright Edelman, founding president of the Children's Defense Fund, as members. In 1993, five African Americans served in his cabinet: Ronald Brown as Secretary of Commerce, Michael Espy as Secretary of Agriculture, Hazel O'Leary as Secretary of Energy, Jesse Brown as Secretary of Veteran Affairs, and

Joycelyn Elders as Surgeon General. Clinton also appointed many African American judges, and he was the first American president to visit Africa. In 1996, Clinton became the first Democratic president to win a second term since Franklin Roosevelt. The economic boom during William Jefferson Clinton's presidency (1993-2000) benefited African Americans. The overall poverty rate for African Americans had declined from 39.1 in 1992 to 26.5 in 1997, the lowest in history. In addition, the high school graduation rate increased, and Black college enrollments rose substantially. The progress made by African Americans during Clinton's presidency declined upon the election of George W. Bush. Few African Americans received appointments in the new administration. The most visible African American appointees included Colin Powell and Condoleeza Rice who had held appointments under George Bush Senior.

African Americans and George W. Bush Presidency

The U.S. Supreme Court granted the disputed election to Republican George W. Bush, allowing him to become president despite numerous reports of voter fraud and disfranchisement of African American voters especially in Florida. Democrat Al Gore won the support of 90 percent of African American voters and also received about a half million more popular votes than Bush. The U.S. Civil Rights Commission, chaired by Mary Frances Berry, declared: "African American voting districts were disproportionately hindered by antiquated and error-prone equipment like the punch card ballot system." African Americans highly opposed George W. Bush's presidency, despite his appointment of high profile African Americans to his administration such as Colin Powell and Condolezza Rice.

General Powell was selected by President George W. Bush to serve as his Secretary of State in January, 2001. Powell was the first African American to hold this high office in the U.S. government. He stepped down from the position after President Bush's reelection to a second term. His four-year tenure as Secretary of State was marked by disagreements with other administration officials over policy. Regardless of these disagreements, Secretary Powell remained a loyal servant of the Bush Administration and an eloquent spokesman for the Administration in international affairs. Powell left his position as Secretary of State with the admiration and respect of people around the world. The following quotation from a February 20, 2004 address at Princeton University provides an excellent example of Colin Powell's statesmanship:

"We must build a better future even as we deal with the security challenges before us. That is how we'll overcome those challenges, because it's not enough to fight against a negative, like terrorism. We must focus on what inspires us, on what brings the good people of the world together. We've got to fight for the positive—for liberty, for freedom, for democracy."

Following his retirement from the military, Secretary Powell wrote his best-selling autobiography, *My American Journey,* which was published in 1995. Additionally, he pursued a career as a public speaker, addressing audiences across the country and abroad.

During Bush's second term, Condoleezza Rice replaced Colin Powell and became the 66th Secretary of State on January 26, 2005. As she stated at her confirmation hearing, "we must use American diplomacy to help create a balance of power in the world that favors freedom. And the time for diplomacy is now." Prior to becoming Secretary of State, Rice served as Assistant to the President for National Security Affairs, commonly referred to as the National Security Advisor.

Bush also appointed Dr. Louis W. Sullivan, President of Morehouse College of Medicine, as Secretary of Health and Human Services. Other

African American appointees included Dr. Kay Cole James, the office of Personnel and Civil Service; Michael Powell, Chairman of FCC Federal Communication Commission; Larry Thompson, Assistant Deputy to Department of Justice; Ron Paige, Secretary of Education; and Alfonso Jackson , Secretary of Housing and Urban Development.

Conclusion

African Americans participated in the political process as voters and electors due to achievements made in the voter registration drives throughout the South. From the late 1960s Black Power Movement to the 21st Century, African Americans became more dominant in urban politics, as their voting power increased. African American mayors were elected in major cities such as Cleveland, Dallas, Houston, Los Angeles, Philadelphia, and Atlanta, just to mention some.

Carl Stokes became the first African American elected mayor in a large city. He served as mayor in Cleveland, Ohio. By 1984, there were 225 African American mayors in urban areas. African Americans were also elected sheriffs, constables, justices of peace, and to state legislative assemblies. On the national level, in 1969, the Congressional Black Caucus was founded, and by the mid-1980s, its membership had increased to 21. By 1985, African Americans in Congress were elected as chairpersons of seven House committees. In the 1990s, African Americans increased their membership in Congress. The presidents appointed African Americans to high level cabinet positions. The appointment of conservative Clarence Thomas to the Supreme Court was ground breaking. The first African American Secretaries of State, Colin Powell and Condelezza Rice, made history. Overall, African Americans had made profound political progress leading into the 21st Century.

Review Questions

1. What is the Congressional Black Caucus?

2. What factors helped African Americans to become mayors of major cities beginning in the late 1960s?

3. What was the significance of the Jackson presidential campaigns?

4. What achievements did African American women make in national politics in the 1970s?

5. How were African Americans involved in the Carter administration?

6. Compare and contrast African American officials in the Ford, Nixon, and Reagan administrations.

7. What political offices did African Americans acquire during Bush's presidency?

8. What reform occurred in Black education in the midst of political activism?

Chapter 23

African American Economic, Familial, and Social Challenges

This chapter is about the challenges and events from the 1970s to 2000 that affected African Americans. The economic status of African Americans improved, despite disparities in pay and training. More African Americans graduated from high school and college than in previous years. As a result of improvements in education, African Americans acquired more technical and professional positions. The standard of living improved for African Americans, as the size of the middle class increased. The African American family was affected by employment trends in the U.S. From the 1970s to 2000, more African American families were headed by women. Furthermore, African American women attained a college education at a higher rate. Overall, the economic and social status of African Americans improved, albeit the family underwent a transformation due to challenges in mainstream society.

In the 1970s, joblessness was prevalent among African Americans. The unemployment rate for African Americans was about 10 percent, compared to five percent for Whites. But while economic expansion in subsequent decades led to improvement in the status of Americans overall, economic differences between African Americans and Whites persisted. In 1970, the median income for African American households was about $22,000, while for White households it was $37,000. In 1999, African American median household income was $27,900, the highest ever recorded, but still far less than for non-Hispanic White households, which was $44,400, and below all other race groups as well. In 1970, five percent of Whites were affluent, compared to only one percent each for African Americans and Hispanics. By 1999, 20 percent of Whites were affluent, compared to eight percent of

Economic and Social Status of African Americans

African Americans and five percent of Hispanics. The rate of affluence for African Americans doubled during the economic boom of the 1990s, from four to eight percent between 1992 and 1999. However, the extent of affluence for African Americans in 1999 was the same as that for Whites in 1977; the rate for Hispanics in 1999 was the same as the rate for Whites in 1970. In 1999, for Whites, there were about three times as many affluent persons as poor persons (20 vs. seven percent); for African Americans (eight vs. 21 percent) and Hispanics (five vs. 20 percent), as the number of affluent persons was only a small portion of the number of poor persons.

After the recessions of the late 1970s and early 1980s, median incomes were about the same. Additionally, Oliver and Shapiro note that racial differences in holdings of financial assets, which are more readily converted into cash during times of emergency than are other assets, are even greater in 1994, the median White household held about $7,400 in net financial assets, whereas the median African American household had only $100; and about three fifths of African American households compared to only about one-quarter of Whites held zero dollars in net financial assets. Despite the economic boom of the 1990s, the racial wealth gap remained very large. These asset differences mean that African Americans and Whites with the same income tended to have different levels

of economic security. African American families not only had lower levels of wealth and economic security, they also had low expectations about their prospects for attaining racial equality in economics.

The last 30 years show that significant strides have been made to insure equal pay for African Americans, although tremendous differences in pay still persist. On average, African American families earned about $61 for every $100 earned by White families in 1970, but the ratio has improved slightly over the decades. Despite all these changes and the narrowing gaps in employment, there is little evidence of employment parity between Whites and African Americans over the last 30 years. In recent years, African Americans have experienced unemployment at more than twice the rate of White Americans.

The types of jobs (white collar, blue collar) that African Americans and Whites held were not as different as they were 30 years ago. In 1970, Whites were twice as likely as African Americans to work in white-collar occupations. Most African American women worked in the service sector, and more than half of African American men were employed in blue-collar jobs in 1970. Substantial gains were made throughout the next three decades, but today the occupational distribution for African Americans and Whites is still different. In 2000, White men and African American men were employed in managerial and professional (white-collar) occupations at 32 percent and 18 percent, respectively. For women, the percentages were 35 percent for White women and 25 percent for African American women.

Over the past 30 years, an African American/White gap materialized in the labor force for the civilian population age 16 and over. Substantial increases occurred in the labor force participation rates for African Americans during that time. In 2000, African Americans and Whites had similar proportions in the civilian labor force, 66 and 67 percent, respectively. However, looking at these figures by gender provides a different perspective. While African American women (64 percent) had higher rates of labor force participation than White women (61 percent), African American men (68 percent) were behind White men (74 percent).

In the 1970s, significant changes were made in many of the school systems throughout the United States. Racial segregation officially ended and the integration of public schools began to take shape. In 1970, only 34 percent of African Americans over 25 had completed high school. Substantial efforts to improve the education of all students took place throughout the 1980s and 1990s, culminating in the narrowing of the large gap between White and African American high school graduation rates. In 2000, the high school graduation level doubled to a record high, nearly 80 percent. However, despite the improving rates for high school completion, we face a sobering reality that a college diploma is perhaps the equivalent requirement for success that a high school diploma was 30 years ago. And in higher education, we still find tremendous racial disparities in levels of educational performance, educational attainment, college enrollment, and college graduation rates between African Americans and Whites. By looking at these statistics, we find that the picture of educational differences is quite similar for higher education today, as it was for primary education in the past. In 1970, only 16 percent of young African American Americans were attending college. That figure rose to 28 percent in 1990. By 2000, many more African Americans were attending college, although they still lagged behind Whites. Compared to 1970 (five percent), three times as many African Americans age 25 and over had earned at least a bachelor's degree in 2000. However, this record proportion of 17 percent was still lower than that of comparable Whites, 28 percent.

In terms of income levels by education, persistent differences existed between African Americans and Whites. In 1970, college educated African Americans made about two-thirds of what college educated Whites earned. In 2000, differential earnings existed for college educated African Americans and Whites. The median income in 2000 for Whites with a bachelor's degree or more was $41,700. For African Americans with a bachelor's degree or more, the median income was $36,600. Concerns persist regarding affluence and poverty status differences for African Americans and Whites. These trends reinforce the fact that little improvement has been made in the relative economic status of African Americans since the 1970s. By 1987, eight percent of African American households were earning $50,000 or more compared to five percent in 1969.

The National Urban League, in *The State of African American America 2004: The Complexity of African American Progress*, unveiled its first "Equality Index," a statistical measurement of the disparities that exist between African Americans and Whites in economics, housing, education, health, social justice, and civic engagement. (Assigning Whites a weighted index value of one, the Equality Index value of less than one means African Americans are doing worse than Whites in a category, while a value of one or more means African Americans are doing equal or better). The report concluded that despite substantial progress, the status of African Americans was .73, or 73%, when compared to their White counterparts. "African American progress has been precarious since the civil rights era," said Marc H. Morial, President and

CEO of the National Urban League. "While there have been increases in business formation, home ownership and educational attainment, equality gaps remain between African Americans and Whites, particularly in the area of economics." As indicated:

1. Fewer than 50% of African American families own their own homes vs. over 70% of Whites.
2. African Americans are denied mortgages and home improvement loans at twice the rate of Whites.
3. African American males' mean income is 70% of White males ($16,876 gap), and African American females' mean income is 83% of their White counterparts ($6,370 difference).

In 2001, the Bush Administration adopted as its highest priority a very large personal income tax cut that primarily benefited the highest-income families. As a result, it provided proportionately less tax relief to racial/ethnic minorities than to Whites. Given the tax cut, the fact that the economy slipped into recession in early 2001 and the increased spending on defense and domestic security in response to the attacks of September 11, 2001, the federal surplus quickly disappeared. This leaves the current administration and Congress, even if they had the political inclination to move forward, little in the way of federal funds to launch major policy initiatives to reduce poverty in general, or ones designed to reduce racial/ethnic disparities in particular. Recessions tend to increase the economic gap between African Americans and other groups because African Americans' unemployment rates are more responsive to the business cycle.

Status of the African American Family

The growth in the number of African American women maintaining families is largely a result of other increases. A rise in the divorce rate, a low remarriage rate for African American women, and an increase in the number of births occurring to African American unwed mothers are correlated with the disproportionate number of African American female single-parent families. In general, female-headed families are the fastest growing segment of the poor population. One reason African American female-maintained families like their White counterparts have attracted considerable attention is due to concomitant problems associated with female headship. A major concern of these families is financial. In 1982, the growing proportion of African American families headed by women accounted for 70 percent of all African American poor families in this country. In 1960, only 22 percent of

African American families were headed by women; this figure had risen to 46 percent by 1982. The strain encountered by African American families maintained by women is not solely financial in nature. Studies reveal that female heads of families are more likely to be victims of physical and mental illness than their married counterparts. Clearly, African American women who maintain families are not the only family members experiencing the ill effects of a family structure in which no male is present. African American children in families headed by women also are faced with poverty and related social anomalies. Presently, the poverty rate for all African American children under the age of 18 is higher than at any time since 1967. Growth in the number of African American women maintaining families is largely a function of still other increases. A rise in the divorce rate, a low remarriage rate for African American women, and an increase in the number of births occurring to African American unwed mothers are correlated with the disproportionate number of African American female single-parent families.

African Americans have been by far the largest non-White racial or ethnic group in the United States. Unfortunately, African Americans have also suffered the most persistent forms of individual and institutionalized racial discrimination. In recent years, because of increases in immigration and slowing birth rates for the African American population, other groups have risen in size comparable to African Americans. America can no longer be viewed as simply a dichotomous African American and White society. Instead, it reflects a multicolored racial and ethnic mosaic, representing people from every conceivable background and heritage in the world. African Americans face unique challenges in this increasingly complex America.

In 1970, the African American population numbered 22.6 million, representing about 11 percent of the total U.S. population. Other non-White racial groups were also much smaller in size. In 2000, African Americans numbered 35.5 million, or roughly 13 percent of the population. This reflected a 57 percent increase over the last 30 years. While African Americans increased in number, the majority of the African American population continued to live in the South (54 percent). About 19 percent of African Americans lived in the Northeast, as well as the Midwest (19 percent). Only eight percent lived in the West. These regional proportions have stayed virtually the same over the last three decades.

Many African Americans continued to live in the same states as well. The five states with the largest African American populations in 2000 were New York (3.2 million), California (1.5 million), Texas (2.5 million), Florida (2.3 million), and Georgia (2.2 million). These states were similar to the largest states in 1970, with the exception of Illinois being replaced by Florida in the top five. Most African Americans (53 percent) also continue to live inside the central cities of metropolitan areas. But this is down from 1970, when the African American population base in central cities was 60 percent. In 2000, 35 percent of African Americans lived in the suburbs (outside central city in metropolitan areas), compared to only 19 percent in 1970. This shift in the African American population from central cities to suburbs occurred due to the corresponding shift of the manufacturing industry and job base from older urban centers.

The African American population remained younger than the White population. In 1970, 42 percent of African Americans were under age 18, compared to 33 percent of Whites. In 2000, that figure was 32 percent versus 24 percent. The median age (30 years) of the African American population in 2000 was five years younger than the U.S. population as a whole. But this gap was smaller than it was in 1970, when the median age of African Americans (22 years) was about seven years younger. African Americans are living longer than before, but still only eight percent of the African American population is over the age of 65, compared to seven percent in 1970. In comparison, 14 percent of non-Hispanic Whites were older than 65 in 2000 and 10 percent in 1970.

The number of African American families increased. There were 8.7 million African American families in 2000 compared to 4.9 million in 1970. In 2000, about half (48 percent) of all African American families were married-couple families, a decline from 68 percent in 1970. Most other African American families in 2000 (44 percent) were maintained by women without husbands present, and eight percent were maintained by men without a wife present. African American families were larger than non-Hispanic White families: 16 percent of African American families had five or more members in contrast to 11 percent of non-Hispanic White families. A slightly higher percentage of African American women than men aged 25 and over had earned at least a bachelor's degree (16 percent and 14 percent). For non-Hispanic Whites, the opposite was true: 31 percent of men and 25 percent of women had at least a bachelor's degree. Seventeen percent of African American men and 24 percent of African American women worked in managerial and professional specialty occupations. Forty-eight percent of all African American married-couple families had incomes of $50,000 or more. About 46 percent of African American householders were homeowners.

The marital status of African Americans also changed over time. In 1970, of African American males aged 15 and over, 57 percent had never been married, 36 percent was married,

four percent was widowed and three percent was divorced. For African American females, these figures were 54 percent, 28 percent, 14, and four percent, respectively. Among African American men aged 15 and over in 2000, 45 percent had never been married, 39 percent was married, three percent was widowed and 10 percent was divorced. Among African American women, the corresponding rates were 42 percent, 31 percent, 10 percent, and 12 percent, respectively.

Home ownership is an area in which African American families demonstrated enormous growth over the last 20 years. It was during the late 1960s and throughout the 1970s that African American families made significant gains in their transition from renter to homeowner status. In 1980, approximately 49 percent of all African American families owned their homes compared to 38 percent in 1969. However, the rate of homeownership for African American families has consistently lagged behind that of Whites, with the latter owning 67 percent of the houses they occupied in 1980. Much of the disparity between the rate of homeownership for African American and White families can be attributed to higher income levels and the reluctance on the part of financial institutions to lend money to African American families for the purchase of property. The growth in homownership for African American families that occurred during this period resulted from increased salaries and governmental programs, both legal and economic, which promoted homeownership among African American families and other racial groups.

African American family members also made notable gains in life expectancy over the last 20 years. Like Whites, African Americans can attribute these increases to several factors. First, there has been a dramatic improvement in the affordability and availability of health care. Next, a marked decline in infant mortality, although twice the rate of Whites, has affected life expectancy. Finally, a decrease in maternal mortality rates has had a positive effect on life expectancy. Statistics point out the fact that gains made by African Americans in life expectancy were greater than those for Whites. Still, Whites have a life expectancy at birth that exceeds that of both African American males and females. In 1981, life expectancy averaged 66 years for African American males and 75 years for African American females, doubling the life expectancy averages of the earlier decades of the century. Comparatively, life expectancy for Whites in 1981 averaged 71 years for males and 79 years for females.

Furthermore, there remains a disparity in life expectancy for African American males and females at all ages. These differences in life expectancy for African American men and women have had a significant influence on the structure of African American families. The fact that African American females live an average of nine years longer than African American males has numerous implications for the African American family structure. For example, African American women are likely to become single heads of families at some point in the family cycle. While this also holds true for White women, African American women are more likely to assume headship due to widowhood at a younger age. Other factors which contribute to disparities in life expectancy for African American men and women are homicide and suicide rates, which are higher for African American men than African American women.

Aside from advances made by African American families in the areas of education, occupation, income, business development, home ownership, and life expectancy, increases in other social and economic spheres affected African American families immensely. Many of these changes were more subtle in nature. Some of the more conspicuous problems were frequently ignored, and for obvious reasons. One principal reason these "gains" were not emphasized, or even acknowledged, was the belief that opponents, having maligned social and economic programs, would point to liberal social policy as the culprit. Considering the limited knowledge many African American families possessed of the complex social, political, and economic systems, the gains made by African American families are commendable. Undoubtedly, much of this can be attributed to the high achievement and work ethic of African American families. In general, there were far too many factors that militated against positive gains for an inordinate number of African American families.

The Million Man March

The Million Man March emerged from Nation of Islam Minister Louis Farrakhan's call for a "Day of Atonement" that would draw attention to the social and economic problems plaguing African American males. On October 16, 1995, approximately 900,000 African American men congregated in Washington, D.C. to hear speeches from African American luminaries such as Rosa Parks, Jesse Jackson, and Maya Angelou. Farrakhan provided the keynote address. He asked African American men to assume responsibility for themselves, their families, their communities, and America as a whole, instead of placing the blame for their conditions on outside forces. Primarily organized by former NAACP executive director Benjamin Chavis, it was the single largest gathering of African Americans in history, surpassing in size the 1963 March on Washington.

Despite the numbers, from its inception the march drew severe criticism. It was denounced on the basis of Farrakhan's reputation as an anti-Semitic firebrand. Both men and women within the African American community criticized the males-only policy and the undue emphasis placed on males as leaders within the African American community. This eventually led to the organizing of a Million Woman March in Philadelphia on October 25, 1997. Others ridiculed the Nation of Islam's brand of African American capitalism. And with its emphasis on individual responsibility as the means of racial uplift, it was charged with overlooking the systemic problem of racism within American social, economic, and political institutions.

While the long-term effects of the march have yet to be determined, immediately afterward it reinvigorated African American grassroots activism. It was also seen as an attempt by Farrakhan to move the Nation of Islam into the mainstream of American politics through a development of a secular, coalition-based movement inclusive of the broad spectrum of African American political thought. If the adage, "There is strength in numbers," holds true, a million African American men affirmed their strength Monday by taking part in a march in the nation's capital, Washington, D.C. Although organizers of the march reported participation surpassing the one million mark, the U.S. Park Service reported that 400,000 African American men participated.

The actual march took place on the mall between Washington Monument and Lincoln Memorial, spanning an estimated 23-block radius. The participants of the march, African American men from all over the United States and from of all religious backgrounds, answered the plea of Minister Louis Farrakhan and Benjamin Chavis for one million African American men to participate in what they called a day of "atonement and reconciliation." Farrakhan held several rallies around the United States, giving many men an oppotunity to register in person for the march. Those who didn't register in person were asked to register by phone. All men were asked to make a contribution of ten dollars.

Despite the controversy surrounding the "leaders" of the march, most agreed that the march was a success. The march's purpose, "to bring African American men together as a show of solidarity," was met. This march, similar to the proposed march of 1941 by A. Philip Randolph, was to be the first step in a mission of restructuring the African American family and community. Alex Brown, a University of Houston African American Studies professor and a participant in the march, said: "(Their) prime goal is for African American men to exert themselves and to take control of their own communities. To

bring one million African American men together to show solidarity and strength, not only to the public, but to themselves. African American men together for one goal. To discuss topics of violence, the dismantling of affirmative action, and taking control in their own communities and homes."

Although this march allowed men only, it was not meant to offend African American women or their role within the African American family, Brown said. "(It was) not as a slap or disregard, no disrespect intended. African American men should be the forces within the community and (the) protectors." Tyrone Tillery, University of Houston history professor, said that the march was "a way of re-energizing African American pride, unity, and a way of reclaiming African American manhood within this country."

Many African American men thought the march was a mission of solidarity to symbolize their desire to revitalize and strengthen the African American homes and communities, by starting with the most essential part of the African American family, the African American man. Although the march was supported by many African Americans, it also received a great deal of opposition from certain religious groups, as well as from other African Americans. Their opposition was not to the march itself, but to one of the more well-known contributors in the forefront, Minister Louis Farrakhan, controversial leader of the Nation of Islam. Tillery said, "Unfortunately, his past rhetoric has overshadowed some of the positive things he has to offer the African American community."

Many did not favor Farrakhan as the leader of a march for peace and unity because of his past comments about Whites, Jews and the church. "How can he, in one point, support racism and hate for others (other races), while at the same time promote responsibility?" said a University of Houston student. Supporters and participants of the march, admittedly cognizant of Farrakhan's offensive statements, seemed to look beyond them in search of solutions. "If not Farrakhan, then who will rally for African American men in America?" Tillery said. Farrakhan's past rhetoric left many African American leaders in an ambivalent position. Many did support the idea, but they did not want to be associated with Farrakhan's controversial views. "A lot more people support it privately, rather than those that admit it publicly," Tillery said. Several African American mayors around the country chose not to participate in the march, but Detroit's Mayor Dennis Archer did. "If somebody has a cure for cancer," Archer said, "would you reject it because it was somebody you may not like who came up with it?" Archer's response was felt by many African Americans, which they demonstrated with their participation. The march attracted such greats as award-winning

poet Maya Angelou, music mogul Stevie Wonder, "civil rights matriarch" Rosa Parks, the Rev. Jesse Jackson, rappers DJ Jazzy Jeff and The Fresh Prince, and basketball star Shaquille O'Neal, among many others. "This march, for young people, symbolized a tremendous amount of potential," said Shawn Riley, a student at Howard University.

The Million Woman March

Modeled after the Million Man March, the Million Woman March in 1998 included African American women from around the nation. It convened in Philadelphia to show solidarity and to spotlight issues ignored by some mainstream women's groups. Hundreds of thousands of women were expected to take part in the rally meant to strengthen bonds in the African American community and lift women's spirits. However, unlike the men's rally, which drew support from leaders such as the Rev. Jesse Jackson, the women's march was organized by women from all walks of life fed up with crime, unemployment, teen pregnancy and other social problems. "The success of the march will depend on all of the African American women who attend," said Phile Chionesu, a grassroots activist, Philadelphia business owner and mother who came up with the idea and organized the march with Asia Coney. "Something had to happen for African American women," Chionesu said. "African American women have taken care of everyone else since the time we've been in this country," she said. "We've taken care of White women, White men, White children... our own men, our own children. And now it's time that we take care of ourselves."

The daylong program of prayer, music and inspirational speeches was designed to help bring about positive change, especially in African American communities. "Oh my gosh. So many. So many," Jo Anne Royster of Arlington, Virgina, said in a hushed tone as she looked out at the crowd. By train, car, plane and hundreds of buses, African American women answered the call of grass-roots organizers and converged on the city for the march that ended at the Philadelphia Museum of Art. The marchers began with a sunrise service by the Liberty Bell and then walked along Benjamin Franklin Parkway to the speaker's tent and podium outside the museum.

The march provided a forum for issues that many African Americans believed some women's groups did not address. Among them were human rights abuses against African Americans, the start of independent African American schools, and a demand for an investigation into allegations of CIA involvement in the crack trade in African American neighborhoods. Motivational speakers and musical performances ranging from jazz to traditional African drumming were among the early acts in the tent. Businesswoman Chionesu and march co-founder Asia Coney, a local housing activist, even bypassed established circuits of African American influence in America, including the NAACP, relying instead on the organizing powers of community leaders like themselves. They distributed flyers and posted on the Internet to get out the news about the march. "We (African American women) have a history of doing the impossible," Coney said.

During breaks, marchers chanted "Love and respect" and "M-W-M, M-W-M" for "Million Woman March." Addressing the crowd without a prepared speech, march co-founder Phile Chionesu said: "This is a new day. Prepare yourselves. We are taking back our neighborhoods." Signs proclaimed "I am one in a million" and "African American Women: No more AIDS, abuse, addiction." Women clamored to buy buttons, T-shirts, hats and flags emblazoned with March logos. Congresswoman Maxine Waters of California told the women: "After today, we will never be the same...America, please be placed on notice: We know who we are. We know what kind of power we have. We will act on that power." Winnie Madikizela-Mandela, former wife of South African President Nelson Mandela, also addressed the women. She associated the destiny of African American women with that of African women on the continent and stated:

"We have a shared destiny, a shared responsibility, to save the world from those who would destroy it." Organizers estimated that 2.1 million people filled a mile-long avenue in early afternoon. African American men were also present. Estimates of marchers made by police officers ranged from 300,000 to 1 million. Two years later, going into the 21st Century, African Americans would be presented with the challenge to stand up for their voting rights in the 2000 national election.

Election 2000 and African American Voters

In the 2000 presidential election, 1.9 million Americans cast ballots that went uncounted. "Spoiled votes" is the technical term used. About one million of them—half of the rejected ballots—were cast by African Americans, although African American voters make up only 12 percent of the electorate. Florida's Gadsden County had the highest percentage of African American voters in the state and the highest spoilage rate. One in eight votes cast there in 2000 was never counted. Many voters wrote in "Al Gore." Optical reading machines rejected these because "Al" is a "stray mark."

By contrast, in neighboring Tallahassee, the capital, vote spoilage was unnoticeable; every vote counted. In Tallahassee's White-majority county, voters placed their ballots directly into optical scanners. If they added a stray mark, they received another ballot with instructions to correct it. In other words, in the White county, make a mistake and get another ballot; in the African American county, make a mistake, your ballot is tossed out. The U.S. Civil Rights Commission investigated the spoiled ballots and concluded that of the 179,855 ballots invalidated by Florida officials, 53 percent were cast by African American voters. In Florida, an African American citizen was 10 times as likely to have a vote rejected as a White voter. One television network stated that Florida's African American voters, newly registered and lacking education, had difficulty with their ballots. Civil Rights Commissioner Christopher Edley appointed the dean of Boalt Hall School of Law at UC Berkeley to examine the Florida case. His team discovered the distressing fact that Florida was typical of the nation. Philip Klinkner, the statistician working on the Edley investigations, concluded: "It appears that about half of all ballots spoiled in the U.S.A. about one million votes - were cast by non-White voters." This "no count," as the Civil Rights Commission labeled it, was no accident. In Florida, for example, technicians had warned Governor Jeb Bush's office well in advance of November 2000 of the racial twist in the vote-count procedures. Given that more than 90 percent of the African American electorate votes Democratic, had all the "spoiled" votes been tallied, Gore would have won Florida, not to mention increase his popular vote total nationwide. Given that more than 90 percent of African Americans favored Gore over Bush, Gore would have won Florida by at least 40,000 votes.

Gore lost Florida's presidential vote because electoral officials declared invalid more than one out of every ten ballots cast by African Americans throughout the state. In some counties, nearly 25 percent of ballots cast by African Americans were set aside as invalid. In contrast, officials rejected less than one out of every 50 ballots cast by Whites statewide. If African American ballots had been rejected at the same minimal rate as White ballots, more than 50,000 additional African American votes would have been counted in Florida's presidential election. These were the results of a statistical study commissioned by the United States Commission on Civil Rights and a subsequent analysis published in the *Journal of Legal Studies* (January 2003). Independent studies by Professors Phil Klinkner of Hamilton College and Anthony Salvanto of the University of California, the *New York Times* and the *Washington Post* confirmed the finding of major racial disparities in ballot rejection rates.

Although individual ballots did not contain racial identifications, these findings were confirmed with data that later became available for some 6,000 Florida precincts, including voter sign-in sheets with racial identifications and the cumulative numbers of valid and rejected ballots. Analysis showed that 11 percent of ballots were rejected in precincts whose voters were 90% or more African American, compared to just two percent of ballots in 90%+ White precincts. Statistical analyses that examined the relationship between ballot rejection and racial composition for all 6,000 precincts yielded similar results.

The Civil Rights Commissioners filed a dissenting report that contained no evidence contradicting the findings of major racial disparities in ballot rejection. The dissenters' alternative argument that disparities were due to factors such as racial differences in education and income were refuted by analyses showing that major racial disparities persisted even after statistically considering education, literacy, age, income, poverty, ballot design, voting technology, first time voting, and the race or party of the election supervisor. Not surprisingly, most supervisors and counties with the highest ballot rejection rates were Democrat, given that these were also the most heavily African American counties.

Moreover, John Lott, the analyst who conducted a statistical study for the dissenters (who was found to have created a sock puppet, Mary Rosh, on the Internet to heap praise on his work and even review one of his books), deserted the argument presented in the dissenter's report. Instead, he claimed that the burden of ballot rejection fell upon African American Republicans, who were just five percent of African American voters. Lott asserted that African American Republicans "are 54 to 66 times more likely than the average African American to produce non-voted ballots." If this claim were true, then the rate of ballot rejection for African Americans was 540 percent to 660 percent—an impossible five to six ballots turned aside for every ballot cast. Lott's work indicated just how desperately the dissenters and their political allies tried to conceal what actually happened in Florida.

Conclusion

African Americans faced economic and social challenges attributed to advances made after the Civil Rights movement. In the 1970s when the Black Power movement had been popularized, African Americans moved to urban centers in large numbers. They acquired jobs that enabled them to improve their quality of life. They faced competition from Whites for the same jobs and often received less pay. In the 1980s, the economy waned and, as a result, unemployment among African Americans increased. The prosperous years of the 1990s during Bill Clinton's presidency saw the standard of living for African Americans improve. They earned higher wages and more entered the professional field. However, despite gains, salaries for African Americans lagged behind those for Whites. In the 21st Century, African Americans have experienced minor improvement in their economic status. African Americans were affected by the economy. It became easier for African American women to secure jobs compared to their men. By the 1980s, the ratio of household headed by African American women had increased to the extent that the majority of the households were headed by them.

In the 1990s, the Million Man March and Million Woman March brought issues that affected African Americans to the forefront. Both marches attracted the nation's interest with emphasis on the African American family, as well as economic and social issues affecting African Americans. The Million Man March revealed a growing tendency for African Americans to assume collective responsibility for their destiny. The Million Woman March attracted attention to issues involving African American Women.

At the beginning of the 21st Century, African Americans became embroiled in the election of 2000 when many African American voters were disfranchised. Thus, in the midst of dealing with economic and social issues, African Americans had to become more politically astute. They helped draw attention to voters' violations that enabled George H. W. Bush to be placed in office by the Supreme Court. The new century would present new challenges for African Americans.

Review Questions

1. What was the significance of the Million Man March?

2. How did the African American family transform from the 1970s to the 21st Century?

3. What was the agenda of the Million Woman March?

4. What economic challenges did African Americans encounter in the new century?

5. How did education for African Americans change from the 1970s to the new century?

6. What methods were used by African Americans to improve their quality of life in the new century compared to the 1970s?

Chapter 24

African Americans in Entertainment and Media Industry

This chapter surveys African Americans influences on popular culture in entertainment from the 20th Century to the new era. Progress in race relations due to the modern civil rights movement enabled African Americans to enter new areas in the entertainment field and media industry. During this period, African Americans progressed in the musical field, theater, motion pictures, radio, and in television as stars in comedies, dramas, musicals, and talk shows. Rap music and dance reflecting African American culture became popularized. The nation witnessed the talents of African Americans in the media thorough these media.

African Americans had long resented negative stereotypical images of their race in entertainment. In the 19th Century, Black face minstrel shows portrayed African Americans as docile, irresponsible, happy-go-lucky, wide-grinning buffoons who laughed loudly, with rolled eyes, danced, played the banjo, ate watermelon, and sang

songs to make the White audience laugh. Bert Williams and George Walker were the princes of Black face comedy who popularized the cake-walk, which mimicked the antebellum plantation dance. In 1896, Williams and Walker appeared on stage in *The Gold Bug*. Many African American artists also made public appearances as musicians and performers. Henry F. Williams was multi-talented as violinist, cornetist, and composer. Williams played in the famous Jubilee Orchestra of Boston as well as in the Gilmore Band. Thomas Green Bethune, known as "Blind Tom," was the most famous African American pianist for this period. He could play any musical piece from memory. The Blues that resonated with the experiences of African Americans became a popular form of music during the period. During the 1890s and early 1900s, African Americans continued to explore their many talents in the area of entertainment. As the period ended, African Americans continued to excel in diverse artistic fields.

The Harlem Renaissance Movement in the early 20th Century exposed the many talents of African Americans in all fields of entertainment such as music, dance, and song, as well as in the theater. In 1924, African American actor and bass singer Paul Roberson starred in dramatist Eugene O'Neill's plays, *All God's Chillun Got Wings* and *The Emperor Jones*. He continued to be a major actor, appearing on stage in *Black Boy* (1926) and *Porgy* (1928) and in eleven motion pictures. Other well known African American artists in the earlier years of the century included Hattie McDaniel, the first African American actor to receive an Oscar Award; Bill Bojangles Robinson and Lena Horne, leading stars in the movie *Stormy* Weather; as well as Dorothy Dandridge, Paul Roberson, Harry Belafonte, and Sidney Poitier, among many others, who laid the foundation that enabled African Americans to acquire recognition in entertainment. As the movie industry and television progressed during the period, African Americans became more dominant as major participants. Nat King Cole and Flip Wilson were among the first African American performers to have their own television series and, as a result, made it possible for others to follow in their paths.

African Americans in Television

In 1980, Black Entertainment Television (BET) became the first and only television network in the United States primarily devoted to the attraction of African American viewers. BET was the brainchild of Robert L. Johnson, who developed the idea for the network in 1979 while serving as vice president for governmental relations at the National Cable Television Association. Johnson, an African American, noted in 1989 that BET "should be for Black media what Disney is to the general media or what Motown was to music." Johnson argued in 1989 that industry racism had stunted BET's growth. In particular, he noted that many cable operators have been slow to carry BET (e.g., BET was carried on only 1,825 of the nation's 7,500 systems in 1989), and that BET has been saddled with some of the lowest subscriber fees in the industry (e.g., BET earned only about five cents per subscriber in 1989, while other cable services typically earned between 15 to 20 cents per subscriber). Some analysts agreed with Johnson's charges of industry racism, but they noted that many of BET's problems were due to the network's lack of resources and Johnson's corresponding inability to adequately market it.

Launched with a $15,000 investment, the Black-owned, basic-cable franchise had grown into a diversified, $61 million media enterprise by late

1993. Despite this rather phenomenal growth, however, BET's audience continues to be overshadowed by larger cable industry players (e.g., Turner Broadcasting Systems [TBS], Home Box Office [HBO], and ESPN). Formerly based in majority-Black Washington, D.C., BET has added about two million subscriber homes per year since 1984, reaching more than 40 million cable households in 2,500 markets by 1995. Moreover, the network has more than tripled its revenues since 1985; it reported profits for the first time in 1986, when it finally hit A.C. Nielsen ratings charts and attracted major advertisers. In 1991, BET Holdings, Inc.—BET's parent company—became the first Black-owned company to be traded on the New York Stock Exchange.

From the very beginning, the heart and soul of BET programming were based on the music video. Predating MTV by a year, BET has offered as much as 18 hours of music videos a day, prompting many to perceive the 24-hour network as essentially a Black-oriented music video service. Thus, while MTV was being criticized in 1983 for excluding Black artists from its play list (Tina Turner and the interracial group English Beat excepted), many viewers were tuning into BET for such offerings. Indeed, the network's flagship program, VideoSoul, has become a household name in many Black communities. But as BET grew, the network began to diversify its program offerings and image. By its tenth anniversary in 1990, the network had initiated several original programs/projects, including For the Record, featuring members of the Congressional Black Caucus; Teen Summit, a Saturday noon show for youth; Black Agenda 2000, a series of fora on issues of interest to the Black community; Conversation with Ed Gordon, an interview program with contemporary newsmakers; Inside Studio A, concerts and interviews taped before a live audience; Personal Diary, one-on-one interviews with prominent Blacks; On Stage, plays written and performed by Blacks; and Our Voices, a daily talk show.

More recent BET program schedules have included Comic View, a stand-up comedy review; Screen Scene, a Black-oriented entertainment journal; Jazz Central, a Jazz music program; and Rap City, a rap video program. From time to time, BET also airs sporting events featuring teams from historically Black colleges and universities and rounds out its schedule with reruns of popular Black-oriented shows such as Sanford and Son, What's Happening, Frank's Place and Roc. News, and public affairs programs tend to be relegated to the weekends. Industry observers have applauded Johnson's efficient management style and his aggressive plans to expand the company's product base and consumers. Johnson currently owns 52 percent of BET, while HBO, Tele-Communications Inc. and Great

American Broadcasting each own 16 percent.

By 1995, BET Holdings owned and operated a broad array of Black-oriented media products, including Black Entertainment Television, the basic-cable network; YSB (Young Sisters and Brothers), a magazine targeted at Black youths; *Emerge*, a magazine offering analysis and commentary on contemporary issues facing Black America; Action Pay-Per-View, a national, satellite-delivered, pay-per-view movie channel based in Santa Monica, California; BET International, a provider of BET programming throughout Africa and other foreign markets; Identity Television, a London-based cable service targeting Afro-Caribbean viewers; BET Productions, a subsidiary providing technical and production services to outside companies; BET Radio Network, a radio service providing news and entertainment packages to affiliated stations across the United States; and BET Pictures, a joint venture with Blockbuster Entertainment Corporation to produce and distribute Black, family-oriented films. Thus, in considering the accomplishments of BET in the entertainment and television industry, it has made it possible for African American entertainers to receive exposure in the industry. Particularly, African American comedians have benefited from BET that served as a medium to introduce their talents.

African American Actors and Comedians

Many American comedians provide comic relief, but few touch on heated issues that effect society. However, some Black comedians manage to find comic humor in most day-to-day situations. Comedians use comedy as a vehicle to discuss how they feel about life. African American comedians gather their material from real life situations. African American comedians not only talk about daily life, they also talk about the oppressive life in which they live and use this as a basis for much of their comedy.

Dick Gregory was one of the first non-Sambo like comics. He along with other comedians such as Bill Cosby broke the minstrel tradition, which presented stereotypical Black characters. Gregory is a stand-up comedian who targets Black issues such as poverty, segregation, and racial discrimination. He is also a public spokesperson who would often blast the injustice and hypocrisies of segregation in front of White audiences, and often leaving them in stitches. Gregory, whose style is detached, ironic, and satirical, came to be called the "Black Mort Sahl" after the popular White social satirist. Gregory's comedy focuses on current events as well as racial issues.

Richard Pryor is perhaps best known for dealing candidly with controversial topics and bringing African American comedic traditions and culture to mainstream audiences. Pryor single handily raised stand-up comedy to the level of what is now considered a performance art. He also influenced a generation of performers such as Chris Rock and D.L. Hughley. Pryor's comedy was so controversial that in the late 1960s and early 1970s, he departed from the conventions of stand-up comedy and pursued a career in film. His comedy was frequently about his experiences as an African American, discussing issues such as racism, sex, and street life. Richard Pryor's comedy was often presented in a rather confrontational, in your-face manner much like Dick Gregory's. Richard Pryor often used profanity in order to convey his point.

Bill Cosby along with Dick Gregory helped African American comics make the transfer from Sambo and minstrel buffoonery to excellent comedians. Cosby accomplished this by discussing social and political concerns in a positive manner with a humorous twist. He is one of the few African American Comedians who refuse to tell racist jokes and use profanity. Even without the use of profanity and racial jokes, Cosby is one of the most successful political comedians ever. Cosby has been one of the world's most beloved comedians and TV stars for more than 30 years, and he makes it without using profanity on stage.

The national media have called Chris Rock the new Eddie Murphy or Richard Pryor. He is one of the smartest, funniest, and most widely appealing comedians ever to make it from being a comedy club-opening act to a household name. Rock has been performing stand-up comedy for more than 12 years. He performs in concerts for sold-out crowds. Chris Rock, like Richard Pryor, touches on many issues that affect African Americans. His ultimate goal is to educate his audiences while dispelling certain stereotypes. Chris Rock will use profanity to convey his point just like Richard Pryor, and he does not play towards political correctness. "There's really nothing I wouldn't go near," Rock admits. "But I wouldn't disrespect God. You can joke about anything, it's just who you diss. I would never diss God. That's not going to happen."

D. L. Hughley is not a popular household comic like Chris Rock or Bill Cosby; however, he does approach political comedy much similar to the way Chris Rock does. Unlike Chris Rock Hughley's comedy is not filled with anger and excessive profanity along with vulgarity. He is a positive role model in the Black community and believes that many problems in our society stem from the lack of fathers within the community. Hughley was recently featured in the movie "Kings of Comedy" where he talks about "Going back home" (the old culture of African Americans). Unlike, Rock's humor where his goal is to dispel stereotypes, Hughley's comedy concentrates on first recognizing them and being able to laugh about them.

Comedy television shows such as "Comic View" and "Def Comedy Jam" allowed Black comedians to take an uncompromising look at all aspects of Black life in America, something they were not often allowed to do either on network television or in film. These outlets allowed Black comics to develop themselves, without needing the acceptance or support of White fans. "At that time, comedy was on a very high rise, especially Black comedy with 'Def Comedy Jam' and BET's 'Comic View,'" Cedric says. "Those shows were new and they were fresh, and they made it possible for African Americans to come into people's homes every night." In addition to comedy shows, African Americans made history by having their own talk-shows during the period of talk-show frenzy.

African Americans in Talk-Shows

Oprah produces and hosts The Oprah Winfrey Show through Harpo Productions. It is seen by 26 million viewers a week in the United States, broadcast in 106 countries, and is the highest-rated talk show in television history. As producer and host of "The Oprah Winfrey Show," Oprah enlightens, entertains and empowers millions of viewers around the world. Oprah began her broadcasting career at WVOL radio in Nashville while still

in high school. At the age of 19, she became the youngest person and the first African American woman to anchor the news at Nashville's WTVF-TV. She then moved to Baltimore's WJZ-TV to co-anchor the six o'clock news and moved on to become co-host of their local talk show, People Are Talking.

In 1984, Oprah moved to Chicago to host WLS-TV's morning talk show, AM Chicago, which became the number one talk show just one month after she began. In less than a year, the show expanded to one hour and was renamed The Oprah Winfrey Show. In 1986, The Oprah Winfrey Show entered national syndication and has remained the number one talk show for 15 consecutive seasons, receiving 34 Emmy Awards. Oprah made her acting debut in 1985 as "Sofia" in Steven Spielberg's The Color Purple and received both an Academy Award nomination and a Golden Globe nomination for her efforts.

Oprah is the chairperson of Harpo, Inc., Harpo Productions, Inc., Harpo Films, Inc., Harpo Video, Inc. and Harpo Studios, Inc. Her contributions can be felt beyond the world of television and into areas such as publishing, music, film, philanthropy, education, health and fitness, and social awareness. Oprah has been honored with the most prestigious awards in broadcasting, including the George Foster Peabody Individual Achievement Award (1996), the IRTS Gold Medal Award (1996) and the

National Academy of Television Arts & Sciences' Lifetime Achievement Award (1998).

In September of 1996, Oprah began Oprah's Book Club, an on-air reading club designed to get the country excited about reading. Each of the books selected for Oprah's Book Club to date has become an instant bestseller. In September of 1997, Oprah launched Oprah's Angel Network, a campaign encouraging people to open their hearts a little wider and help those in need. Since its launch, Oprah's Angel Network has collected over $3.5 million in spare change to create college scholarships for students in need and has funded nearly 200 Habitat for Humanity homes.

In 1997, Oprah was named Newsweek's most important person in books and media and TV Guide's "Television Performer of the Year." In June of 1998, she was named one of the 100 most influential people of the 20th Century by Time Magazine. In 1998, Oprah starred as "Sethe" in the critically acclaimed Beloved based on the Pulitzer Prize-winning novel by Toni Morrison. Oprah has been lauded for her performances in the ABC made-for-television movies The Women of Brewster Place, There Are No Children Here, and Before Women Had Wings with Ellen Barkin. Through Harpo Films, Oprah has a long-term deal with the ABC Television Network to produce Oprah Winfrey Presents telefilms. Both

Before Women Had Wings and The Wedding were among the highest-rated, critically acclaimed television movie broadcasts of the 1997-1998 season. In November of 1998, Oprah announced the formation of a company, Oxygen Media LLC, which includes Harpo Group LLC, GBL LLC—controlled by Geraldine Laybourne and CWM LLC—Carsey-Werner-Mandabach. Oxygen Media includes a women's cable network which launched on February 2, 2000 and is integrated with Oxygen's online properties for women. Oprah's first production for Oxygen was Oprah Goes Online, a 12-part "course" giving a step-by-step look at all things online. Oprah was joined by her friend, Gayle King, and millions of women viewing across the country to experience first hand the way the Web will change women's lives.

In November of 1999, Oprah received one of the publishing industry's top honors, the National Book Foundation's 50th Anniversary Gold Medal, for her influential contribution to reading and books. In April of 2000, Oprah's Angel Network began the Use Your Life Award and now gives $100,000 every Monday on The Oprah Winfrey Show to people who are using their lives to improve those of others. Projects under the Oprah Winfrey Presents banner include Amy and Isabelle, based on the best-selling novel by Elizabeth Strout and starring Academy Award-nominee Elisabeth Shue; the award-winning Tuesdays With Morrie, based on the best-selling novel by Mitch Albom and starring Academy Award-winner Jack Lemmon and Emmy Award-winner Hank Azaria; David and Lisa, starring Academy Award-winner Sidney Poitier; the mini-series, The Wedding, based on Dorothy West's novel; and Before Women Had Wings, adapted from a novel by Connie May Fowler. In September of 2000, Tuesdays With Morrie received four Emmy Awards—Outstanding Made for Television Movie, Lead Actor (Jack Lemmon), Supporting actor (Hank Azaria), and Single-Camera Picture Editing (Carol Littleton). The movie has also received awards from the Screen Actors Guild (Jack Lemmon), Producers Guild of America (Oprah Winfrey and Kate Forte), and Directors Guild of America (Mick Jackson).

In addition, in April of 2000, Oprah, along with Hearst Magazines, introduced O, The Oprah Magazine, a monthly magazine that is the personal-growth guide for the new century. Oprah's magazine is credited as being the most successful magazine launched in recent history. O, The Oprah Magazine gives confident, smart women the tools they need to explore and reach for their dreams, to express their individual styles, and to make choices that will lead to happier and more fulfilled lives. O, The Oprah Magazine is another medium through which Oprah can connect with her viewers and provide possibilities for

transforming their lives. In January of 2001, Oprah was hailed as *Newsweek's* "Woman of the Century." She has also received seven Emmy Awards for Outstanding Talk Show Host and nine Emmy Awards for Outstanding Talk Show. In addition, Oprah also has an exclusive agreement to produce feature films for the Walt Disney Motion Pictures Group. The first of these films was Touchstone Pictures' Beloved in which she also starred.

Oprah's commitments extend to her initiation of the National Child Protection Act in 1991; she testified before the U.S. Senate Judiciary Committee to establish a national database of convicted child abusers, and on December 20, 1993, President Clinton signed the national "Oprah Bill" into law. She has established scholarships for hundreds of students and has donated millions of dollars to higher education institutions, such as Morehouse College, Spelman College and Tennessee State University. Oprah also serves as the National Spokesperson for A Better Chance, an organization that provides students, predominantly from inner city school districts, the chance to attend many of the nation's finest schools.

Montel Williams is another accomplished African American talk show host whose achievements are noteworthy both in television and in the community. The "Montel Williams Show" is one of the most popular talk shows on the air. Montel has received an Emmy for the most outstanding talk show host. Although many Americans recognize him in this capacity, Montel is also an actor, producer, author, motivational speaker to millions of youth, counselor, and former award-winning marine and intelligence officer. Montel's shows have had topics such as families torn apart by drugs and racism and his attempts to reunite those families, uniting family members who have never met one another, and uniting families torn apart by unfaithfulness. Montel offers counseling sessions, drug rehabilitation programs and weight loss programs to former guests who need help.

Montel had a wide range of experiences before becoming a talk show host. He joined the United States Marines in 1974. While in the marines, he studied Mandarin Chinese and received a degree in general engineering, with a minor in International Security Affairs. He served as a special duty intelligence offer, specializing in cryptology. While stationed in Guam, Montel received a degree in Russian. He served on board the USS Sampson during the United States invasion of Grenada, along with his other service. Some of the medals he received include an Armed Forces Expeditionary Medal, a Naval Expeditionary Medal, a Navy Commendation Medal, and two Meritorious Service Awards (few people win more than one). It is possible that his military service affected his later television career,

because in 1988 he began to counsel the wives and families of servicemen under his command. Williams was then asked to speak to Kansas City youths about leadership and overcoming obstacles. After that, for three years he traveled the country and spoke to teenagers, parents, teachers and business leaders. He resigned his naval commission during the time he spoke to three million teenagers.

Montel believes that each person should take responsibility for his/her own actions, and there is no limit to what a person can accomplish, even if a person has been a victim of circumstances when younger. He is the author of the book, *Mountain Get Out Of My Way*, which teaches self-respect, restraint and responsibility. According to Montel, "If you have faith, you can move mountains . . . . If you have faith in something bigger than yourself—in God, community, family, whatever, then anything is possible. Faith alone will give you the strength to clear any obstacles in your way. I don't believe that things happen by mistake. If you ask me, things happen because you make them happen."

Montel, also a father, believes that if parents taught children "simple restraint, we could solve half the problems young people face today." He has received other recognitions besides for his marine service. In 1988, the U.S. Chamber of Commerce gave him its Special Services Award. Past winners have included Ronald and Nancy Reagan and George and

Barbara Bush. He has also won awards for helping to improve the mental health of children through advocacy and education. As an actor, Montel starred in the television action adventure, "The Peace Keeper." As a producer, he developed and starred in the one-hour drama, "Matt Waters." He also played a marine in "JAG" and was in "Touched By An Angel."

Oprah and Montel have made history as first African Americans to have and sustain a talk show. They made it possible for other African Americans, however unsuccessful, to have talk shows. The form of entertainment provided by them appealed to mainstream White society. Thus, African Americans became creative in making gains in other aspects of entertainment such as in music and the arts.

African American Hip Hop Culture and Rap Music

In exploring entertainment, rap music has to be examined. Furthermore, rap music cannot be understood without studying what is known as the 'Hip Hop' culture. Rap is an integral part of this subculture that did not evolve or exist in isolation from its other major components. 'Hip Hop' culture was also comprised of graffiti, break dancing, and the attitude and dress of the people who subscribed to the mores and traditions of this subculture. Bronx in New York City

served as the origin for the 'Hip Hop' culture. Steven Haver in his book, *Hip Hop; the Illustrated History of Break Dancing, Rap Music and Graffiti*, states that there were three major events which took place in the Bronx that led to the birth of this subculture. First, in 1959, Parks Commissioner Robert Moses began building an expressway through the heart of the Bronx. As a result, the middle class Italian, German, Irish, and Jewish neighborhoods disappeared overnight. In addition, businesses and factories relocated and left this borough. These exiting middle classes and businesses were replaced by poor Black and Hispanic families. Accompanying these poor people were crime, drug addiction, and unemployment. The second major event which occurred once again under the direction of Parks Commissioner Robert Moses would siphon off a majority of what was left of the middle class in the Bronx. This event occurred in 1968 with the completion of a 15,382 unit co-op apartment complex on the northern edge of the Bronx near an expressway. This project fostered and accelerated the Bronx middle class exodus from comfortable and well-kept apartments. As a result of the skyrocketing vacancy rates, reputable landlords began selling out to professional slumlords. As a consequence of this action, the Bronx deteriorated into a neighborhood with many unkempt and vacant buildings. The Bronx in this deteriorating condition fell prey to the third major event which led to the direct development of the graffiti aspect of the 'Hip Hop' culture. This event occurred in 1968 and coincided with Robert Moses' second major project in the Bronx, the Co-Op City. This third event involved a group of seven teenage boys who began terrorizing the vicinity around the Bronxdale Project on Bruckner Boulevard in southeast Bronx. This may not seem important, but this group of teenagers laid the groundwork for a surge of street gang activity that would overwhelm the Bronx for the next six years. This group at first called itself the Savage Seven; but as more members joined, the group changed its name to the Black Spades. Overnight, street gangs appeared on every corner of the Bronx. Afrika Bambaataa (Bam) had a tremendous effect on rap music and the 'Hip Hop' culture was a member and leader of the Black Spades at one time. As a matter of fact, many rappers in the 'Hip Hop' subculture were gang members at some time in their lives.

Gangs in New York reached their peak in 1973, according to Hager. The Black Spades, one of the largest street gangs in New York, started to decline after this period. According to Bam, some gangs got into drugs, others got wiped out by rival gangs, while others became so large that members did not want to be involved anymore. Bam went on to say that girls got tired of the gang life and wanted to start to raise children. Times were changing;

with the advent of the 1970s people were getting into music and dancing and going to clubs. One legacy of the gangs which affected the 'Hip Hop' culture was gang graffiti. Nobody really knows how graffiti evolved, but they have been around for a long time. They go as far back as during World War II when someone wrote "Kilroy was here" in a startling number of places in our country and abroad. During the 1950s street gangs used graffiti for self-promotion, marking territorial boundaries and intimidation. However, around 1969, something changed and graffiti became a way of life with its own code of behavior, secret gathering places, slang, and esthetic standards for hundreds of New York City youths, according to Hager. It was TAKI 183 who started graffiti during this era or who made it famous. TAKI 183 was a teenager from Greece named Demetrius. Demetrius was first influenced when he saw "Julio 204" written on a street. Julio was a teenager who lived on 204th Street. Demetrius assumed the nickname Taki and placed it in front of the street on which he lived, 183rd Street. Thus, the tag name TAKI 183 was created. Demetrius proceeded to write his tag name in as many places as he could find.

Graffiti writing was mainly done with spray paint until the invention of the magic markers in the 1960s. The magic marker helped the spread of graffiti writing because it was easier to conceal and at the same time left an indelible mark on just about any surface as did the spray paint. At first, graffiti writing was limited to just artists writing their tag names. Some examples of some famous tag names in New York City other than TAKI 183 were SLY II, LEE 163d, PHASE 2, and TRACY 168. There was a large group of graffiti writers who attended DeWitt Clinton High School located across the street from a Transit Authority storage yard. The subway system was a main target of the early graffiti writers. A common meeting place was a coffee shop near DeWitt on W. Mosholu Parkway. As the graffiti aspect of the 'Hip Hop' subculture developed, graffiti writing groups started to form. One of the most revered and earliest groups to form was the Ex-Vandals. Another famous group was the Independent Writers who had Super Kool as a member. Independent writers indicated their affiliation with their group by writing 'INDS' after their tags or signatures. Another graffiti writing group that deserves mentioning is a group called Wanted which was founded by TRACY 168 in 1972.

Tracy was a streetwise White kid who was so tough that he was allowed to hang out with the Black Spades. What made the group the Wanted unusual was that it had a permanent clubhouse in the basement of an apartment complex on the corner of 166th Street and Woodycrest Avenue in the Bronx. At its peak in the 1970s

the Wanted had over 70 members. Some other important graffiti writing groups which existed in New York City were the Magic, Inc., the Three Yard Boys, the Vanguards, the Ebony Dukes, the Writers Corner 188, The Bad Artists, the Mad Bombers, the Death Squad, the Mission Graffiti, the Rebels, the Wild Style, the Six Yard Boys, and the Crazy 5. Membership was not exclusive; some graffiti artists belonged to several groups.

Graffiti reached a new peak of activity during 1976 when whole subway car murals started to appear more frequently. The graffiti artist Lee Quinones became well known for his subway car murals. The Transit Authority did not view these murals as works of art. In 1977, the Transit Authority established a giant subway car wash at its Coney Island train yard at an annual cost of $400,000. This discouraged many graffiti artists who were into subway train murals. At this subway car wash, the cars were sprayed with large amounts of petroleum hydroxide. After that, the graffiti murals and writings were buffed off. The graffiti artists referred to the spray as 'Orange Crush' which they named after the defoliant 'Agent Orange' that was used in Vietnam. The smell from this spraying caused many people who came into contact with it to become nauseous. Some graffiti artists tried to counter this process known as 'buffing' by using a better quality of spray paint which they covered with a clear enamel. This was not effective because the Transit Authority found out that in order to counter this new technique, all they had to do was run the trains through the 'buffing' process several more times. Lee Quinones had a better solution to the 'buffing' process. Quinones abandoned painting his murals on the subway trains and started painting his murals on handball courts. It should be noted that handball court painting originated with TRACY 168, but it was Quinones who was known primarily for painting these courts. Quinones' court murals mingled cartoon imagery with a strong moral sensibility.

In 1980, graffiti art began to receive the recognition it deserved. Two key events happened that would have a lasting effect on graffiti art. The first occurred in June of 1980 with the Times Square Show. It was the first time that new aspiring artists would come in contact with and display their art work with graffiti artists. One of the most notable contacts was between Keith Haring and Fred Brathwaite (Brathwaite began to be known as 'Fab Five Freddy.' Students might recognize this name as the name of the person who hosts 'Yo! MTV Raps!'). It was after this show that Keith Haring began to produce the graffiti art for which he became famous. The other major event which was to occur in 1980 happened in December. Richard Goldstein, author of the first pro-graffiti story in a *New York* magazine in 1973, wrote an extensive article in the *Village Voice* on new graffiti writers. This article was important for two reasons. First, Goldstein countered the myth that graffiti writers were an antisocial element. Goldstein felt that some of the graffiti artists who wrote on subway walls and tenement walls were bright individuals who were just expressing themselves in the environment in which they lived. Second and most important, Goldstein in this article was the first to link graffiti and rap music together. His assumption that graffiti and rap music originated from the same cultural conditions was a valid assumption. In fact, some prominent graffiti writers went on to record rap records and play an influential role in the development of the rap music industry: for example, PHASE 2, FUTURA, and Fab Five Freddy (Brathwaite).

Although 'Hip Hop' subculture and rap music seemed to have originated in the United States in the Bronx, Jamaican music also had a tremendous effect on American rap music. One style of Jamaican music that needs to be explored is known as 'toasting.' Dick Hebdige, in his book, *Cut 'N' Mix* described Jamaican 'toasting' as when the Jamaican disc jockeys talked over the music they played. This style developed at dances in Jamaica known as "blues dances." "Blues dances" were dances which took place in large halls or out in the open in the slum yards. "Blues dances" were a regular feature of ghetto life in Jamaica. At these dances, Black America R&B records were played. Jamaicans were introduced to these records by Black American sailors stationed on the island and by American radio stations in and around Miami which played R&B records. Some favorite R&B artists were Fats Domino, Amos Melburn, Louis Jordan, and Roy Brown. There was a great demand for the R&B type of music; but, unfortunately, there were no local Jamaican bands which could play this type of music as well as the Black American artists. As a result, 'sound systems' (comprised of DJs, roadies, engineers, bouncers) which were large mobile discotheques were set up to meet this need.

The major player in the 'sound systems' was the DJ. Some notable Jamaican DJs were Duke Reid, Sir Coxsone, and Prince Buster. They were performers as well as DJs. For example, Duke Reid dressed in a long ermine cloak with a pair of Colt 45s in cowboy holsters with a cartridge belt strapped across his chest and a loaded shotgun over his shoulder. This outfit was topped off with a gilt crown on his head. Just as there were to be DJ battles (competition) in the Bronx, they would occur first in Jamaica with one DJ trying to out play another DJ. As in both 'battles,' here in the U.S. and Jamaica, the competition scaled down to who had the loudest system and the most original records and technique. It was not uncommon for

things to get out of hand and for fighting to erupt during these DJ battles at the Jamaican "blues dances" once the crowds got caught up in this frenzy. It was said that Duke Reid would bring the crowd under control by firing his shotgun in the air.

At first, Jamaican toasting began when DJs would 'toast' over the music they played with simple slogans to encourage the dancers. Some of these simple slogans were "Work it, Work it" and "Move it up." As 'toasting' became more popular, so did the lengths of the toasts. One of the first big 'toasting' stars was a Jamaican named U Roy (his real name was Ewart Beckford). Another technique which developed along side 'toasting' was called 'dubs.' 'Dubbing' was when the record engineers would cut back and forth between the vocal and instrumental tracks while adjusting the bass and the treble. This technique highlighted the Jamaican 'toasting' even more.

There are four areas which Jamaican 'toasting' and American rap music have in common. First, both types of music relied on pre-recorded sounds. Second, both types of music relied on a strong beat by which they either rapped or toasted. American rap music relied on the strong beat of hard funk, and Jamaican 'toasting' relied on the beat from the Jamaican rhythms. Third, in both styles, the rappers or toasters spoke their lines in time with the rhythm taken from the records. Fourth, the content of the raps and toasts were similar in nature. For example, as there were boast raps, insult raps, news raps, message raps, nonsense raps, and party raps, there also existed toasts that were similar in nature.

According to Dick Hebdige, in his book, *Cut 'N' Mix*, 'break dancing' would be replaced in the 'Hip Hop' culture by dance moves known as the 'electric boogie' moves. Most of these moves would call for dancers to snap and twitch muscles in time to the music. Some of the most popular moves of this style of dance were the Tick, the Mannequin or Robot, the King Tut, the Wave, the Pop, the Float, and the Moonwalk which was made famous by the great Michael Jackson. In fact, many of Michael's dance moves were this style of dancing. Michael in an interview with Oprah Winfrey gave credit to the Moonwalk and several of his moves to dancers he observed in clubs and on the streets. These moves had originated from dancers into the 'Hip Hop' culture. The 'electric boogie' moves, according to Hebdige, were replaced in 1982 by a type of dancing known as 'free style' in which dancers would improvise their own moves.

When one examines the dress of the 'Hip Hop' culture, it is quite evident that one major factor affecting the dress of this subculture has been the dances. Whether the dancer was doing 'break' moves, 'electric boogie' moves, or 'free style' moves, loose fitting clothing was a prerequisite in

order to do them. Also, comfortable shoes would be needed, and sneakers seem to have filled this need. A question may arise about why young male students wear their pants hanging down by their hips. This style did not result from the dance styles of the 'Hip Hop' culture but from a more dubious source, one that many of these young male students are completely unaware of. This style originated in the prisons. Unfortunately, there is a high percentage of young minorities that are incarcerated at some point in their lives. Once behind these locked doors, prison officials usually remove inmates' belts for obvious reasons. As a consequence, inmates would walk around with their pants around their hips. Once these young inmates were released and returned to their old neighborhoods, they brought with them this style of wearing their pants around their hips. This style became popular with young males without their realizing they were emulating a style that had originated in prison. If these young males had known the origin of this style, it may not have become so popular.

Even though rap is proportionally more popular among Blacks, its primary audience is White and lives in the suburbs, according to David Samuels, in his article in the November 11, 1991 issue of *The New Republic*. The article is titled "The Rap on Rap: the 'Black Music' that Isn't Either." Samuels attempts to substantiate this fact by revealing that the number one selling record in 1991 according to Billboard Magazine was Niggaz4life, a celebration of gang rape and other violence by the group N.W.A. (Niggers With Attitude). Billboard Magazine in the summer of 1991 started to use 'Soundscam,' a much more accurate method of counting record sales by scanning the bar codes of records sold at the cash register instead of relying on big-city record stores to determine the most popular record. Samuels went on to state that the more rappers were packaged as violent Black criminals, the bigger the White audience became.

The first rap record to make it big was "Rapper's Delight" released by the Sugar Hill Gang on Syliva and Joey Robinson's Sugar Hill label. Mr. David, in his article, said that "Rapper's Delight" (a nonsense rap), "White Lines" (a rap with an anti-drug theme), and "The Message" (about ghetto life in the Black neighborhood) were designed to sell records to Whites and had a less favorable reaction in the streets where rap was created, according to Russell Simmons, president of Def Jam Records. Simmons recalls an incident when Junebug, a famous DJ of the time, was playing "The Message" and Ronnie DJ put a pistol to his head and said "Take that record off and break it or I'll blow your f——g head off." The whole club stopped until he broke the record and put it in the garbage. Run-D.M.C. was the first Black rap

group to break through to a mass White audience with its albums titled Run-D.M.C and King of Rock. These albums led the way that rap would travel into the musical mainstream. Even though members of Run-D.M.C. dressed as if they came right off the street corner, this was not the case. Run and D.M.C came from middle class families; they were never deprived of anything, and they never ran with a gang. One could never tell this by their dress or from the raps they made. Run-D.M.C. records were produced under the Def Jam label which had as one of its founders a Jewish punk rocker named Rick Rubin. Russell Simmons, Run's brother, was to later take control of the Def Jam label in 1989. However, this cannot take away from the fact that this so-called militant rap group was at one time produced by a White person. Furthermore, one of the most militant rap groups, Public Enemy, was also produced by Rick Rubin. Just as Run-D.M.C. came from middle-class families, so did Public Enemy. Members of Public Enemy grew up in suburban Long Island towns with successful middle-class professional parents.

As rap music evolved and became popular, women tended to be the targets of male rap lyrics and generally were not portrayed in a favorable light. Rap music producers also seemed to be hesitant to produce female rap artists. David Thigpin in his article, "Not for Men Only; Women Rappers are Breaking the Mold with a Message of their Own," offers two reasons for this reluctance. One is that rap producers were apprehensive about signing female rappers because they feared tampering with their proven formula of success of producing macho male rappers. The other is that rap producers did not feel that female voices could supply the requisite loudness and abrasiveness that they felt was a major feature of rap music. A New York City female rap trio by the name of Salt 'N' Pepa would provide the rap music industry with the incentive to produce more female rappers with the success of its debut album, Hot, Cool, & Vicious, which sold over a million copies. Besides the fact that people like what they heard, Russell Simmons who was quoted in Thigpen's article offers another explanation. Simmons stated: " There are more women buying rap records who would like to relate to women artists, and there are more guys who want to hear a women's point of view."

With the advent of female rappers also came new rap messages which transcended the boasting that was so common with male rappers. For example, Salt 'N' Pepper rapped over soul-tinged R&B melodies with teasing, street-savvy raps about maturity, independence from men, and sexual responsibility. Another female rapper, Monie Love, tried not to be too serious with her rap messages. Queen Latifah's raps were

about women being optimistic and having pride in themselves and tended to counter male rappers' lyrics which tended to express a poor opinion of women. However, there are some female rappers like BWP (Bytches with Problems) who voice a vengeful brand of radical Black feminism. BWP's raps dealt with such issues as date rape, male egos, and police brutality. BWP showed that they could be just as boastful as male rappers with their lyrics on the record 'In We Want Money' when they stated: "Marry you? Don't make me laugh! Don't you know, all I want is half!" Another female rapper who deserves mentioning because of her forceful attack on misogyny is Yo-Yo with her record 'You Can't Play with My Yo-Yo.'

Rap music began in a poor Black neighborhood in New York City, the Bronx. It quickly spread from one major urban center to another where there was a large population of Blacks. Music on early rap records sounded like the Black music of the day, which was heavy funk or more than often disco music. The basic function of rap music was to serve as dance music, as did the Jamaican 'toasting' music from which it originated. One major criticism that the older generation has had about rap music centers on how it is very difficult to understand what the rapper is saying. David Samuels quotes Bill Stephney's (Stepheny who is considered by many to be the smartest man in the rap business) reaction to first hearing rap music to address this point on how difficult it is to understand young rappers. Stephney said: "the point wasn't rapping, it was rhythm, DJs cutting records left and right. It was the rappers role to match the intensity of the music rhythmically. No one knew what he was saying. He was just rocking the mike."

These stations fail to take into account that rap music when it began was basically distributed through cassette recordings and has now grown to such a point that there are record companies that cater almost exclusively to rap music. Yet, when national advertisers wish to reach the 18-24-year-old group, they would employ a rap artist. Second, in my opinion, rap music is truly an American minority creation which deserves more credit and recognition as an art form rather than as a fad which should just fade away with time. Hopefully, my students will come to this same conclusion.

Although hip-hop includes graffiti art, break dancing, and rap music, the name connotes more than the sum of these parts. Hip-Hop is a means of creative expression that gives voice to young, ethnic, urban populations. Says historian Tricia Rose, "Hip-Hop is a cultural form that attempts to negotiate the experiences of marginalization, brutally truncated opportunity, and oppression within the cultural imperatives of African American and Caribbean history, identity, and community." In 1959, the

city of New York began to construct the Cross Bronx Expressway. Designed to connect New Jersey and Long Island with Manhattan, the freeway project reflected the needs of White suburban commuters. By causing the destruction of numerous Bronx businesses and apartment complexes, the expressway project finished what the decline of federal assistance programs had begun, catapulting the Bronx into destitution. Longtime White residents fled to the suburbs, and slumlords bought up the devalued apartments that flanked the dusty and noisy construction sites.

A power outage in New York in 1977 and the looting and disorder that followed turned public attention toward the Bronx, and the borough became a national symbol of the inner city crisis. Bronx residents, primarily African and Caribbean Americans, received little external support as they attempted to live amid an economic wasteland. Hip-Hop culture emerged as a new, creative, and flexible value system in a landscape stripped of value. Although neighborhoods were ugly and neglected, fashion and art could embody pride, beauty, and, self-respect.

Teenagers improvised. Black and Hispanic youths who had no dance halls and community spaces began dancing in the streets—first to disco, then to Jamaican-influenced DJ remixes, and then to rap. DJs tapped into street lights to drive their booming sound systems. Young musicians, whose under-funded schools could provide no instruments, used stereo technology to make new sounds. Young artists painted on walls and subway cars instead of canvases. Break dancing, rap, and graffiti art were all, in a sense, need-induced innovations, and each enriched the others. Graffiti artists designed posters, stage sets, and fashions for local DJs and rap musicians; break dancers followed the rhythms of rap.

Many of hip-hop's progenitors were trained in skills such as printing and radio repair, which quickly became obsolete in post-industrial New York. Unable to secure the kind of jobs that had abounded ten years before, these craftspersons found artistic outlets for their workplace skills; graffiti replaced letterpress printing, rap replaced radio repair. Hip-Hop helped to ameliorate the archaic conditions of the inner-city as the world approached the computer age. Hip-Hop culture emphasized the new social allegiances of "crews" or "posses." Often inter-ethnic, always pan-familial, crews and posses resembled gangs. Although a premium was placed on musical and artistic activities, gang-like rivalries characterized inter-group relations. Dancers and rappers held showdowns, competing against opponent performers, and graffiti artists sometimes defaced the murals of rivals. Hip-Hop culture included ongoing battles for local status, and creative conflicts often erupted into physical

fights. In the early 1980s, hip-hop culture exploded into the American mainstream. Break dancing and rap gained nationwide popularity through movies, documentaries, music videos, and albums. The rampant merchandizing that followed led some observers to suggest that the social and political power of hip-hop died with commercialization.

From the beginning, however, hip-hop artists maintained an often ambivalent relationship to consumer culture. Rap musicians both flouted and celebrated popular commodities. Although graffiti artists painted commercial icons such the Smurfs and Kodak film boxes, they often subordinated such images to their own massive, dynamic signatures. Break dancers imitated Hollywood robots. Hip-Hop fashion mocked luxury companies such as Gucci, yet sometimes celebrated conspicuous consumption. Members of hip-hop culture neither panned nor unconditionally embraced White consumer society, although often they called attention to its artifice. As rap artists accrued wealth and notoriety, the political impact of the hip-hop ethos increased. Some rappers like Public Enemy and NWA (Niggas With Attitude) penetrated public consciousness with aggressive dissent that unnerved many members of the White establishment. Writer Kristal Brent Zook suggests "that there are persistent elements of Black Nationalist ideology which underlie and inform both rap music and a larger 'hip-hop' culture. These elements include a desire for cultural pride, economic self-sufficiency, racial solidarity, and collective survival." At the end of the 20th Century, hip-hop continues to represent the cultural movement that originally developed in the Bronx. Hip-Hop sensibilities, however, prevail across the nation and around the globe, comprising social conscience as well as artistic innovation.

What is hip hop? What are some of the common stereotypes and generalizations by which hip hop is conceived? Is it a music that is for only one group of people? Does hip hop promote violence and negativity? Many people claim that it is a disgraceful, meaningless din. Antagonists often claim that hip hop is offensive to many groups of people. The fact is that so many artists out there are in the industry simply for the love of the art. These artists are not "sellouts" that are only in the industry for the money and fame. Also, there are many artists out there in the hip hop world that promote positive behavior. As time goes on, hip hop culture will continue to integrate many different racial and ethnic groups. It is now socially acceptable for people of all races to enjoy the many aspects of hip hop.

Hip hop was popularized in the late 1970s. DJ Afrika Bambataa, credited as being the first rapper ever, was the first to "talk" to his music. His unorthodox style quickly became very popular in the disco and funk clubs. "Rap" was the term given to the music. As more and more rappers appeared, the term MC, or Master of Ceremonies, was associated with rappers. Afrika Bambaataa ran a sound system at the Bronx River Community Center. As Bob Marley was a spokesperson for reggae, Bam was an ambassador and spokesperson for the 'Hip Hop' culture. Afrika Bambaataa was the name of a famous 19th Century Zulu chief; the name means Affectionate Leader. Bam took his role as a leader in the 'Hip Hop' culture seriously. In 1975, Bam founded an organization known as the Zulu Nation. The major function of this organization was to replace gang rumbles and drugs with rap, dance, and the 'Hip Hop' style.

Break dancing actually originated a few years prior to DJ Afrika Bambataa. Break dancers (B-Boys and B-Girls) would dance during the breaks in the music while steady beats were played. Eventually, rap and break dancing united and hip hop began. The area in which hip hop first became a popular music was the Bronx. The Bronx is often labeled as the birthplace of hip hop. In its early stages, hip hop was mostly among Blacks and Hispanics. As hip hop has evolved over the past 20 some odd years, its fan base has dramatically broadened. Not only has its area of influence broadened, but the race and ethnicities of hip hop lovers have also.

Groups such as A Tribe Called Quest and The Roots welcome this ethnic mixing in their music. On the contrary, most "gangster rappers" do not promote this mixture. They preach about racial tension, thereby further distancing the possibility of tranquility between races.

The best hip hop out there is what's called "underground." Most rappers are underground at first. Unfortunately, underground hip hop is not extremely prosperous. Mainstream artists differ from underground rappers because they are exposed to all of the fame and luxuries provided by society. Many underground rappers become frustrated because of the lack of exposure. Too many of the most famous rappers "cop out" by making music that caters to mainstream American consumers. All of a sudden, they become tough, hard knock thugs; thus, the name gangster rappers. This is the image that sells. Gangster rappers' lyrics lack substance and meaning. The theme of their music becomes repetitive. All of their songs deal with and only with the following elements: sex, drugs, violence, and racism.

Mos Def and Talib Kweli are two very talented rappers who have stayed true to their underground roots while gaining stardom in the hip hop world. Their insightful lyrics reflect their intelligence. Their stories reflect everything from the day-to-day troubles of living in New York City to the troubled state of the world today.

They rap about astronomy and the ancient faiths of Christianity and Islam. The beats they use also show the heavy influence that Jazz has had on hip hop. They tend to not use hard, loud, monotonous beats. Another group that shows its recognition for Jazz is The Roots. Instead of a DJ who plays records, The Roots have a guitar player and a drummer. I can tell you from experience that having a drummer and a guitar player truely enhances their live performances.

The sudden sensation of White and Asian rappers is concrete evidence that hip hop is rapidly integrating people of all races. Eminem, a White rapper from Detroit, has taken hip hop by storm. His hit single, "My Name Is," has become extremely popular worldwide. The Mountain Brothers are a fairly recent group of Asian rappers from Philadelphia. They have the potential to become one of the best groups in hip hop.

Many People understand "Hip-Hop" as a culture or a way of life that started from the roots of activities such as Graffiti, Breakdancing and block-parties in New York City. Although this is somewhat accurate, the 'Hip-Hop Culture' should not be confused with Hip-Hop music. A Rhythm and Blues record may be covered with Hip-Hop culture but would not necessarily be identified as Hip-Hop music. It contains essentially three ingredients, these being Breaks, Beats and Scratches. This has evolved over the years; for example, Breaks used to be snippets of James Brown records and short soul samples—this has changed to people like Parliament and Funkadelic, and the previous short samples have been replaced by major chunks of the original song mixed into the new record. Scratches have been almost totally removed due to the demise of the DJ in Hip-Hop records. This may have more to do with rappers realizing that they can do without a DJ in most cases and still make the same money. Beats, however, have not changed dramatically and, therefore, are the heart of Hip-Hop music.

A real Hip-Hop beat is difficult to describe but is usually slightly offbeat with a rolling, slightly "Jerky" feel to it (an expert on rhythm arrangements could probably give me a more technical description). The best way to find out a true Hip-Hop beat is to listen to records such as BDP's "Criminal Minded," early Schooly D records, along with early Run-DMC and Eric B & Rakim's "Paid in Full."

Rap can be roughly defined as words spoken rhythmically. In modern days, it can be added that these words are spoken over a beat. With its origins in Africa, it should be understood that Rap has been around a lot longer than Hip-Hop's 17 years.

A rapper may rap over a soul backing track, or even a heavy metal rock track, but this could not be Hip-Hop music. The artist may have originated through Hip-Hop culture, but the music he is making is Soul/Rap or Rock/Rap fusion, not Hip-Hop. For a record to be a Hip-Hop record, it would need to have primarily Hip-Hop beats. A Hip-Hop artist will rarely make every track using Hip-Hop beats (this is one thing that has changed over the years). Artists like LL Cool J will make an album with a half and half mixture of R'n'B and Hip-Hop, although he is regarded as a Hip-Hop artist. A few rappers still stay true to the Hip-Hop game, such as KRS-One, but they are in the minority. A new problem is the emergence of Rappers who rap over breaks and beats; and whilst it could be argued that the records are Hip-Hop, the beats are not as complex as Hip-Hop beats used to be. Whether you consider an artist as a Hip-Hop artist or simply a rapper is open to personal tastes; but, essentially, the artist needs to use Hip-Hop beats frequently in order to be truly considered Hip-Hop.

A Hip-Hop record does not need to contain any rapping at all, and likewise a rap record may not contain any Hip-Hop beats. Chart Rappers, Rock/Rap fusion and some Gangsta rappers should not be confused with genuine Hip-Hop rappers such as KRS-One. We should also not confuse Hip-Hop culture with the music—it often goes hand-in-hand, but frequently it does not, especially with the emergence of music such as Swingbeat. A suprising number of younger rap fans don't seem to know the difference. Hip-Hop music is the soul of young Black America as well as the youth of all colors around the world. For it to be merged with other music and diluted to a point where Hip-Hop ceases to exist in its own right would be extremely unfortunate.

Conclusion

African Americans made significant gains in entertainment from the 1980s to the present. Oprah Winfrey and Montel Williams established names for themselves as talk show hosts. As a result of their achievements in television, many other African Americans had the oppor-tunity to have talk shows. African Americans also gained leading roles in television drama and comedy series. Major shows on national network portrayed the lives of African Americans. Such progress would not have been possible without the accomplishments of African American predecessors in the movies and theater.

In addition to television, African Americans made significant contributions in music. Rap music evolved in the late 1970s; and by the 1980s, it was very popular among the new X generation and Hip hop culture. Rap became synonymous with Black culture along with breakdancing. This form of music also affected the dress style of young African Americans. The trend on Rap music continues to the present and remains very visible among the African American audience. It is clearly evident that Rap music remains an important form of artistic musical expression for Hip Hop generation in the 21st Century.

Review Questions

1. How did Oprah Winfrey's television career materialize in the 1980s?

2. What is Black Entertainment Network (BET), and how was it founded?

3. What is Rap music and how was it started? Who were the first major Rap artists?

4. How did Montel Williams' television career begin, and what factors led him in this direction?

5. What is Hip Hop culture, and what are its features?

6. Compare and contrast comedians Dick Gregory and Bill Cosby?

Bibliography

Abrams, Harry N. 1987. *Harlem Renaissance: Art of Black America.* New York, N.Y.: The Studio Museum in the Harlem.

Adelsberger, Bernard. Men of the Old 24th Fight for its Honor: Reject Army's Assessment of Performance in *Korea Army Times* 56:29 August 7, 1995.

Adler, Jeffrey and David Colburn. 2001. *African American Mayors: Race, Politics and the American City.* Chicago: University of Illinois Press.

Information on African American Collegian. Available online at: *African American Mosaic: Liberia.* http://lcweb.loc.gov/exhibits/African/afam003.html.

Information on African Americans in Twentieth Century. Available online at:
http://www.liu.edu/cwis/cwp/library/african/2000/1970.htm
http://www.liu.edu/cwis/cwp/library/african/2000/1980.htm
http://www.liu.edu/cwis/cwp/library/african/2000/1980.htm
http://www.liu.edu/cwis/cwp/library/african/2000/1990.htm

Alferdteen, Harrison, ed. 1991. *Black Exodus: The Great Migration from the American South.* Jackson: University Press of Mississippi.

Allen , Norm R. Jr.. Winter 1995. "Farrakhan and the Million Man March." *Free Inquiry.* Vol. 16.

Allen, Robert L. 1993. *The Port Chicago Mutiny.* New York, N.Y.: Penguin.

Alt, William E. 2002. *Black soldiers, White Wars: Black Warriors from Antiquity to the Present.* Westport, Conn.: Praeger.

Anderson, James. 1988. *The Education of Blacks in the South. 1860-1935.* Chapel Hill, NC: University of North Carolina Press.

Anderson, Jervis . 1986. *A. Philip Randolph: A Biographical Portrait.* Berkeley, CA: University of California Press.

Anderson, Paul Allen. 2001. *Deep River: Music and Memory in Harlem Renaissance Thought.* Durham, NC: Duke University Press.

Andrews, William L. "African American Literature." Encyclopædia Britannica's Guide to Black History. 2005. Encyclopædia Britannica. 5 June 2005
<http://search.eb.com/Blackhistory/article.do?nKeyValue=343805>

Armstrong, Julie Buckner. 2002. *Teaching the American Civil Rights Movement: Freedom's Bittersweet Song*. New York : Routledge.

Arthur Knight.2002.*Disintegrating the Musical: Black Performance and American Film*. Durham, NC: Duke University Press.

Ayers, Edward. 1984. *Vengeance and Justice: Crime and Punishment in the Nineteenth Century American South*. New York: Oxford University Press.

Badger, Tony and Brian Ward.1996.*The Making Of Martin Luther King and the Civil Rights Movement*. NewYork.: New York University Press.

Baker, Houston A. 1988.*Afro-American poetics: revisions of Harlem and the Black Aesthetic*. Madison: University of Wisconsin Press.

Baker, John. "Effects of the Press on Spanish-American Relations in 1898." 19 Feb. 2002. 10 June 2005 <http://www.humboldt.edu/~jcb10/spanwar.shtml>

Barbeau, Arthur E., Bernard C. Nalty, and Florette Henri. 1974.*The Unknown Soldiers: African-American Troops in World War I*. Philadelphia: Temple University Press.

Barker, Lucius J. . 1999.*African Americans and the American political system*. Upper Saddle River, N.J. : Prentice Hall.

Barnes,Denise..*"Million Man March Still Echoes in Many Ears." The Washington Times*. April 16, 1996.

Bassett, John Earl, 1992. *Harlem in Review: Critical Reactions to Black American Writers, 1917*-Cranbury, NJ : Associated University Press.

Beech,Wendy M..*"Keeping it in the Family". Black Enterprise*. Vol. 29, November 1998.

Beifuss, Joan Turner Beifuss.1985. *At the River I Stand : Memphis, the 1968 Strike, and Martin Luther King*. Brooklyn, N.Y.: Carlson Publisher.

Bell, Alan and Paul Stekler.1984.*Hands that picked cotton [video recording]: Black Politics in today's rural south*. New Orleans: Stekler.

Billingsley, Andrew.1968. *Black Families in White America* .Englewood Cliff, N.J: Prince Hall.

Information on black ghettos. Available online at: http://college.hmco.com/history/readerscomp/rcah/html/ah_010200_blackghet tos.htm

Information on Black Panther Party. Available online at: http://www.marxists.org/history/usa/workers/black-panthers/

Blomquist,Brian..*"Million Man March official says Financial vow to city will be Met." The Washington Times*. April 16, 1996.

Bontemps, Arna. 1984. *The Harlem Renaissance Remembered*. New York: Dodd, Mead.

Bornstein, George and Tracy Mishkin. 1998. *The Harlem and Irish Renaissances: language, identity, and representation*. Gainesville, FL: University of Florida Press.

Bositis, David A.1998.*Black Elected Officials*: A Statistical Summary. Washington,D.C.: Joint Center for Political and Economic Studies.

Bowers, William T. and others. 1996. *Black Soldier, White Army: The 24th Infantry Regiment in Korea*. Washington,D.C.: Center of Military History, U. S. Army.

Boyd, Herb and Howard Dodson. 2003. *The Harlem Reader: A Celebration of New York's Most Famous Neighborhood, from the Renaissance Years to he Twenty-first Century.* New York: Three Rivers Press.

Brandt, Nat.1996. *Harlem at War: The Black Experience in WWII.* Syracuse, NY: Syracuse University Press.

Brian Dooley.1998. Black *and Green : the Fight for Civil Rights in Northern Ireland and Black America.* Chicago : Pluto Press.

Broderick, Francis L. and August Meier. 1965. *Negro Protest Thought in the Twentieth Century.* Indianapolis : Bobbs-Merrill Co.

Brooks,RoyL.1992.*Rethinking The American Race Problem.*Berkeley, CA: University of California Press.

Brotz,Howard.1970. *The Black Jews of Harlem; Negro Nationalism and the Dilemmas of Negro Leadership.* New York: Schocken Books.

Brown, Tony , James Cannady, and Sheryl, J. Cannady.1991.*The Black Eagles [video recording] / from WNET.* New York, N.Y.: Tony Brown Productions, Inc.

Brundage, W. Fitzhugh. 1993. *Lynching in the New South: Georgia and Virginia, 1880 -1930.* Urbana, Illinois: University of Illinois Press.

Bryer, Jackson R., Maurice Duke, and Thomas M. Inge.1978. *Black American Writers: Bibliographical Essays.* New York: St. Martin's Press.

Bullock, Penelope L. *The Afro-American Periodical Press, 1838-1909.* Baton Rouge: Louisiana State University Press, 1981.

Bussey, Charles M. 1991. *Firefight at Yechon: Courage and Racism in the Korean War.* Washington, D.C.: Brassey's.

Button, James W. 1978. *Black Violence: Political Impact of the 1960s' Riots.* Princeton, N.J.: Princeton University Press.

Button, James W.1989. *Blacks and Social Change : Impact of the Civil Rights Movement in Southern Communities.* Princeton, N.J.: Princeton University Press.

Calverton, V.F., ed. 1929. *Anthology of American Negro Literature.* New York: Modern Library.

Campbell, Will D.2003.*Robert G. Clark's Journey to the House: a Black Politician's story.* Jackson: University Press of Mississippi.

Carawan, Candie and Guy Carawan.1963. *We shall Overcome: Songs of the Southern Freedom movement.* New York: Oak Publications.

Carmichael, Stokey & Charles V. Hamilton.1967. *Black Power: The Politics of Liberation in America.* New York: Vintage Book.

Carson, Clayborne, Emma J. Lapansky-Werner, and Gary B. Nash. 2005. *African American Lives: The Struggle for Freedom, Volume II-Since 1865.* New York: Pearson Education, Inc.

Carter, Allene G .2003.*Honoring Sergeant Carter: Redeeming a Black World War II Hero's legacy.* New York: Amistad.

Information on Civil Rights Movement in America. Available online at:

http://encarta.msn.com/encyclopedia_761580647/Civil_Rights_Movement_in_t he_United_States.html

http://encarta.msn.com/encyclopedia_761580647_2/Civil_Rights_Movement_in _the_United_States.html

http://www.civilrights.org/research_center/civilrights101/economicjustice.html

http://college.hmco.com/history/readerscomp/rcah/html/ah_017100_civilrights m.htm

http://en.wikipedia.org/wiki/American_civil_rights_movement

http://www.sparknotes.com/history/american/civilrights/context.html

http://www.uiowa.edu/~socialed/lessons/CivilRights.htm

http://www.umich.edu/~eng499/concepts/power.html

http://www.watson.org/~lisa/blackhistory/civilrights-55-65/freeride.html

Choper,Jesse H."Why the Supreme Court should not have decided the presidential election of 2000."*Constitutional Commentary*. Vol. 18, 2001.

Clayborne, Carson.1981. *In Struggle : SNCC and the Black Awakening of the 1960s.* Cambridge, Mass.: Harvard University Press.

Clayton,Dewey M.2000. *African Americans and the Politics of Congressional Redistricting.* New York: Garland Publishing.

Cohen, William. 1991. *At Freedom's Edge: Black Mobility and the Southern White Quest for Racial Control, 1861-1915.* Baton Rouge, Louisiana: Louisiana State University Press.

Coleman, Leon. 1998. *Carl Van Vechten and the Harlem Renaissance: A Critical Assessment* New York: Garland Publisher.

Collins,Patricia Hill. "Intersections of race, class, gender, and Nation: some implications for African American family studies." *Journal of Comparative Family Studies*. Vol. 29, 1998.

Converse, Elliott V. III.1997. *The Exclusion of Black Soldiers from the Medal of Honor in World War: The Study Commissioned by the United States Army to Investigate Racial Bias in the Awarding of the Nation's Highest Military Decoration.* Jefferson, N.C.: McFarland & Co.

Cooper, Anna Julia . 1990. *A Voice From the South: Edited with an Introduction by Mary Helen Washington.* New York: Oxford University Press.

Cooper, Wayne F. 1987. *Claude McKay :Rebel Sojourner in the Harlem Renaissance.*

Couto, Richard A. 1991. *Ain't Gonna Let Nobody Turn Me Round : The Pursuit of Racial Justice in the Rural South.* Philadelphia : Temple University Press.

Cronin, Gloria, ed. 1998. *Critical Essays on Zora Neale Hurston.* New York: G. K. Hall; London: Prentice Hall International.

D'Souza, Dinesh.1995. *The End of Racism : Principles for a Multiracial Society.* New York : Free Press.

David Carroll Cochran.1999. *The Color of Freedom: Race and Contemporary American Liberalism.* Albany, GA : State University of New York Press.

David Toop.2000. *Rap Attack: African Rap to Global Hip-hop.* London: Serpent's Tail.

Davis, Lenwood G. 1981. Black A*thletes in the United States: A bibliography of Books, Articles, Autobiographies, and Biographies on Black Professional Athletes in the United States, 1800-1981.* Westport, Conn.: Greenwood.

Davis, Thadious M. 1986. *Afro-American Writers before the Harlem Renaissance.* Detroit.: Gale Publishers.

Davis,Richard A. "The Norm of Legitimacy in the African American Family. "*The Western Journal of African American Studies.* Vol. 22, 1998.

Dawson, Michael C. 2001. *Black Visions: The Roots of Contemporary African American Political Ideologies.* Chicago: University of Chicago Press.

De Jongh, James. 1990. *Vicious Modernism: Black Women and the Literary Imagination.* New York:Cambridge University Press.

Defrantz, Thomas F. 2002. *Dancing Many Drums: Excavations in African-American Dance.* Madison, Wisconsin: University of Wisconsin Press.

Detwiler, Frederick G. *The Negro Press in the United States.* Chicago: University of Chicago Press, 1922.

Diawara, Martha.1993. *Black American Cinema.* New York: Routledge.

Dittmer, John.1993.*Essays on the American Civil Rights Movement.* College Station: Texas A&M University Press.

Doyle, William. 2001. *An American Insurrection: The Battle of Oxford, Mississippi, 1962.* New York: Doubleday, 2001.

Draper, Alan .1994. *Conflict of Interests: Organized Labor and the Civil Rights Movement in the South, 1954-1968.* Ithaca, N.Y. : ILR Press.

Dray, Philip. 2002. *At the Hands of Persons Unknown: The Lynching of Black America.* New York: Random House, 2002.

Dudley, William, ed. 1997.*African Americans: opposing viewpoints.* San Diego, Calif.: Greenhaven Press.

Dumas,Kitty. August 1992. "The Year of the African American Woman." *African American Enterprise.* Vol. 23.

E. Marvin Goodwin.1990. *Black migration in America from 1915 to 1960: An Uneasy Exodus.* Lewiston : E. Mellen Press.

Earley, Charity Adams. 1989. *One Woman's Army: A Black Officer Remembers the WAC.* College Station, Texas: Texas A&M University Press.

Egar, Emmanuel Edame 2003. *Black Women Poets of Harlem Renaissance.* Lanham, Md.: University Press of America.

Elliott, Jeffrey M. 1986. *Black Voices in American Politics.* San Diego: Harcourt Brace Jovanovich.

Ellis,Walter,Jones,Clara B. 2001. "The African American Family: Strengths, Self-Help, and Positive Change."*The Western Journal of African American Studies.* Vol. 25, 2001.

Information on The Employment of Negro Troops. Available online at: <http://www.army.mil/CMH-pg/books/wwii/11-4/chapter1.htm>

Erhagbem, Edward O.1991.*The American Negro Leadership Conference on Africa;*

A New African-American Voice for African in The United States 1962- 1970.
Boston, Mass: African Studies Center, Boston University.

Events in the South and Civil Rights. Available online:
http://www.infoplease.com/spot/civilrightstimeline1.html

Fauntroy, Michael K.2000. *The Erosion of Home Rule in the District of Columbia: The Impact of Partisan Politics, City-suburban Politics, and Congressional Intervention, 1973-1998.* Doctoral Dissertation, Washington, D.C.: Political Science, Howard University at Washington, D.C.

Fayer, Steve, Sara Flynn and Henry Hampton.1991.*Voices of Freedom : An Oral History Of the Civil Rights Movement from the 1950s through the 1980s.* New York : Bantam Books.

Fernandez, John P. 1975. *Black Managers in White Corporations.* New York : Wiley.

Ferguson, Blanche E. 1966. *Countee Cullen and the Negro Renaissance.* New York, Dodd, Mead.

Fischer, Perry E. 1993.*Blacks and Whites, Together through Hell: U.S. Marines in World War II.* Turlock, Ca: Millsmont Publisher.

Fleming, Harold C.1996. *The Potomac Chronicle : Public policy & Civil Rights   from Kennedy to Reagan.* Athens, GA : University of Georgia Press.

Fleming, Robert E. 1987.James Weldon Johnson. Boston, MA: Twayne Publishers.

Fligstein, Neil. 1981. *Going North: Migration of Blacks and Whites from the South, 1900 –1950.* New York: Academic Press, 1981.

Flowers, Sandra Hollin.1996.*African American Nationalist Literature of the 1960s. Pens of Fire.* New York :Garland Publishing.

Foner, Philip S. 2002.*The Black Panthers Speak.* New York: Da Capo Press.

Ford, Shirley A.1983.*A Community Development Approach to Increasing the Participation of Low Income Blacks in the Electoral Process in Washington.* Master's Thesis, Washington, D.C.: Political Science, Howard University at Washington, D.C

Franklin, John Hope and Alfred Moss, Jr. 2000. *From Slavery to Freedom: A History of African Americans.* New York: McGraw Hill.

Gaines, Kevin. 1996. *Uplifting the Race: Black Leadership, Politics and Culture in the 20th Century.* Chapel Hill: University of North Carolina Press.

Gardner, Michael R. 2002. *Harry Truman and Civil Rights: Moral Courage and Political Risks.* Carbondale, IL: Southern Illinois University Press.

Garrow, David J. 1989. *Birmingham, Alabama, 1956-1963 : The Black Struggle for Civil Rights.* Brooklyn, N.Y.: Carlson Publisher.

Garrow, David J. 1989. *We shall Overcome : The Civil Rights Movement in the United States in the 1950's and 1960's.* Brooklyn, N.Y.: Carlson Publisher.

Garrow, David J. Garrow.1999. *Bearing the Cross: Martin Luther King, Jr., and the Southern Christian Leadership Conference.* New York : Quill Publisher.

Garrow, David J.1981. *The FBI and Martin Luther King, Jr.: From Solo to Memphis.* New York : W.W. Norton.

Garrow, David J.1989. *Atlanta, Georgia, 1960-1961: Sit-ins and Student Activism.*

Brooklyn, N.Y.: Carlson Publisher.

Gary Null.1995. *Black Hollywood: The Performer in Motion Pictures*. New York: Carol Publishing Group.

Gates, Henry Louis, Richard Newman, and Marcia Sawyer, eds. 1996. *Everybody say freedom: everything you need to know about African-American history*. New York: Plume.

Gatewood, Willard B., ed. 1971.*Smoked Yankees and the Struggle for Empire: Letters from Negro Soldiers, 1898-1902*. Urbana, Illinois: University of Illinois Press.

Gatewood, William B., Jr. *Black Americans and the White Man's Burden, 1898-1903*. Urbana: University of Illinois Press, 1975.

Information on George Henry White. *Available online at:* http://www.spartacus.schoolnet.co.uk/USAWhiteGH.htm.

Graham, Hugh Davis. 1994. *Civil Rights in the United States*. University Park, PA: Pennsylvania State University Press.

Goodwin, E. Marvin. 1990. *Black Migration in America, 1915-1960*. Lewiston N.Y.: Edwin Mellen Press.

Grant, William R., Bill Jersey, Sam Pollard, and Richard Wormser. The Rise and Fall of Jim Crow. "Fighting Back (1896–1917)." PBS. Thirteen/WNET, New York. 8 Oct. 2002.

Grant, William R., Bill Jersey, Sam Pollard, and Richard Wormser. The Rise and Fall of Jim Crow. Fighting Back (1896–1917). *PBS. Thirteen/WNET*, New York. 8 Oct. 2002.

Grant,Nancy L.1990. *TVA and African American Americans:Planning for the Status Quo*. Philadelphia : Temple University Press.

Gray, Herman . 2004. *Watching Race: Television and the Struggle for Blackness*. Minneapolis: University of Minnesota Press.

Greene, Larry A. and Lenworth Gunther. "World War I and the Great Migration, 1915–1920." The New Jersey African American History Curriculum Guide: Grades 9 to 12. 23 Apr. 2003. New Jersey Historical Commission, New Jersey Department of State. 14 June 2005. Information available online at: <http://www.njstatelib.org/NJ_Information/Digital_Collections/AAHCG/unit 9.html>

Gropman, Alan L.1998.*The Air Force Integrates, 1945-1964*. Washington.DC: Smithsonian Institution Press.

Hale, Grace. 1998. *Making Whiteness: The Culture of Segregation in the South, 1890-1940*. New York: Pantheon Books.

Hamer, Jennifer.2001. *What It Mean to Be Daddy:.Fatherhood for African American Men Living Away from Their Children*. New York:Columbia University Press.

Hamilton, Dona Cooper.1997. *The Dual agenda : Race and Social welfare Policies of Civil Rights Organizations*. New York : Columbia University Press.

Hansen, Drew D. 2003. *The Dream : Martin Luther King, Jr., and the Speech that Inspired a Nation*. New York : Ecco.

Hargrove, Hondon B..1985. *Buffalo Soldiers in Italy: Black Americans in World War*

II. Jefferson, N.C.: McFarland Publisher.

Information on the Harlem Renaissance. Wikipedia, The Free Encyclopedia. 25 May 2005. Wikipedia. 5 June 2005. Available online at: <http://en.wikipedia.org/wiki/Harlem_Renaissance>

Harris, Joseph E. 1994. *African-American Reactions to War in Ethiopia, 1936- 1941*. Baton Rouge: Louisiana State University Press.

Harris, Trudier. 1987. *Afro-American writers from the Harlem Renaissance to 1940*. Detroit, MI.: Gale Research Co.

Harrison, Hubert H. 2001. *A Hubert Harrison reader / edited with introduction and notes by Jeffrey B. Perry*. Middletown, Conn.: Wesleyan University Press.

Haskins, James.1999. *Distinguished African American Political and Governmental Leaders*. Phoenix, Ariz.: Oryx Press.

Haynes,Karima A. "Will Carol Moseley Braun be the first African American woman senator?." *Ebony*. Vol. 47, June 1992.

Hemingway, Al. Airman Down in Korean hills: Interview with Former Pilot Thomas Jerome Hudner, *Jr. Military History* 12:54-60 June 1995.

Henderson, Gwendolyn, Roses Lorraine Elena Roses, Elizabeth Ruth, and Mae Randolph. 1990. *Harlem Renaissance and Beyond: literary biographies of 100 Black women*. Boston: Harvard University Press.

Henri, Florette and Richard Joseph Stillman. 1970. *Bitter Victory: A History of Black Soldiers in World War I*. Garden City, NY: Doubleday.

Henry, Charles P.1990.*Culture and African American Politics*. Bloomington: Indiana University Press.

Herman, L..1999. *Community, Violence, and Peace : Aldo Leopold, Mohandas K. Gandhi, Martin Luther King, Jr., and Gautama the Buddha in the Twenty-first Century*. Albany, N.Y.: State University of New York Press.

Higgs, Robert. 1977. *Competition and Coercion; Blacks in the American Economy, 1865-1914*. New York: Oxford University Press.

Higham, John. 1955. *Strangers in the Land: Patterns of American Nativism, 1860-1925*. New Brunswick: Rutgers University Press.

Hine, Darlene Clark , ed. 1993. *Black Women in America: An Historical Encyclopedia: Volume II*. New York:Carlson Publishing.

Hine, Darlene Clark, William C. Hine, and Stanley Harrold. 2004. *African Americans: A Concise History*. Upper Saddle River, New Jersey: Pearson Education, Inc.

Hine, Darlene Clark, William C. Hine, and Stanley Harrold. 2003. *The African American Odyssey: Volume Two, Since 1865*. Upper Saddle River, New Jersey. Prentice Hall.

Hine, Darlene Clark.1979. *The Rise and Fall of the White Primary in Texas*. Milwood, N.Y: K.T.O Press.

Hines,Revathi I. The Silent Voices: 2000 Presidential Election and the Minority Vote in Florida. *Western Journal of African American Studies*. Vol. 26, 2002.

Hogan, Lawrence. 1984. *A Black National News Service: The Associated Negro Press and Claude Barnett, 1919–1945*. Rutherford: Farleigh Dickinson University Press;

London: Associated University Presses.

Horton, James Oliver and Lois Horton. "African American History." Encarta Online Encyclopedia. 2005. Microsoft. 14 June 2005 . Available online at: <http://encarta.msn.com/encyclopedia_761595158/African_American_History. html>http://brownwatch.squarespace.com/display/ShowPage?moduleId=17311

Huggins, Nathan Irvin. 1971. *Harlem Renaissance.* New York, Oxford University Press.

Hughes, Langston. 1993. *The Big Sea.* New York: Hill and Wang.

Hughes, Alan. Making strides, but losing ground? African American, woman- owned firms growing, but at a slower pace than other groups. *Black Enterprise.* Vol. 32, April 2002.

Hull, Gloria T. 1987. *Color, sex & poetry: three women writers of the Harlem Renaissance.* Bloomington: Indiana University Press.

Hunter, Tera W. 1997. *To 'Joy My Freedom: Southern Black Women's Lives and Labors After the Civil War.* Cambridge: Harvard University Press.

Hutchinson, George. 1995. *The Harlem Renaissance in black and white.* Cambridge, Mass.: Belknap Press of Harvard University Press.

Information on Important Cities in Black History. Available online at: <http://www.factmonster.com/spot/bhmcities1.htmlI

Information on Influence of Black Music (Motown Sound). Available online at: http://www.essays.cc/free_essays/e2/blc13.shtml

Jacob U. Gordon. 2000. *Black leadership for social Change.* Westport, Conn.: Greenwood Press.

James Edward Mock. 1981. *The black political executives and black political interests, 1961- 1981.* Doctoral Dissertation, Knoxville, Tennessee: Political Science, University of Tennessee at Knoxville.

Jennings, James. 1992. *Race, Politics, and Economic Development: Community Perspectives.* New York: Verso.

Information on Jesse Jackson. Available online at: http://encarta.msn.com/encyclopedia_761557067/Jackson_Jesse_(Louis).html

Jewell, Sue. K. 1988. *Survival of the African American Family: The Institutional Impact of U.S. Social Policy.* New York: Praeger Publishers.

Johnson, Jesse J. 1974. *Black Women in the Armed Forces, 1942-1974.* Hampton, Va.: Johnson.

Jordan, William G. *Black Newspapers and America's War for Democracy, 1914–1920.* Chapel Hill, NC: University of North Carolina Press, 2001.

Kemble, Jean. 1997. The Harlem Renaissance: a guide to materials in the British Library / by Jean Kemble. London: Eccles Center for American Studies

Kevern Verney. 2000. *Black Civil rights in America.* New York : Routledge.

King, Mary C. " Are African-Americans losing their footholds in better jobs?" *Journal of Economic Issues.* Vol. 32, 1998.

Kramer, Victor A., Robert A. Russ, eds. 1997. *Harlem Renaissance re-examined.* Troy,

N.Y.: Whitson Publisher.

Krasner, David, 2002. *A Beautiful Pageant: African American theatre, drama, and Performance in the Harlem Renaissance.* New York: Palgrave Macmillan.

Lee, Ulysses .1966. *The employment of Negro troops.* Washington, D.C.: Office of the Chief of Military History, U.S. Army.

Lemann, Nicholas. 1991. *The Promised Land: The Great Black Migration and How it Changed America.* Knopf Publisher.

Leonard Steinhorn.1999. By *the Color of Our Skin: The Illusion of Integration and the Reality of Race.* New York : Dutton.

Levy, Peter B. 1992.*Documentary History of the Modern Civil Rights Movement.* New York : Greenwood Press.

Levy, Peter B. 1998. *The Civil Rights Movement.* Westport, Conn.: Greenwood Press.

Litwack, Leon. 1998. *Trouble in Mind: Black Southerners in the Age of Jim Crow.* New York: Alfred A. Knopf.

Lloyd Hogan.1984. *Principles of Black political economy.* .Boston, MA : Routledge & Kegan Paul.

Information on World War II. Available online at:
http://www.coax.net/people/lwf/ww2.htm

Loevy, Robert D. 1997. *The Civil Rights Act of 1964: The Passage of the Law That Ended Racial Segregation.* Albany, NY: State University of New York Press.

Logan,Sadye L.2001. The Black Family:Strengths, Self-Help,and Positive Change. Boulder, CO:Westview Press.

Long, Michael G.2002. *Against Us, But For Us : Martin Luther King, Jr. and the State.* Macon, Ga.: Mercer University Press.

Loverro, Thomas. 2003. *The Encyclopedia of Negro League Baseball.* NY: Checkmark Books, 2003.

Lusane, Clarence.1994.*African Americans at the crossroads: the restructuring of Black leadership and the 1992 elections.* Boston, MA: South End Press.

Information on Malcolm X. Available online at:
http://encarta.msn.com/encyclopedia_761552252/Malcolm_X.html

Malik Simba.1977. *The black laborer, the black legal experience and the United States Supreme Court with emphasis on the neo-concept of equal employment.* Doctoral Dissertation, Minneapolis, Minnesota, Political Science, University of Minnesota, Minneapolis.

Mandle,Jay R.1992.*Not Slave, Not Free:The African American Economic Experience since the Civil War.* Durham, NC: Duke University Press.

Marcelle Size Knaack.1986. *Post-World War II fighters, 1945-1973.* Washington, D.C.: Office of Air Force History, U.S. Air Force.

Mark A.Reid.1993. *Redefining Black Film.* Berkeley: University of California Press.

Information on Martin Luther King. Available online at:
http://www.core-online.org/history/martin_luther_king.htm
http://www.lucidcafe.com/library/96jan/king.html

Martin, Tony .1991.*African fundamentalism: a literary and cultural anthology of Garvey's*

Harlem Renaissance. Dover, Mass.: Majority Press.

Mason, Gilbert R. 2000. *Beaches, Blood, and Ballots : A Black Doctor's Civil Rights Struggle*. Jackson : University Press of Mississippi.

Meacham, Jon .2001.*Voices in our Blood : America's Best on the Civil Rights Movement*. New York: Random House.

Meier, August. 1970. The Transformation of Activism: Black Experience. Chicago: Aldine Publishing Company.

Mervyn M. Dymally.1971. *The Black politician: his struggle for Power*. Belmont, Calif., Duxbury Press.

Meyer, Stephen Grant. 2000. *As Long as They Don't Move Next Door: Segregation and Racial Conflict in American Neighborhoods*. Lanham, Maryland: Rowman & Littlefield.

Miller, Richard. "The Golden Fourteen, Plus: Black Navy Women in World War One." *Minerva* 13 (Fall/Winter 1995): 713.

Information on million woman march. Available online at: http://www.cnn.com/US/9710/25/million. woman.march2/ htm1.

Moore, Brenda L. e.1996. *To serve my country, to serve my race : The story of the only African American WACS stationed overseas during World War II*. New York: New York University Press.

Moreland, Laurence W. and Robert P. Steed. 2002. *The 2000 Presidential Election in the South: Partisanship and Southern Party Systems in the 21ˢᵗ Century*. Westport, Conn.: Praeger.

Morrison, Minion K.C.1987.*Black Political Mobilization: Leadership, Power, and Mass Behavior*. Albany: State University of New York Press.

Morton, Cynthia. 1989. *Afro-American Women of the South and the Advancement of the Race, 1895-1925*. Knoxville: University of Tennessee Press.

Motley, Mary Penick. 1975. *The Invisible Soldier: The Experience of the Black Soldier, World War Two*. Detroit: Wayne State University.

Murphy, Brenda Murphy, ed. 1999. *The Cambridge companion to American women Playwrights* .Cambridge [England]; New York: Cambridge University Press.

Nalty, Bernard C. 1995. *The right to fight : African-American Marines in World War II*. Washington, D.C.: History and Museums Division, Headquarters, U.S. Marine Corps.

Nalty, Bernard C. 1986. *Strength for the Fight: A History of Black Americans in the Military*. New York: Free Press, 1986.

National Association for the Advancement of Colored People. 1919. *Thirty Years of Lynching in the United States, 1889-1918*. New York: NAACP.

National Urban League. Research Dept.1992. *Abridging the Right to Vote: A Study of State Restrictions and Black Political Participation*. New York: National Urban League.

Information on the Negro League. Available online at: <http://search.eb.com/Blackhistory/article.do?nKeyValue=3007Neverdon-

Information on Nixon and Civil Rights. Available online at: http://www.lexisnexis.com/academic/2upa/Aaas/CivilRightsNixon.asp

Nwachukwu Frank Ukadike.2002. *Questioning African Cinema*. Minneapolis: University of Minnesota Press.

Palmer, Colin A. 1998. *Passageways: An Interpretive History of Black America: Volume II: 1863-1965*. New York: Harcourt Brace College Publishers.

Parker, Frank R. 1990. *Black Votes Count: Political Empowerment in Mississippi after 1965*. Chapel Hill: University of North Carolina Press.

Patrick B. Miller, Therese Frey Steffen, Elisabeth Schäfer-Wünsche.2001. *The Civil Rights Movement Revisited: Critical Perspectives on the Struggle for Racial Equality in the United States*. Hamburg Lit Piscataway, NJ: Distributed in North America by Transaction Publishers.

Perpener, John O. 2001. *African-American Concert Dance: the Harlem Renaissance and Beyond*. Urbana: University of Illinois Press.

Information on the Plight of the African American. Available online at: http://www.pbs.org/wgbh/amex/1900/filmore/reference/interview/lewis_plightframer.html.

Plummer, Brenda Gayle. 1996. *Rising Wind: Black Americans and U.S. Foreign Affairs, 1935-1960*. Chapel Hill, NC: University of North Carolina Press.

Pohlman, Marcus D. 2003. *African American Political Thought*. New York: Routledge.

Pride, Armistead and Clint C. Wilson II. 1997. *A History of the Black Press*. Washington, DC: Howard University Press.

Pride, Armistead and Clint C. Wilson II. A History of the Black Press.

Rabinowitz, Howard. 1978. *Race Relations in the Urban South, 1865-1890*. New York: Oxford University Press.

Rampersad,Arnold and James Trotman. 1995. *Langston Hughes: The man, his art, and his Continuing Influence*. New York: Garland Publisher.

Reed, Adolph, Jr. 1986. Race, Politics and Culture; Critical Essays on the Radicalism of the 1960s. Westport, Conn.: Greenwood Press.

Reed, Bill .1998. *Hot Harlem :Profiles in African-American Entertainment*. Los Angeles, CA : Cellar Door Books.

Information on rise and fall of Jim Crow. Available online at: <http://www.pbs.org/wnet/jimcrow/stories_events_spanish.html>

Rishell, Lyle. 1993. *With a Black Platoon in Combat: A Year in Korea*. College Station, TX, Texas A&M University Press.

Robert D. Loevy.1997. *The Civil Rights Act of 1964: the passage of the law that ended racial segregation*. Albany, NY: State University of New York Press.

Rose, Robert A..1976."Lonely eagles": the story of America's Black Air Force in World War II. Los Angeles : Tuskegee Airmen, Western Region.

Rowan, Carl T. 1993. *Dream Makers,Dream Breakers: The World of Justice Thurgood Marshall*. New York: Welcome Rain.

Rudwick, Elliott W. 1982. *W.E.B. DuBois: Voice of the Black Protest Movement*. Urbana: University of Illinois Press.

Sandler, Stanley. 1992. *Segregated Skies: All-Black Combat Squadrons of WWII*.

Washington, DC: Smithsonian Institution Press.

Information on Jazz. Available online at:
  <http://search.eb.com/Blackhistory/article.do?nKeyValue=110142>

Scott, Ann Firor. Most Invisible of All': Black Women's Voluntary Organizations. *Journal of Southern History*, 56 (1):12.

Scott, Emmett J. 1969. *Scott's Official History of the American Negro in the World War, 1919*. New York: Arno Press, 1969.

Scott, William R. 1993. *The Son's of Sheba's Race: African-Americans and the Italo-Ethiopian War, 1935-1941*. Bloomington, IN: Indiana University Press.

Scott,Matthew S. Two decades in the African American. *African American Enterprise*. Vol. 25, October 1994.

Information on segregation in America. Available online at:
  http://encarta.msn.com/encyclopedia_761580651_2/Segregation_in_the_United_States.html

Silvera, John D..1969.*The Negro in World War II*. New York: Arno Press.

Sitkoff, Harvard . "Racial Militancy and Interracial Violence in the Second World War," *Journal of American History* 58, no. 3 (1971): 663-83.

Sitkoff, Harvard. 1981. *The Struggle for Black Equality, 1954-1980*. New York: Hill and Wang.

Smallwood, Arwin D..1998.*The Atlas of African-American History and Politics: From the Slave Trade to modern times*. Boston: McGraw-Hill.

Snowden,Lonnie R. Social Embeddedness and Psychological Well-Being Among African Americans and Whites. *American Journal of Community Psychology*. Vol. 29, 2001.

Information on the Spanish-American War and Buffalo Soldiers. Available online at:
  http://www.nps.gov/prsf/history/buffalo_soldiers/spanish_american_war.htm>

Starling,Kelly. "The Million Woman March: Historic Gathering Reaffirms the power of Sisterhood.*" Ebony*. Vol. 53, December 1997.

Information on state of African Americans. Available online at:
  http://www.uapb.edu/source/features/features_state_of_African Americanamerica.html.
  http://www.webbschool.com/theoracle/october/welfare.htm\
  http://www.whitehousehistory.org/05/subs/05_c19.html
  http://www.whitehousehistory.org/05/subs/05_c19.html
  http://www-mcnair.berkeley.edu/2000journal/Kelley/Kelley.html

Theilman, John and Al Wilhite. 1991. *Discrimination and congressional campaign Contributions*. New York: Praeger.

Thomas Borstelmann.2001. *The Cold War and the color line : American race relations in the global arena*. Cambridge, Mass.: Harvard University Press.

Thompson, James. 1981. *True Colors: 1004 Days as a Prisoner of War*. Port Washington, NY, Ashley Books, 1989: The story of a black POW during the Korean Conflict. Originally published as *Camp 5*. Laguna Beach, CA: Voyager

Press.

Thompson,Bennie Gordon. 2003. African *Americans and political participation: a reference handbook.* Santa Barbara, Calif.: ABC-CLIO.

Tinney, James S. and Justine J. Rector. 1980. *Issues and Trends in Afro-American Journalism.* Washington, DC: University Press of America, Inc.

Town, Stuart W. 2002. *We Want Our Freedom : Rhetoric of the Civil Rights Movement.* Westport, Conn.: Praeger.

Tracy, Steven C. 2001. *Langston Hughes and the Blues.* Urbana: University of Illinois Press.

Trotter, Joel William, Jr. 2001. The *African American Experience: Volume II From Reconstruction.* New York: Houghton Mifflin Company.

Tryman, Mfanya Donald. 1982. *Afro-American mass political integration: a causal and deductive model.* Washington, D.C.: University Press of America.

Information on Tuskegee Airmen. Available online at: http://www.kent/wednet.edu/KSD/SJ/TuskegeeAirmen/Tuskegee_HomePage.html

Information on Twentieth Century African-Americans. Available online at: <http://www.liu.edu/cwis/cwp/library/african/2000/century.htm>

Van Deburg, William L.1997.*Modern Black Nationalism: from Marcus Garvey to Louis Farrakhan.* New York: New York University Press.

Walters, Ronald W.1990.*An Introduction to Black Politics* [video recording].Lexington, KY: Production & Engineering.

Walters, Ronald W. 1999. *African American Leadership.* Albany: State University of New York Press.

Walters, Ronald W. 1988. *Black Presidential Politics in America: A Strategic Approach.* Albany, N.Y.: State University of New York Press.

Walton, Hanes, Jr. 2003.*American Politics and the African American Quest for Universal Freedom.* New York : Longman.

Washington, Robert E. 2001. *The Ideologies of African American Literature: From the Harlem Renaissance to the Black Nationalist Revolt.* Lanham, Md.: Rowman & Littlefield Publishers.

Watson, Steven. 1995. *The Harlem Renaissance: Hub of African American Culture, 1920– 1930.* New York: Pantheon, 1995.

Weisbrot, Robert. 1990. *Freedom Bound: A History of America's Civil Rights Movement.* New York: W.W. Norton.

Westin, Alan F. 1964. *Freedom Now : The Civil Rights Struggle in America.* New York: Basic Books, Inc.

Wexler, Sanford.1999. *An Eyewitness History of the Civil Rights Movement.* New York. Checkmark Books.

William T. Bowers.1996. *Black soldier, white army : the 24th Infantry Regiment in Korea.* Washington, D.C.: Center of Military History, U.S. Army.

Williamson, Joel. 1984. *The Crucible of Race: Black-White Relations in the American South*

Since Emancipation. New York; Oxford University Press.

Wilson, Joe Jr. 1999.*The 761st "Black Panther" Tank Battalion in World War II: An illustrated history of the first African American armored unit to see combat.* Jefferson, N.C.: McFarland.

Wintz, Cary D., ed. 1996. *Black writers Interpret the Harlem Renaissance.*New York: Garland Publisher.

Wintz, Cary D., ed. 1996. *Analysis and Assessment, 1940-1979.* New York: Garland Press.

Withers, Ernest C. *Negro League Baseball.* Harry N. Abrams, 2004.

Wolseley, Roland Edgar. 1971. *The Black Press, U.S.A.* Ames, Iowa: Iowa State University Press.

Wolters, Raymond. 1975. *The New Negro on Campus: Black College Rebellions of the 1920s.* Princeton, NJ: Princeton University Press.

Information on World War I: A Historic Context for the African-American Military Experience. Available online at:<https://www.denix.osd.mil/denix/Public/ES-Programs/Conservation/Legacy/AAME/aame3.html https://www.denix.osd.miKrl/denix/Public/ES-Programs/Conservation/Legacy/AAME/aame3.html

Information on World War I and Postwar Society. Available online at: <http://memory.loc.gov/ammem/aaohtml/exhibit/aopart7.html>

Wynn, Neil A. 1975. *The Afro-American and the Second World War.* New York: Holmes & Meier Publishers.